MICROSOFT FRONTPAGE 97:
HTML AND BEYOND

MICROSOFT FRONTPAGE 97:
HTML AND BEYOND

Gus Venditto

Henry Holt & Company, Inc.
New York

MIS:Press
A Subsidiary of Henry Holt and Company, Inc.
115 West 18th Street
New York, New York 10011
http://www.mispress.com

Copyright © 1997 by MIS:Press

Printed in the United States of America

All rights reserved. No part of this book may be reproduced or transmitted in any form or by any means, electronic or mechanical, including photocopying, recording, or by any information storage and retrieval system, without prior written permission from the Publisher. Contact the Publisher for information on foreign rights.

Limits of Liability and Disclaimer of Warranty

The Author and Publisher of this book have used their best efforts in preparing the book and the programs contained in it. These efforts include the development, research, and testing of the theories and programs to determine their effectiveness.

The Author and Publisher make no warranty of any kind, expressed or implied, with regard to these programs or the documentation contained in this book. The Author and Publisher shall not be liable in any event for incidental or consequential damages in connection with, or arising out of, the furnishing, performance, or use of these programs.

All products, names and services are trademarks or registered trademarks of their respective companies.

First Edition—1997

ISBN 1-55828-527-X

MIS:Press and M&T Books are available at special discounts for bulk purchases for sales promotions, premiums, and fundraising. Special editions or book excerpts can also be created to specification.

For details contact: Special Sales Director
                        MIS:Press and M&T Books
                        Subsidiaries of Henry Holt and Company, Inc.
                        115 West 18th Street
                        New York, New York 10011

10 9 8 7 6 5 4 3 2 1

Associate Publisher: *Paul Farrell*

Executive Editor: *Cary Sullivan*   **Production Editor**: *Anthony Washington*
Editor: *Debra Williams Cauley*   **Technical Editor**: *Simon St.Laurent*
Copy Edit Manager: *Shari Chappell*   **Copy Editor**: *Sara Black*

DEDICATION

To Dorothy, for happiness beyond measure.

ACKNOWLEDGMENTS

Many people helped the preparing this book. A few stand out.

Chris Peters, Robert Crissman, Jr. and Steven Lurie were especially helpful. Most importantly, they led the teams that produced such a great product but they are also very eloquent in explaining how it works.

Richard Enriquez contributed greatly to the book with the spectacular color images from MetaTools' photo library that you'll find on the CD-ROM.

Many special thanks to Simon St. Laurent for adding insight into FrontPage97 and the web in general. And to Debra Williams Cauley for working so hard on so many topics, and to Anthony Washington for grace under pressure.

Contents in Brief

Introduction 1
Chapter 1: The Anatomy of a Web Site 7
Chapter 2: Building Your Web Site on Solid Ground .29
Chapter 3: Web Site Building Blocks 47
Chapter 4: The Two Faces of FrontPage 65
Chapter 5: Fast Starts with Wizards and Templates . .93
Chapter 6: The Essential Tools for Text, Graphics, and Links 119
Chapter 7: Adding Color to Your Web 147
Chapter 8: Fine-Tuning Image Properties 163
Chapter 9: Creating and Perfecting Graphics with Image Composer 181
Chapter 10: Layout Magic with Tables 217
Chapter 11: Organizing a Site with Frames 237
Chapter 12: Creating Forms to Gather Information . .253
Chapter 13: Organizing a Site with Time-Saving WebBots 275
Chapter 14: Running a Discussion Group 287
Chapter 15: Adding Sound, Video, and Animation . .303
Chapter 16: Developing with JavaScript and VBScript 329
Chapter 17: Connecting with Office 97 and Remote Databases 351
Chapter 18: Perfecting Your Web Site 367
Index 393

CONTENTS

Introduction 1

Part I
Planning Your Web Site

Chapter 1: The Anatomy of a Web Site 7

The Structure of the Web 7
    The Internet: Networks Serving People 8
    The Difference between an Internet and an Intranet 9
    Connecting to the Internet 10
    Passing through Gateways 12
    The IP Address System 12
Are You a Static or a Dynamic Address? 13
    Names on the Internet 15
    The Meaning of a URL 17
The Rules of the Web 19
    HTTP: The Reason Links Work 20
    HTML: The Code behind Web Pages 21
    MIME: The Secret behind the Magic 24
    ActiveX, Java, and the Next Big Thing 26

Chapter 2: Building Your Web Site on Solid Ground 29

What You Need from a Web Server 30
   The Stripped-Down Web Host 30
   The Well-Equipped Web Host 31
   The Ideal Web Host 33
   Will Your Pages Be Public or Private? 36
   The FrontPage Personal Web Server 37
Choosing a Home for Your Site 37
   Total Control: Master of Your Own Host 38
   Sharing a Corporate Network 41
   Shopping for Web Host Services 42

Chapter 3: Web Site Building Blocks 47

HTML Pages: The Foundation of Your Site 47
   Finding the HTML Files at a URL 48
   Links: Local and Remote References 50
   Tags: Basic and Extended 52
   Extended Tags: Risky Business 55
Graphic Formats That Color the Web 57
   GIF: Fast and Flexible 58
   JPEG: For Quality and Realism 59
Other Ways of Interacting 60
   Multimedia of All Kinds 61
   Scripts That Communicate 61

Part II
Building Your Web Site

Chapter 4: The Two Faces of FrontPage 65

FrontPage Explorer: The Big Picture 66
Opening Webs in FrontPage Explorer 67

Contents

Explorer's Graphical Overview 68
Fine-Tuning Your Web View 71
   Showing Links among Pages and URLs 71
   Revealing Repeated Links 72
   Showing Links inside Pages 73
Folder View Versus Hyperlink View 74
   Switching from Hyperlink to Folder View 74
   Managing Server Folders with Explorer 75
   Keeping Your View Accurate 76
   The Secret Ingredients in a FrontPage Web 76
   Sharing and Controlling Access to Webs 79
   Testing Your Net Connection 84
   Changing HTML, Graphics, and Multimedia Editors 84
FrontPage Editor: Your Web Page Toolbox 85
   Moving Between the Editor and Explorer 85
   FrontPage Editor's Graphic Preview 86
   Tricks and Traps 87
Personal Web Server: At Work Behind the Scenes 89
   Giving Others Access with the Web Server 90
   Setting Personal Web Server Permissions 90

Chapter 5: Fast Starts with Wizards and Templates 93

Build a Web in 60 Seconds 94
   Where WebBots Fit in 94
   The Difference between a Wizard and a Template 94
Whipping Up New Webs in Explorer 96
   Naming Your New Web 98
   Choosing the Right Wizard 101
   The Difference between Wizards in Explorer and Editor . 101
   The Wizards of Explorer 102
Jump Starting New Web Pages 108
   Opening Up FrontPage Editor Templates 108
Publishing a New Site 114
   Step One: Prepare the Server 115

Step Two: Publish the Site 116
Working with Child Webs 117
Publishing to Sites without FrontPage 117
Naming Your Home Page 118

Chapter 6: The Essential Tools for Text, Graphics, and Links 119

Getting the Hang of It: Drag, Drop, and Preview 119
    Avoiding Lost Files 121
    Faster Than a Printout: Page Previews 122
Formatting Text with Styles 125
    HTML Text Styles 125
    Changing Text Styles 126
    HTML List Styles 127
    Changing List Styles 128
Formatting Text with Fonts 130
    Selecting Font Sizes 130
    Selecting Fonts 132
    Removing a Font Format 133
Adding Graphics to a Page 133
    Inserting Clip Art in a Page 134
    Alternative Image Settings 135
    Controlling a Graphic's Size 137
    Aligning an Image 138
    Image Borders 139
Adding Links to a Page 140
    Clickable Graphics Versus Image Maps 140
    Bookmarks: Linking Inside a Page 141
    Linking to Other Pages in a Web 143
    Linking to Other Web Sites and URLs 145

Chapter 7: Adding Color to Your Web 147

Colors around the Web 147
    How Colors are Conveyed on the Web 148

HTML Color Tags 149
A Master Scheme for Your Webs 150
  Creating a Color Scheme You Can Reuse 151
The Elements You Can Color 152
  Selecting Background Images 153
  Selecting Background, Text, and Link Colors 155
  Adding Color Highlights to Text 156
  Custom Colors 158
  Reusing Someone Else's Color Scheme 159
  Adding Color to Horizontal Lines 160

Chapter 8: Fine-Tuning Image Properties 163

Adding Image Effects in FrontPage Explorer 163
  Blending Images: Transparent GIFs 164
Creating Clickable Image Maps 169
  Preparing to Add Hot Spots to an Image 170
  Step-by-Step: Creating an Image Map 171
Designing with Text 175
  Designing with Fonts on Intranets 177
Choosing the Best Image Editor 177
  Selecting Your Own Image Editor 178

Chapter 9: Creating and Perfecting Graphics with Image Composer 181

Overview of Image Composer 181
  Loading Image Composer 183
  Getting to Know Image Composer 183
  Right-Sizing Images before You Begin 185
  Zooming and Panning for a Better View 187
Sprites: Objects within Images 187
  Moving and Resizing Sprites 189
  Selection Sets and Groups of Sprites 191
Creating New Sprites 192
  Text Sprites 192

Fitting Text into a Space 193
Creating a Shadow Effect with Text 195
Arranging Text 195
Creating New Shapes 197
Adding a Sprite with the Shape Tool 197
Adding 3D Effects with Shapes 202
Special Effects with Color Lift 203
Adding Impact with Artistic Effects 204
Controlling Color Effects with Patterns 204
Sending Sprites behind Other Sprites 206
Changing a Single Color 206
Warps and Filters 207
Adding Color with Paint Tools 210
Touching Up with Paint 212
Saving Sprites, JPGs, and GIFs 213

Chapter 10: Layout Magic with Tables 217

Gaining New Perspective on Tables 217
Creating a Table 221
   Adding Rows and Columns 222
   Deleting Rows and Columns 223
Controlling the Size of a Table 223
   Adjusting the Width of a Cell 225
Controlling the Appearance of Tables 226
   Aligning Tables on a Page 226
   Aligning the Contents of a Cell 227
   Cells That Span Other Cells 228
   Adding and Removing Borders 229
   Cell Padding 231
   Cell Spacing 232
Nesting Tables inside Tables 233
   Inserting Tables within Tables 233
   Splitting Cells within Table Cells 234
Getting Creative with Tables 234

Chapter 11: Organizing a Site with Frames 237

Understanding Frame Tags 237
    The Structure behind Frames 239
    How Frame Tags Work 239
    The Importance of Good Sources 242
Creating Pages with Frames 242
    Starting the Frames Wizard 243
    Choosing among the Frame Templates 244
    Adding New Columns and Rows 245
    Adding Source Files 247
    Displaying an Alternate Page 248
    Wrapping Up and Revising 249
    Fixing HTML Frame Tags 249
    Editing and Refreshing Pages 251

Chapter 12: Creating Forms to Gather Information 253

Forms Processing Basics 253
Creating a Form 254
    Inserting Form Fields 255
    Editing the Fields 256
Controlling the Data You Collect 257
    Form Field Properties 258
    Text Box Properties 259
    Scrolling Text Box Properties 260
    Check Box Properties 261
    Radio Button Properties 261
    Drop-Down Menu Properties 262
    Push Button Properties 263
Configuring the Forms Handler 264
    Selecting a Forms Handler 265
    Sending the Results to a File 266
    Splitting the Results 267
    Thanking Clients and Explaining Failures 268

Validating Data before You Collect It 269
Validating Text Entries 270
Validating Radio Buttons 271
Validating Drop-Down Menus 271

Part III
Enhancing Your Site

Chapter 13: Organizing a Site with Time-Saving WebBots 275

WebBot Components 275
   Editing WebBot Component Properties 276
Reusing Pages and Graphics 277
   One Navigational Toolbar for Every Page 277
   Keeping Information Current 278
   Inserting the Include WebBot 279
Putting Your Site on a Schedule 279
   Inserting the Include WebBots 280
   Keeping Visitors Informed about Updates 281
Providing a Search-the-Site Button 282
   Inserting the Search WebBot 284
Displaying an Overview of Your Site 285
   Inserting the Table of Contents WebBot 285

Chapter 14: Running a Discussion Group 287

Talk Show Basics 287
   Where Newsgroups Fit In 288
   The Drawbacks of a Discussion Web 290
Creating a New Discussion Web 291
   Selecting the Discussion Web Wizard 291
   Controlling Access to Protected Discussions 296
   Fine-Tuning the Pages in a Discussion Web 298

Chapter 15: Adding Sound, Video, and Animation 303

Defining Multimedia 303
   Planning Multimedia Applications 304
   Planning Multimedia: Client Issues 304
   Planning Multimedia: Download Issues 305
   Planning Multimedia: Server Issues 305
Distributing Multimedia at a Web Site 307
   Playing with MIME 307
   Plug-In Player Overview 308
   Adding Files That Require a Plug-In 311
   ActiveX Control Overview 312
   Adding Files That Require an ActiveX Control 314
   Java Applets for Multimedia 316
Short and Silent Animations 319
   Adding Shockwave Presentations .320
   Microsoft GIF Animator 320
   Creating a GIF Animation 322
Adding Sound to a Page 324
   Playing Sound in the Background .325
   Basic Text Animation with Marquees 325
Inserting Video Files 326

Chapter 16: Developing with JavaScript and VBScript .329

The Politics of Scripting Languages 329
   The ActiveX Environment 331
   Embracing Java within ActiveX 332
   Where JavaScript and VBScript Fit In 333
   Adding Scripts to Your Web Pages 334
   Choosing between JavaScript and VBScript 334
Adding JavaScript to Web Pages 335
   Overview of JavaScript 335

Displaying an Alert Message with JavaScript 337
Redirecting Browsers to a New URL with JavaScript 340
Adding VBScript to Web Pages 342
Overview of VBScript 343
Displaying an Alert Message with VBScript 345
Redirecting Browsers to a New URL with VBScript 348

Chapter 17: Connecting with Office 97 and Remote Databases 351

Receiving Files from Co-Workers 351
Receiving Files from Office 97 352
Saving Excel Spreadsheets with the Internet Wizard 353
Connecting Web Sites to Databases 356
Microsoft's IDC Format for SQL Queries 356
Creating IDC Files with the Database Connector Wizard 357
Activating Your IDC Query 360
Customizing Your HTX Database Results 361
Publishing Pages Data Directly from Microsoft Access 363
Saving Access Tables to HTML Files 364

Chapter 18: Perfecting Your Web Site 367

Working Smarter 367
Use the Best Editor for the Job 367
Learn from Others 369
Annotate Your Tags 371
Keeping a To-Do List 374
Moving Your Site to a New Server 376
Fixing Image Maps for Servers without FrontPage Extensions .378
Moving Files to Servers without FrontPage Extensions 380
Managing Change at Your Site 383
Replacing Text in Every Page 384
Changing Text That Changes Often 386
Gaining More from Your Hard Work 389
Register Your Site with Search Engines 389

Add Your URL to Your E-mail 390
Create a Temp Web for Housecleaning 391

Index 393

INTRODUCTION

Web sites have become more than interesting attractions on the information super-highway. They have become important tools for business. Any information that can be delivered in an office memo or printed report will get there faster and at lower cost if it's published directly to a Web site. No paper is required.

But simple documents are just the beginning. Web sites are becoming a vehicle for sharing recorded speeches and promotional films. A Web site can be used to communicate ideas and exchange information. You can register users to a company database or poll customers on their preferences for future products. You can even create a discussion group, inviting visitors to post messages for others to read and respond to.

Microsoft FrontPage 97 represents a turning point for Web publishing. It allows anyone to tap all the tools available for online document publishing, but it also helps you step into the next generation of the Web, where Web sites will be interactive. Whether you want to control more of a user's experience using scripting languages or you want to give them access to larger pools of information by providing database queries, FrontPage 97 can help you get there faster.

In writing this book, I assumed that readers have a general familiarity with computers and Windows. You don't need to be an expert, but you should know your way around basic applications like word processors. I assumed that you know files are stored in documents and hard disks are organized into folders (and you may even know folders used to be called directories before Microsoft changed the terminology). And I assumed that you are using either Windows 95 or Windows NT (required for Microsoft FrontPage 97) and have access to a Web server that's on the public Internet or a private organization's intranet.

Because many readers have a general idea of how the Internet works but may need to fill in a few gaps to master the world of Web publishing, the book begins with an overview of essential concepts. If you are experienced with the Internet, you can skip Chapter 1 and maybe even Chapter 2. These two chapters explain the specifications that have made publishing on the Web possible and attempt to put it all in perspective. If you don't know an intranet from the Internet, you'll find the answers in these two chapters. Even if you are well versed in basic Internet terminology, you may find that the chapters answer a few questions that remain.

The book is designed to help you gradually acquire the basic skills required for mastering FrontPage 97. The early chapters examine the interface and explain the general concepts. With each chapter, new skills are added. By chapter 6, you'll have learned enough to create a well-designed Web site that's on a par with thousands of other sites. But we're just starting.

You'll learn how to create images that gain attention and forms that capture information from people who visit your site. And you'll learn how to organize material using frames. By this point, your site will be approaching state-of-the-art status, ready to be considered for "cool site of the day" awards. But we're not done yet.

Chapter 14 will guide you through the process of creating a message board that can be open to the public or restricted to users who register and record a password. Chapter 15 will help you decide whether multimedia clips—animations, Java applets, sound files, or full-motion video—are worth adding to your pages and, if they are, how to do it while reducing the burden on your site's resources. In Chapter 16, you'll learn how to create basic scripts in JavaScript and VBScript in just a few minutes even if you've never written a computer program before. Chapter 17 will walk you through the process of connecting your Web site to Office 97 files and remote databases, so visitors to your site can submit queries to the database and review search results.

Whether you want to move straight through the entire program, from primers to the graduate courses in sequence, or you just want to browse, you'll find the help you need to master Web technology with FrontPage 97. I also believe you'll find that you're equipped for the next generation of Web technology. As a consultant and as director of product testing for *Internet World* magazine, I've worked with hundreds of products that are pushing the standards for the Web into the future. I've tried to distill that experience into the hundreds of tips and recommendations that appear throughout the book.

Introduction

The Internet and intranets are clearly moving from the HTML document standard that created the Web into a world where scripts and multimedia files are the norm. The following pages will help you bridge that gap at the pace that makes the most sense for you.

Gus Venditto
Director, IW Labs, *Internet World* magazine
President, C.V. Creative, Inc.
Westchester, New York

PART I
PLANNING YOUR WEB SITE

CHAPTER 1
THE ANATOMY OF A WEB SITE

Microsoft FrontPage has dozens of tools to help you build Web pages, polish them with colorful special effects, and add spice with multimedia. As you become proficient with the software, you'll be able to build attractive Web pages in minutes and keep them up to date with very little effort.

In fact, it's so easy that many people get caught up in the process of fine-tuning Web pages without giving a second thought to how the Internet works. That's a mistake, because your Web site will be more valuable if you keep the Web's underlying structure in mind as you create your pages.

Whether you've spent years mastering the intricacies of the Internet or have just discovered this new universe, to do a good job of planning your Web pages and tweaking them with new technologies in the coming years, you'll want to make sure you're making the best choices on where your Web pages are created and published.

This chapter provides an overview of the Internet and intranets. It will help you understand the technologies needed to create a Web site, and some of the opportunities you can explore once you've got a basic site in place.

THE STRUCTURE OF THE WEB

The *World Wide Web* is actually a technique for publishing that uses the Internet to move documents around. At times, people talk about the Web and the Internet as though they're interchangeable, but they're not. The Web is just one of many ways to use the Internet.

Once a computer is connected to the Internet, it can take part in the World Wide Web, either to view pages or to publish them. You need a browser, such as Netscape Navigator, Mosaic, or Microsoft Explorer, to view Web pages. The browser uses TCP/IP to find pages that have been published on the Web, download the pages, and display them on your computer.

Any computer connected to the Internet has the potential to publish pages that others see on the World Wide Web, as long as the right connections are in place. At its simplest, publishing a Web page is no different from creating a word processing document on your hard disk. Instead of using a word processor, you'll use FrontPage to create your documents. And, instead of printing documents on paper to share them with others, you'll let others display the documents in a Web browser on their own computers.

But creating a Web page alone is not enough to be part of the Web. Other computers need to be able to find the computer on which you've stored your pages. You need to store the file on a computer that is part of the World Wide Web or, if you're creating a Web site only for members of your organization, you'll need access to a directory that is part of your company's intranet.

The following chapters will explain the techniques you can use to build and polish your own Web site. But before you start building castles in the sky, make sure you know how to use the Internet, so others can view your work.

The Internet: Networks Serving People

The *Internet* is a complex organism with a very simple goal. At its heart, the Internet is a technique for connecting networks of computers. A backbone of data communication lines forms the links among the millions of smaller networks.

When a single user makes a connection to the Internet, he or she becomes a *node* on a network. This node is on the Internet if the network is connected to the rest of the Internet. Once you become part of any of these networks, you can reach any other network and any other node on the network. In theory, any single computer on the Internet can establish a connection with any other computer. In chat rooms, for example, anyone who logs in can send messages to any other user, in complete privacy;

these two computers are communicating directly across the Internet even though they are on totally different networks.

However, the Web uses a *client-server* design, which is a way of saying that when two computers are connected on the Web, they're not equal. The *client* makes requests and receives material. The *server* dispenses information.

The Difference between an Internet and an Intranet

If your organization has an intranet, you'll have a choice over where your Web pages will be placed: on your company's intranet or on the public Internet.

Intranets are identical to the Internet, except that they're private. A corporation sets up an intranet to use the Internet for some of its network, but it places barriers at key junctions so that only authorized members of the organization can take part in the private intranet. Before the Internet became popular, when an organization wanted to connect users who worked in different buildings, it needed to create a wide area network. It needed to lease telecommunications lines to carry the data traffic from one location to another and it needed to either buy or lease expensive hardware for routing all the traffic. When users needed to communicate with people outside the company, for e-mail or to read through public databases, the company needed to add another connection for Internet access.

As the Internet has grown, corporations have found that it can carry much of the traffic generated by their own computer users. The expensive setup needed to link each of the company's offices can be eliminated because the Internet, a public network, carries the traffic. Firewalls and proxy servers can create barriers between the company's private intranet and the public Internet.

In creating Web pages for an intranet or the Internet there are really only two considerations:

- Who is the audience? If it's limited to members of your organization, you'll have a different message than if it's the world at large.

- Where will you store your files? To build a Web site for an intranet, you'll need to make sure the computer you're using is accessible to everyone in the organization; your company's network administrators will need to confirm this. To build a Web site for the public Internet, either you'll need to have your company's administrators set aside space for you on a Web site or you'll need to rent space using a Web-hosting service.

Fortunately, you won't need to worry about the software you'll use or the types of graphics you'll show. Web sites on the Internet and intranets use the same types of software. That means you can use your computer to view the Internet's public World Wide Web (as long as your network gives you that permission) and you can also view Web pages created for viewing only by members of your organization. As a Web publisher using FrontPage, you can place some of your pages on the public Internet and other pages on the private intranet.

Connecting to the Internet

The Internet can connect any computer that can communicate with TCP/IP (Transmission Control Protocol/Internet Protocol). Just about any computer you can think of, short of a teenager's game player, can make this connection. PCs, Macs, UNIX workstations, minicomputers, laptops, and even some handheld portables can communicate using TCP/IP.

Computers don't always come with this connection (though many do). In most cases, you can plug in the communications equipment and install the software necessary to make the connection to put a system on the Internet.

Modems, ISDN adapters, and LAN (local area network) cards are the most common ways to send and receive the actual computer bits. Software on the computer ensures that the connection runs TCP/IP. On a Windows 95 or NT system, there are two or three pieces of software needed to establish the TCP/IP connection:

- Hardware drivers that recognize the modem or adapter card; these are set up when the hardware is installed and can be configured with the Windows Control Panel.

- A dialer is needed if the communications equipment is a modem or ISDN adapter (see Figure 1.1). The dialer sends instructions to the hardware to establish the connection. A dialer is not needed if the system is a network card; the network connection is established automatically when you turn on the computer.

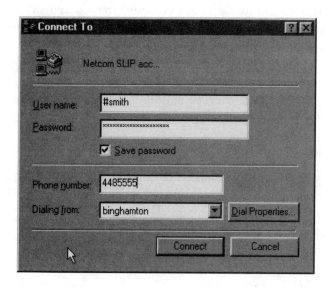

Figure 1.1 The Windows dialer connects to the Internet with a modem or ISDN adapter.

- Winsock software (short for "Windows sockets") makes the connection between the incoming data and the software you'll run. This file, called **WINSOCK.DLL**, comes with Windows 95 and NT; it's stored in the main Windows directory.

All three pieces of software must be properly configured to establish an Internet connection with Windows 95 or NT. Only then will TCP/IP software, such as a browser or e-mail manager, be able to reach the Internet. And, of course, the hardware must be working and able to connect with another computer that is already on the Internet.

Passing through Gateways

While it's common for people to talk about the Internet as a way to connect computers, this is actually an oversimplification of what really happens.

To reach the Internet, your computer has to actually connect with communication devices, known as *switches*, that act as a gateway to other computers on the Internet. If you're connecting with a modem, another modem answers the phone and then passes the connection over to a switch; if you're connecting via network, you may connect to devices known as *routers*, *bridges*, or *hubs*, but they perform the same switching function. Your Internet connection is constantly being switched from one computer to another over a gateway as you select different Web sites or other Internet services.

To keep track of the millions of Internet connections that are active at any given moment of the day, every computer and routing device needs an IP (Internet Protocol) address. The gateway identifies your computer with a unique IP address and connects you to other computers using their IP addresses.

The IP Address System

Because every system on the Internet is identified by an IP address, it can be useful to understand how the addresses are assigned. When browsers display the pages at a Web site, the server software records the IP address of the system. That means you'll be able to know a little bit about the people who visit your site, if you have an understanding of how IP addresses are assigned.

An *IP address* is actually a series of four numbers, separated by periods. For example, 198.105.232.1 is the IP address of one of Microsoft's FTP servers, a computer Microsoft provides for distributing software. The IP address system uses a hierarchy that reveals a bit about the organization that owns the address. The first part of the number (that's *198* in Microsoft's case), indicates the network number, the largest grouping of computers on the Internet. The last number (that's *1* in the example), identifies a specific system in that network. A system of three classes, ranging from Class A to Class C, is used to allocate IP addresses.

- In a Class A network, the highest level, the first part of the number is reserved for one organization; the organization is free to assign the remaining three parts. The organization has more than 16 million individual IP addresses under its control, and so a Class A network is available only to very large organizations. IP addresses that start with a number ranging from 1 to 126 are in the Class A network.

- In a Class B network, the first two numbers are assigned and the organization assigns the last two parts, for a total of 64,516 addresses. Universities and large corporations are the most typical owners of Class B networks. IP addresses that start with a number ranging from 128 to 191 are in the Class B network.

- In a Class C network, the first three numbers are assigned and the organization assigns only the last part, providing just 254 individual IP addresses. Class C networks are the smallest grouping possible in the Internet; many are owned by small companies or departments within a large corporation. IP addresses that start with a number ranging from 192 through 223 are in a Class C network.

Few organizations have as many IP addresses as they'd like. You can't simply request ten more after you run out; you have to register a completely new Class C network. As a result, the process of obtaining a new IP address can be a challenge when you plan your new Web site.

ARE YOU A STATIC OR A DYNAMIC ADDRESS?

Because IP addresses are such a valuable resource, Internet service providers and network administrators usually control the pool of addresses and assign them a user only when they actually connect to the Internet. Many users connect to the Internet with a different IP address each time. When they connect, their name is assigned to that IP address and when the connection ends, the IP address goes back in the pool of addresses so it can be assigned to the next user who needs it.

In planning your Web site, one of the first things you need to consider is if the computer you'll use has a permanent IP address. If you're not sure, you need to find out.

WARNING

A system that obtains its IP address dynamically cannot be used as a Web server because other Internet users would not be able to find the site reliably.

If you're not sure if you have a permanent or a dynamic IP address, you can check the Windows 95 or NT Control Panel setting for networks:

1. Click the **Start** button to open the Taskbar.
2. Select **Settings/Control Panel**. The Control Panel opens, displaying a variety of icons.
3. Double-click on the **Network** icon. The Configuration folder should be displayed; if not, select the **Configuration** tab. A window opens, showing the networking components installed for your system.
4. Double-click on the **TCP/IP** listing. A window will open with six folders; each represents a different set of properties.
5. Select the **IP Address** tab. This display will show clearly whether the system obtains its IP address dynamically or whether it has its own address, as shown in Figure 1.2.

CHAPTER 1—The Anatomy of a Web Site

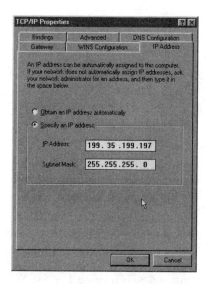

Figure 1.2 The Network icon shows when a system has its own IP address.

You can run Microsoft FrontPage on any Windows 95 or NT system. It doesn't matter if your system has a dynamic or a static IP address for preparing Web pages, but only a system that has a static IP address can be a Web server.

Names on the Internet

The Internet wouldn't be very useful if mere mortals needed to memorize the hundreds of IP addresses they use online in an ordinary day. If you know the IP address of a Web server, you can type it into your browser's command line. (Go ahead and try the IP address used in the previous pages; type **ftp://198.105.232.1** on your browser's command line.) But who wants to work like that?

To help us humans in our never-ending struggle to keep computers under our control, a naming convention was established. Domain name servers are Internet computers that handle the thankless job of matching names with IP addresses. They contain enormous databases identifying Web servers and other hosts (such as mail servers and FTP servers) by name and number.

When you type the name of a Web site at your browser, the browser asks a domain name server to look up the IP address for that name, a process called *resolving an address*. If the Web site is properly registered, the Web site's IP address is *resolved*, meaning that the correct address is found and sent back to the browser. The browser then contacts the computer at that address to display the Web pages. If the Web site's name was typed incorrectly or the Web site is not listed at the domain name server, then the browser reports a problem.

The database of Internet names and addresses is maintained by Internic, an organization that maintains a Web site at

www.internic.net

You can learn the domain name server that controls any Web name by visiting Internic's site. When your browser displays the site, select the **Directory and Database Services** and run a Whois query. Figure 1.3 shows the listing at Internic's Web site for microsoft.com.

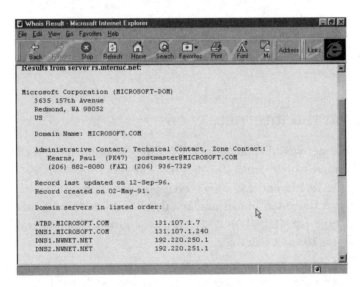

Figure 1.3 The Internic listing shows the IP addresses for a site's domain name servers.

The IP addresses displayed on the Internic report are not the actual location of the Web site; they are the location of the domain name server where the Web site is registered. The domain name server will refer all requests to the Web site to the right computer. That means any computer on the network can work as a Web site, as long as it has a static IP address and it is properly registered at the domain name server on its network.

In assigning names, Internic allows users to select any domain name that's not in use, but it will add a *zone* (or suffix) according to specific rules. The most familiar zone is *com*, indicating a commercial site. Table 1.1 shows the most common zones.

Table 1.1 Common Domain Name Zones

Zone	What it Means
au	Located in Australia
ca	Located in Canada
com	Commercial organization in the United States
edu	Educational institution in the United States
fr	Located in France
gov	United States government bodies and departments
it	Located in Italy
net	Networking organization, including Internet service providers
org	Professional organization or committee
uk	Located in the United Kingdom

NOTE Initially, domain name zones were three letters and were used to indicate the type of organization that ran the Internet host. Because the Internet was built in America, zones were assumed to be in the United States. When a host was located outside the United States, a two-letter abbreviation was used for the country. Table 1.1 shows only a handful of the many two-letter zones used for country names.

The Meaning of a URL

Domain names are at the center of the Internet's naming scheme, but they're not the last word. A domain name is an umbrella for a variety of resources. It can be used for just one computer or for multiple hosts. The server software in the computer used as the domain host determines which computers perform which functions. You can use a single domain name to create multiple Web sites, and you can store the sites on one computer or spread them out over several computers.

The letters we type to display a Web page are known as a *URL* (universal resource locator). The first part of the URL is always the Internet protocol used to communicate with the host computer. In the URL

```
http://www.whitehouse.gov
```

the first letters—*http*—indicate that the protocol to be used is hypertext transport protocol, the system used to transport pages on the Web. The colon and two slashes are used as punctuation, separating the protocol from the actual address. The letters *www* indicate that the domain is located on the World Wide Web. You wouldn't use those letters if you were accessing pages on a corporate network that was not connected to the World Wide Web. Finally, *whitehouse.gov* is the domain name for a server where the White House maintains its Web site. When you type **http://www.whitehouse.gov**, your browser displays the files published at this server.

A URL can be more precise than just the domain name. You can go right to a specific directory at that domain. For example, if you type the following URL on a browser's address line, it will display pages on a specific topic at the White House Web site, shown in Figure 1.4:

```
http://www.whitehouse.gov/WH/Services
```

If you know the correct URL, you can even display a single file at a Web site. The slashes that appear after a domain name usually indicate a folder (or subdirectory) that was created on the Web server. The Web pages displayed are stored in this folder.

NOTE

As you build your own Web sites, keep in mind that you can direct people to specific pages on your Web using URLs that include the domain name, folders on your Web server, and even individual file names.

CHAPTER 1—The Anatomy of a Web Site

Figure 1.4 A URL can be a domain name or it can refer to specific files at the Web site.

THE RULES OF THE WEB

The World Wide Web is a fairly uninhibited place. No one reviews the pages for accuracy, no one tries to censor content, and no one establishes standards for the information displayed at a Web site. The government is still thinking about whether the Internet requires its own set of laws, but for now, the Internet is as unregulated as a public bulletin board in a town square.

But from a technical perspective, the Web has very strict rules on how documents must be formatted. The World Wide Web Consortium (W3C) is the organization that created these rules, publishes revisions, and considers changes. The W3C keeps the latest specifications on the Web at

`http://www.w3c.org`

Figure 1.5 shows the opening page at the W3C site.

Microsoft FrontPage 97: HTML and Beyond

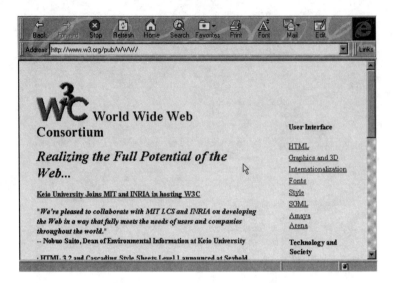

Figure 1.5 The technical specs for the Web are detailed at the W3C site.

You could spend an entire day reading through the volumes of technical papers on display—but you don't have to. The combination of this book and FrontPage software will ensure that you're playing by the rules.

The two most important sets of rules are HTTP and HTML.

HTTP: The Reason Links Work

Links are the spice that makes the Web so interesting. They make it possible for you to jump from any published page or graphic to any other with the click of a mouse. Links perform this magic because Web browsers are able to communicate with Web servers using HTTP, hypertext transport protocol.

HTTP was designed to use the Internet for sending a variety of types of data over the Internet. It was created in the early 1990s specifically to enable the types of Web applications we enjoy today.

The specification is a client-server model, meaning software on the *host* (server) computer will respond to requests from *remote* (client) computers, as long as they conform to HTTP syntax. Web browsers like Microsoft Explorer and Netscape Navigator are, technically speaking,

HTTP clients; they exist for the sole purpose of communicating with HTTP servers like Netscape Enterprise Server, Microsoft Internet Information Server, O'Reilly Web Server, and others.

A central element in the HTTP spec is the ability to transfer files from server to browser with virtually no effort. Unlike earlier online systems, where downloading a graphic file required careful preparation at both ends to ensure the file was transferred properly, the HTTP spec makes it possible to download pictures, text, and multimedia files simply by clicking on a link to a page. The HTTP also establishes the spec that clients (browsers) use to quickly switch from one Web server to another—which is the essence of a link. And they establish the rules for displaying pages automatically, so that when your browser contacts a domain name, the Web server at that computer can begin the process of downloading the text and graphics.

NOTE

Links are a popular way to connect with other pages, but they can become a maddening source of frustration as you build your own Web site. A link must be precise. It's difficult enough to correctly type a URL, but keeping links straight is compounded by the fact that you'll usually create your Web site on one system and then move it to the Web server after you're finished. Fortunately, FrontPage has tools for keeping links untangled when you move a Web site to a different system.

HTML: The Code behind Web Pages

When it became possible for client software to receive pictures and graphics across the Internet, a technique for displaying those pages was needed. HTML, or Hypertext Markup Language, is the coding system that dictates how browsers will display pages.

The Web has become so popular because HTML was so successful in accomplishing its objective. HTML's creators wanted a system that would make it possible for every conceivable computer to be able to share the same documents. It started with the most common type of data on computers—text in ASCII format—and added codes that would control how the text appears. A Web page is a text file that conforms to HTML rules.

In order to be universal, HTML gives the browser software an extraordinary amount of discretion in how it will display a page. There are so many differences among computer systems that Web pages cannot be too specific regarding page display. Specific fonts cannot be required; the browser must use the fonts available on the client computer. Even the space available to display a page can't be known in advance; some monitors have resolutions of 640 by 480 pixels, others have 800 by 600, and others have 1024 by 768. Figure 1.6 shows a Web page displayed at a resolution of 640 by 480. Figure 1.7 shows the same page displayed at a resolution of 1024 by 768.

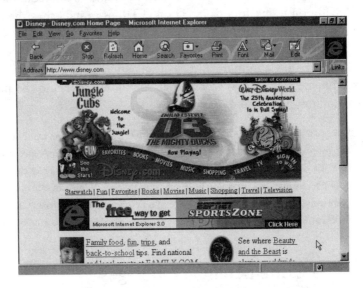

Figure 1.6 The Disney home page at a resolution of 640 by 480.

A typical HTML page contains text that appears on-screen and codes that format the text and display graphics. HTML codes, known as *tags*, can be typed in with any word processor. The coding is very simple to understand for basic tasks, such as adding emphasis to a word or inserting a link. HTML tags that control the appearance of text remain in effect until the tag is turned off; to end a formatting command, a tag that consists of a slash and the formatting tag is inserted after the text. For example, the following HTML code will display the text *Today's news* in the font used for a level three header:

```
<H3>Today's news</H3>
```

CHAPTER 1—The Anatomy of a Web Site

Figure 1.7 The same page as shown in Figure 1.6, but at a higher resolution.

The basic design of HTML is simple to understand, but creating HTML pages in a word processor is a tedious job. All tags must be typed in precisely, you must follow the rules on how to end a tag, and you have to be especially careful when combining special effects, such as displaying part of a headline in italics.

Viewing your work, including changes, is also tedious. You must save your file, leave your word processor, open the page with a browser, and then return to the word processor to try a new effect. FrontPage eliminates the drudgery; you choose HTML designs from a menu, highlight some text, and see the change immediately.

As the Web has grown, HTML has become increasingly complex. Web designers have experimented with innovations that HTML didn't handle at first. Rather than format pages with a handful of simple formats, today's Web pages use new formats that come with a long string of options.

Netscape took the lead by extending HTML in 1995, when it introduced a version of Netscape Navigator that could display Web pages in ways the HTML spec didn't support. Netscape published and explained these new HTML tags at its Web sites, and soon thousands of Web sites were peppering their pages with the special effects, such as background colors and text displayed in tables. Soon after, Microsoft got into the act, adding its own extensions that could be viewed only with Microsoft Explorer. The extensions began to build on each other's efforts. For example, Netscape introduced the first tags for tables, and Microsoft extended the table tags with the addition of background color.

The W3C organization is laboring mightily in an effort to keep up with these innovations. Each of the extensions that Microsoft and Netscape have added to their browsers were submitted to the W3C for consideration as part of the official HTML specification. In time, the W3C will catch up and formalize these new extensions. But in the meantime, the official HTML specification is just a starting point.

As a FrontPage 2.0 user, you don't need to be too concerned with the process of HTML specifications and extensions. FrontPage gives you the ability to use all the HTML extensions used in Netscape Navigator 3.0, Microsoft Explorer 3.0, and earlier versions. And if you want to try new extensions as they're introduced, you can type in those tags—as long as you're careful to follow the syntax precisely.

MIME: The Secret behind the Magic

The most common type of data seen on Web pages is text. Because text files don't require very much data, it made sense for the HTML specification to be based on text, for both formatting the pages and displaying words that appear on screen.

Graphic images and multimedia files, on the other hand, require special handling. The Internet has a technical limit that makes it more difficult to move these types of files.

The Internet was designed as a 7-bit communications network, which means that data move around in packets that are 7 bits long. While many of the newer computers and switches now in use are capable of the more robust 8-bit communications standards, this older standard is still in effect, and it has created a limit on the size of data packets.

This is not a problem for text files; they don't need to be longer than 7 bits. Files created for graphics, sound, or animation, on the other hand, need an 8-bit format. The problem has been solved on the Internet by using encoding systems that convert these types of files from their original 8-bit format to the 7-bit format as it travels over the network and back to the 8-bit format when they're displayed on the receiving system.

The encoding system used on the Web is *MIME*, which stands for Multipurpose Internet Mail Extensions. Web servers and browsers treat everything that's not a text file as a MIME file. The most common MIME files are GIF and JPG graphic files, but there are dozens of other MIME-compliant files being used, including AVI video clips, WAV sound files, VRML virtual reality words, and Shockwave presentations.

Web browsers like Microsoft Explorer and Netscape Navigator come preconfigured to display a wide range of MIME types. Figure 1.8 shows the default setting in Microsoft Explorer for GIF images. You can add new MIME types for any file type that's not already configured. When you add a plug-in or ActiveX control to a Web site, you're updating the MIME configuration with a new type. You're telling the browser which software should be used when this type of file is encountered at a Web site.

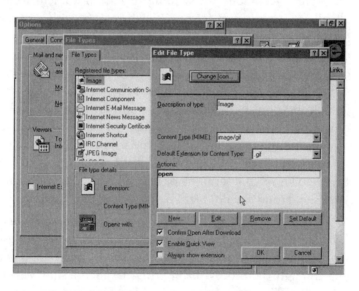

Figure 1.8 Microsoft Explorer displays many MIME file types and lets you add new ones.

As a Web page designer, you should think of MIME as a type of conduit. It makes it possible for you to add many different types of data files to your Web pages. As long as the browsers used to view your Web page have installed a plug-in or helper application for each particular MIME type, the files will play as they should. If they haven't added a MIME type for a particular file type, there's no harm in using the file; users may not be able to see the file, but it won't hurt the rest of the page. Browsers usually display a broken link graphic to indicate a file they don't understand.

ActiveX, Java, and the Next Big Thing

Up to this point, we've seen how the Internet and a private intranet can be used to publish documents, sending files from a server to a browser. The Web was designed as a publishing platform, but clever minds haven't been satisfied with this one-way street. They want to give the clients of Web sites—people running browser software—the ability to interact with Web sites. A few methods are already being used, and more are bound to follow:

- *Forms* are a technique for sending text from a client to a browser. Usually forms are used for a visitor to register with a site or request information from the Web site's publisher. The most common ways of creating forms at Web sites have been CGI and Perl scripts running on a server; these methods require Web publishers to learn a UNIX scripting language. FrontPage doesn't use CGI or Perl; instead, it lets you create forms by selecting menu options with *bots*. The forms are processed by a forms handler program on the server; as a result, you can create forms with FrontPage only if your server is running extension software from Microsoft. (Chapter 2 explains this issue in depth.) If you do know CGI scripting or have a CGI script you want to add to your site, FrontPage does let you insert the script, but it doesn't offer any help in constructing it.

- JavaScript and VBScript are simple languages for creating programs that run in a browser. FrontPage has some simple tools for guiding you through the process of inserting JavaScript and VBScript statements in a Web page. It's not a development environment, but it will help you create some fairly sophisticated scripts simply by selecting menu choices.

- Java applications are programs written in an advanced computer language known as Java that's comparable to C++. The leading browsers

(Netscape Navigator and Microsoft Explorer) can decode these programs and execute them on the client's system. You can insert Java programs into your Web pages using FrontPage's **Insert** command.

- Plug-ins are software programs that work with a browser to extend the browser's commands. Many plug-ins were created to play a certain type of file, such as a movie, virtual reality world, or audio clip. They were initially created for Netscape Navigator, but Microsoft Explorer 3.x can also run Netscape plug-ins. You can insert plug-in data files into your Web pages using FrontPage's **Insert** command.

- ActiveX controls are comparable to plug-ins, but they were written according to Microsoft's ActiveX development environment. Microsoft Explorer 3.x can play ActiveX controls; users who run Netscape Navigator will need to install additional software to run ActiveX controls. You can insert ActiveX programs into your Web pages using FrontPage's **Insert** command. The FrontPage menus will help you insert the control so that links to the page appear correctly, but FrontPage cannot help you create ActiveX controls.

These are the most common ways to make a Web site interactive, but they're certainly not the only ones. The strength of the Web has been its ability to accommodate innovation. Developers are sure to come up with new ways to breathe life into Web pages as time goes on. Fortunately, the design of HTML makes it possible to welcome new technologies as they arrive.

CHAPTER 2

BUILDING YOUR WEB SITE ON SOLID GROUND

A Web site can be filled with dazzling special effects or sober, thoughtful material. It's all up to you. As the manager of a Web site, you can have complete control over the material. Your vision for the site is essential to its success.

FrontPage tools make it possible to realize and maybe even exceed your vision for the site. In designing and polishing your pages, however, you may find that the server where your pages are stored presents obstacles that undermine your progress.

Most people start a Web site using a Web server that's convenient. The site is being offered by a co-worker or the Internet access provider they use. It's main advantage is that it's readily available. Because there are no strings attached, they put together the Web site quickly without spending days to learn all the options. But as the Web site grows, the server's limits become apparent. Multimedia files won't run properly. Forms don't work properly. And the site's address is a problem; it's too long, too confusing, and not memorable.

This chapter will explain the choices available for a Web server. You'll learn the minimum requirements and the special services that can dramatically improve the quality of your site. Then, we'll explore the options available for obtaining the Web services you need, looking at the steps involved in doing it yourself, sharing a corporate network, and renting space from a Web host service.

If you haven't yet decided on a home for your Web site, this chapter will help you decide where to go. And if you're already using a particular Web site, it will help you decide whether you may be better off moving the site to a new server. The process of moving a Web site from one server to another involves some work, but if your current Web server is placing limits on your ability to realize your vision for the site, the effort to move the site will be a very small price to pay. If you're completely satisfied with your current Web server, you may want to skip to the next chapter, but remember that you can always come back if you encounter limits.

What You Need from a Web Server

With technology, all things are possible. But they become possible one step at a time. A Web site is dynamic. You start with simple pages and add new features over time. The simplest type of Web host delivers just disk space on an HTTP server. Adding new features to your site requires work in developing your Web pages, using FrontPage, but it also requires access to resources on the server. You may start out with only limited access to your Web server, but as you enhance your site, you'll need to gain more control.

Before you reach a decision on how to host your site, let's look at what you must have from the Web host. Then we'll look at what you would really like to have.

The Stripped-Down Web Host

At a minimum, your Web site must provide the following.

- HTTP server software.
- A fixed IP address (e.g., 199.35.191.197).
- A domain name that is properly configured at a domain name server (for example, www.smith.com).
- A directory on the server that's been set aside for your Web site (for example, www.smith.com/joe).
- Read, write, and delete privileges for your Web site directory on the server.

When you have access to these five services, you can create a simple Web site. You'll use FrontPage to create HTML files and graphics and then

CHAPTER 2—Building Your Web Site on Solid Ground

copy the files to your Web site's directory. Anyone who has access to this server will be able to view your Web pages with a Web browser. If the Web server is on the World Wide Web, everyone with Internet access can see your pages, as long as they know your Web address or URL. If the server is on a corporate network without access to the Web, your site will be available only on systems that can log into the network.

Any Web host service in business today will be able to provide this minimum amount of service. Your organization's MIS or computer services department may also be able to provide all or part of these services.

In this type of scenario, you're completely at the mercy of the Web administrator. The administrator of the server will provide you with the URL to give to others. And the administrator will need to give you access to Web services like CGI script processing if you want to add interactive forms to your pages.

You may not even have the right to log into the server for updating the files at your convenience; some server administrators are reluctant to grant access privileges to their Web servers. Instead, the administrator takes on the job of copying the files to the proper directories, using the HTML and graphics files you submit. This situation is far from ideal, but it's corporate policy in some organizations.

If this scenario describes your situation, you're certain to find that the limitations will restrict the success of your Web site. Not only will they prevent you from fine-tuning the site, but they'll also create more work because you will not be able to use many of FrontPage's time-saving wizards. One of your top priorities should be to plan to increase the amount of control you have over your Web site.

The Well-Equipped Web Host

Microsoft FrontPage was designed to simplify the work of Web designers and network administrators. As a result, there's one simple feature FrontPage users want added to their "stripped-down host"—Microsoft FrontPage server extensions installed on the Web host system—the extensions are software routines that run on the Web host system, adding services that will be called by FrontPage and launched from code that FrontPage inserts into HTML pages.

The extensions make it possible for you to easily update your Web site with a single command. Without the extensions, you'll need to copy each file individually to the server, using an FTP utility or Telnet software.

When the FrontPage server extensions are installed on your Web host, the work of keeping links between your HTML files and graphics will be much easier. That's because FrontPage is able to coordinate the references to file locations between your system and the server, only if FrontPage is able to synchronize the files on your system with the files on the Web host.

Finally, the FrontPage extensions provide a wide range of services for processing scripts that are normally provided through the CGI (common gateway interface) language. FrontPage comes with automated scripts, called *bots*, which require the extensions. You can use these bots for a wide range of interactive applications, from simple response forms to discussion groups that can run for days at your Web site with little effort from you. Without the extensions, you'll need to learn CGI and insert the scripts into your HTML page. You'll also need to have permission to use the directory on your server where CGI scripts are stored so that you can edit and update your scripts.

The extensions are available for almost all HTTP Web servers on the Internet. The FrontPage CD-ROM includes the following software needed for the most popular servers.

- O'Reilly WebSite
- O'Reilly WebSite Professional for Windows 95 and NT
- Microsoft Internet Information Server 1.0 and 2.0
- Netscape Commerce Server 1.1 for Windows NT
- Netscape Communications Server 1.1
- Netscape Enterprise Server 2.0
- Netscape FastTrack 2.0

The extensions for other servers can be downloaded at no charge from Microsoft's Web site at the URL:

```
http://www.microsoft.com/frontpage
```

You don't need to use a Web host that runs the FrontPage extensions, but you'll be missing out on many of the features within FrontPage if you don't. If your Web host service does not have the extensions, you'll probably want to consider moving the site to one that the Web host services have provided. You can find a list at **http://www.microsoft.com/ frontpage**; see Figure 2.1.

Figure 2.1 Microsoft provides the FrontPage server extensions at its Web site, free of charge.

The Ideal Web Host

If your Web server doesn't have FrontPage extensions and you set out to convince the administrator that they should be installed at his or her earliest convenience, you're likely to face an issue you'll encounter again and again. Server administrators—whether they work at Internet service providers or at corporate MIS departments—don't always look kindly on requests from users. They have their hands filled with requests from management for work that's considered slightly more important, like adding users to the system, finding lost passwords, and restoring accidentally deleted files. They regularly receive requests for new applications and fear the new software will introduce incompatibilities with the software already running. Don't be too surprised when your network administrator is less than thrilled to see this new request.

If you have a network administrator who's happy to add the extensions and is able to supply you with the configuration help you need, you're lucky.

The rest of us need to face the issue of control. You can run a Web site without control over the server, but it's hard. Not only do you miss out on the convenience of running FrontPage extensions, you lose the ability to install new applications. For example, many Web sites are adding video and audio files that require the installation of additional server software, such as Progressive Networks' RealAudio, VDOnet Live Server, or Xing StreamWorks. These programs are servers that stream files in their own unique formats, and they must run on a Web server as a process separate from the HTTP server. You can't install such software without the cooperation of the administrator. The software must be installed on the physical system, and it will require changes to the server configuration.

Even the addition of simple multimedia files that don't require their own server will require the help of an administrator. The HTTP server software must have a MIME listing in the registry of services for each file type you use on your pages. Common file types, like GIF graphics, are part of the minimum installation for any HTTP server. But if you insert a relatively new type of file, such as a WAV sound file, it will not be available to users unless the administrator updates the server's MIME registry. Adding a new MIME type can be either a cumbersome task that the administrator is loathe to perform or an easy job that will be completed in minutes. It depends partly on the workload of the administrator and partly on the Web server used. For example, updating the MIME registry on Microsoft NT Internet Information Server, shown in Figure 2.2, is an awkward tasks that is difficult to do correctly.

Chapter 2—Building Your Web Site on Solid Ground

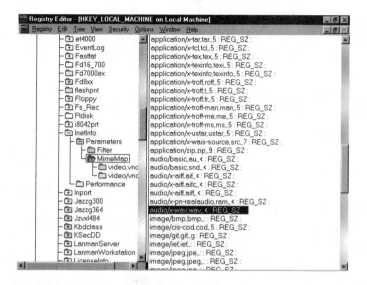

Figure 2.2 Updating the registry in MS Internet Information Server with a new MIME type.

But if the Web server is O'Reilly's WebSite, adding a new MIME type is easy, as shown in Figure 2.3.

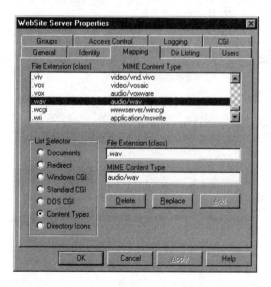

Figure 2.3 Adding a new MIME type to O'Reilly's WebSite.

You can build a simple Web site with only minimal cooperation from your Web administrator. But to reach your maximum potential, you'll need to have a good amount of control over the host's services.

Will Your Pages Be Public or Private?

Pages that are created for the World Wide Web are either completely private or completely public. When the pages are stored on your personal system, they're private since only people who can view your screen are able to see the pages. When you move your pages to a Web server on the World Wide Web, suddenly millions of people can see the pages, since anyone with Internet access and a browser can reach the server where the pages are stored.

In many organizations, however, the company's intranet creates a middle ground. After you move your Web pages to the network's Web server, your Web host will be accessible only to the company's private intranet; only members of the organization who have access to that network can view the pages. In order to place your pages in the public World Wide Web, the server you use must be registered on a domain name server that's part of the Web.

If you need to create a Web site on the public Internet and your organization has not created one, you'll need to use one of the techniques described on the following pages.

It's not uncommon for people who work in large corporations that only have an intranet to buy Web hosting services in order to create a public Web site. You may want to sit down with your company's network administrator before you decide whether you need a Web host.

NOTE
Some organizations find that it's more cost effective to rent Web host services from an outside company rather than install new hardware, new software and new telecommunications services on the company intranet.

You may want to create different types of Web sites for different purposes, publishing some pages on your company's intranet and others on the World Wide Web. Keep in mind that some members of your organization may not have access to the World Wide Web and may be able to see your pages only if they're published on the company's intranet.

Finally, perhaps the most important consideration is the URL for your site. To gain maximum exposure for your site, you'll want to register a name that describes the site and is easy to remember. A Web address like `www.smith.com/news` is more memorable than `www.smith.com/pub/html/mktg/news`. One of the advantages of having control over your Web site is the ability to decide how to construct the URLs. Your ability to register a domain name for a site with Internic is not affected by your choice of a Web host, but you'll probably create separate pages that don't require their own unique domain name if for no other reason than the fact that registering and maintaining a domain name costs money.

The FrontPage Personal Web Server

The FrontPage CD-ROM comes with the FrontPage Persona Web Server, a program that provides the most rudimentary features of an HTTP server. It's performance is not strong enough to enable you to get a Web server off the ground, but it's enough to test the waters. The program is included with FrontPage mainly so that you can test the features in FrontPage that require server extensions on a desktop, before the site is moved to the active Web site.

If you don't have access to a Web site, you can create a kind of "mini-server" environment simply by loading the Personal Web Server and FrontPage together and then using a browser to contact the personal server. You'll quickly see why it's not a good idea to run this program as your Web server: it's much too slow.

Choosing a Home for Your Site

If you're already happy with the Web server you use, congratulate yourself on having solved one big piece of the puzzle and then jump ahead to the next chapter. Everyone else will need to seriously evaluate their options for their Web host, making sure they'll have sufficient control over the resources to allow for continued growth.

The technology behind the Internet and the Web was created in order to encourage the widest number of people to take part. Consequently, there are many ways to build a Web site, but they fall into three general categories:

- *You can take total control.* You'll buy your own computer, set up a direct Internet connection, install a Web server, and build all the pages by yourself with your own software.
- *You can use space on one of your company's servers.* It probably won't add anything to your department's budget, but you'll need to have the cooperation of the LAN (local area network) administrator.
- *You can rent space from a Web host,* paying modest monthly fees that are a fraction of the cost of doing it yourself.

There's no right way to do it. You can structure it any way that suits you and your budget.

Total Control: Master of Your Own Host

Controlling the Web hardware is clearly the most expensive option, but it's also the only way to gain total control. You can add the software you want, when you want. You can add new processing speed, memory, and storage as needed. And you can dedicate the entire system to your Web pages, eliminating the delays that arise when several sites share a system.

One of the biggest fixed expenses in running your own Web server is the telecommunications and access charges for your Internet connection. Many people on a corporate network are able to avoid this expense by tying into the existing Internet connection and incurring expenses only for the computer and Web server software.

If you'll be bringing a new Internet connection to your offices, your first step is to shop for a local Internet Service Provider (ISP). Hundreds of companies are in this business, and many of the companies that sell individual accounts for modem access can also install a dedicated line at speeds appropriate for running a Web server. You can choose from a number of large companies like NetCom, Uunet, and PSI; they provide Internet service on a national scale and employ a small army of trained

CHAPTER 2—Building Your Web Site on Solid Ground

technicians. Or you may find better rates and service through a small company that operates in your area. Contact at least three and ask for bids. The costs are affected dramatically by the bandwidth (or data rate) that will be used to connect your Web site to the Internet.

TIP

The cost of a dedicated Internet connection ranges from about $300 a month for ISDN access but can go as high as $2,000 a month for T3 speed.

The computer system you use for the Web host must be compatible with the Web server software you select. It must also run a network operating system that's compatible with the Web server software (for example, Windows NT). A good choice for users of FrontPage would be Windows NT 4.0 as the network operating system and either Microsoft Internet Information Server or O'Reilly WebSite as the HTTP server software.

The system will need to have at least 24 Megabytes of RAM, over 1 Gigabyte of storage, and a communications adapter needed to reach your Internet connection. For example, if you share the Internet connection with other computers in your office, you probably use a Ethernet 10Base T adapter. If you're setting up the system to connect directly to an Internet service provider over an ISDN phone line (one of the least expensive options for a direct Internet connection), you'll need an ISDN adapter.

Installing your own Web host is not especially difficult as long as you have all the information you'll need from your ISP. In Windows NT, you configure the options from the Control Panel under Networks, as seen in Figure 2.4.

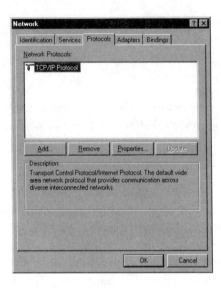

Figure 2.4 Beginning to configure a server in the Windows NT Control Panel.

You'll need to know the host name, network settings (including domain name server, subnet mask, and gateway IP address), and the IP address for this system. If you have all the information at hand as you install the software, the process of connecting and configuring your system should take only a few hours.

The setup software for the networking operating system and Web server will prompt you for the information you'll need when you install it, but you can also add it later, after the operating system is installed.

After you go through this process, you'll be prepared to master every new technology as it comes to the Web. Owning your own Web server is the only way to guarantee that you have complete control over your Web site. The time you spend setting up your own site will be paid back many times over.

Unfortunately, this option is a budget-buster. Most Web masters will need to surrender some control over the Web site in order to stay within their budget.

CHAPTER 2—Building Your Web Site on Solid Ground

WARNING

You'll need to plan for backing up a site if you host it on your own computer. And if your business requires that the Web site be online 24-hours a day, you'll need to make arrangements to have another server mirror the site for constant backup.

Sharing a Corporate Network

Running the system on your company's network is probably the easiest and least expensive option for anyone who has access to a network running the TCP/IP. Of course, you must be sure that the corporate network will reach your audience. The network must have a domain name server on the public Internet if you want your site to be on the World Wide Web.

The computer system will be comparable to the system described in the previous section. You'll need to consider how much of the Web maintenance you provide and how much will be provided by the company's computer support technicians. You'll have more control over the site if you're willing to install the network operating system and server software by yourself, even though you'll probably need help from the network administrator. The job can be made easier if you buy a system sold as a Web server; Dell, Compaq, Sun, and other hardware manufacturers offer this type of configuration. Because the system is sold with all the components you'll need, you won't have to worry about matching the hardware and software.

To establish a system as a Web server running on the company's network, you'll need to ask the administrator of the main network to register your system as a host on the network and to provide you with a name for the system as well as the IP address the server will use. If you run Windows NT on the server, you'll be able to configure the system by running the Networks module in the Control Panel. You'll need to enter the IP address assigned to your location, the name of the primary name server, and the host name for this system. Most of the necessary information will be stored in the TCP/IP Properties dialog box. Figure 2.5 shows a typical Web configuration.

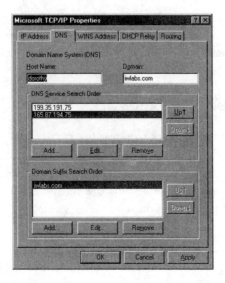

Figure 2.5 Configuring the name for a Web server.

You may try the FrontPage Personal Web Server on a trial basis, but as explained in "The FrontPage Personal Web Server," performance will be a problem. You'll end up wanting a real Web server before long.

Shopping for Web Host Services

The most economical way to provide the Web server for a site on the World Wide Web is to buy host services. You'll need to devote less time to the job of maintaining the system, and you'll spend less on hardware and network access fees.

Fees start at around $15 a month for the most basic services, but advanced options can add hundreds of dollars a month. Even at several hundred dollars a month for a Web host service, you'll probably spend much less than you would to install your own Web host. And you'll spend less time negotiating with your friendly network administrators.

TIP

You will need to have Internet access to maintain your Web site, but you don't need to buy Internet access from the same company who provides your Web host service.

In shopping for host services, be sure that your host has FrontPage extensions installed on the Web server. Fortunately, it's easy to find companies that do: Microsoft publishes a list at its Web site (see Figure 2.6).

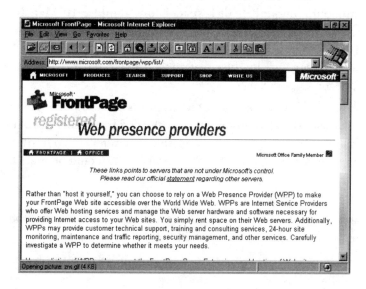

Figure 2.6 Services that provide FrontPage extensions listed at Microsoft's Web site.

Each of the companies listed at this site has a Web site linked to the listing on Microsoft's list, so it's easy to compare the rates and services for a number of companies. You can go directly to the list of host services, which Microsoft calls "Web presence providers," using this URL.

http://www.microsoft.com/frontpage/wpp/list

Don't be shy about comparing the different services. You're likely to be using the service for months or years. Even though it's possible to change your Web host and have a domain name transferred, it's extra work. And many Web host services charge a setup fee when opening the new account. Price is one of your concerns, but some of the following factors can have an impact on your level of satisfaction.

- What is the speed of their Internet connection? This consideration tells you how quickly your Web pages will be able to reach people across the Internet. At the minimum, the host service should use a T1

- connection; some boast T2 or greater. A fractional T1 line is slower, because they share it with others.

- How much disk space is included in the fee? Most services offer a minimum amount of disk space (for example, 10 Megabytes) and charge for space beyond that. Others set no limit. You may not have 10 Megabytes of data now, but you will if your site grows. Also, your site will generate log files that could grow to more than 1 Megabyte if it becomes popular.

- What is the limit on traffic? Many hosts allow a minimum amount of *bandwidth* (the amount of data downloaded by visitors to your site) and charge for data traffic beyond the minimum. If your site becomes popular, a service that has a low monthly fee could be more expensive in the long run.

- Do you need to have your domain name transferred? They should be able to do it for you; some services charge a fee beyond the Internet registration service charged by Internic.

- How much is the setup fee? Fees range from zero to several hundred dollars.

- Do they offer additional servers for your site, such as RealAudio, a video server, or an SQL server? Most Web hosts do not offer these extras, but some do.

- Will they provide virtual hosting? If you want to register your own domain name (example, www.smith.com), you'll need this feature. When a service offers *virtual hosting*, it creates a directory on it's own Web servers that receives traffic to your domain. To everyone on the Web, you seem to have your own server ,but the Web host service actually hosts the domain name on its servers.

- Will they forward e-mail from your Web site's domain to another e-mail account? This feature is useful if you use the site for a specific business purpose but don't want to starting monitoring a new e-mail account.

- Is there adequate tech support? Make sure that tech support will be available when you may need it. Some companies keep banker's hours, and others are on call 7 days a week. You may want to test the

CHAPTER 2—Building Your Web Site on Solid Ground

tech support's responsiveness; if they keep you on hold 20 minutes before you're a customer they won't be any better after you sign up.

The process of establishing your site at a Web host should take a day or two. After you place the order, the service should have your directory space set up within a few hours, but if you need to register a domain name for your site with the Web registration service Internic, you'll have to wait anywhere from a week to a month for the actual site name to be fully registered. Until the registration takes place, you should be able to access your site with a URL that is based on the Web host's domain.

TIP

Microsoft FrontPage is so much easier to use when your Web server runs the FrontPage extensions that you may want to switch to a Web host service that uses the extensions, even if you already have a Web site running with a host service.

The process of moving your Web site from one Web host service to another is not difficult. If your site is active, you'll want to be sure that you open the new account before you close the old one to guarantee that the new service is up and running in time. You can move your files from the old site in one of two ways.

- Use an FTP utility to download files from the old site and then upload them to the new site. You'll need to use this technique if you did not use FrontPage for the existing pages.

- Use FrontPage's **Copy Web** command to transfer the pages to the new site.

The new Web host service should be able to transfer a domain name from one server to the new one in a day or two. You may incur a separate charge for this service, or it may be included in the setup fee.

45

CHAPTER 3
WEB SITE BUILDING BLOCKS

Many Web sites seem so impressive that you might think the technology is complex and forbidding. Nothing could be further from the truth. The essential structure of a Web site is very simple.

This chapter will explain the basic building blocks of a Web site. You'll become familiar with the file types that are essential to a Web site and the optional components that you can use to dazzle your audience.

Because FrontPage spares you from many of the technical details of Web construction, you may be tempted to ignore this chapter. And if you're experienced in Web design, you may find the material is too basic. But it's essential to understand how Web sites are constructed so that you don't become tangled in threads of your own making.

HTML PAGES: THE FOUNDATION OF YOUR SITE

HTML is everywhere on the Web. Every Web site, from the smallest to the largest, is created with files in HTML format. Although new technologies for multimedia and interactivity are being introduced every day, none of them dares to undermine the stature of HTML. These new file types are essentially subservient to HTML. Browsers can reach them only after first displaying an HTML file and selecting a link—often called a *hyperlink*—written in HTML code.

Millions of users running Web browsers are able to display HTML pages, so if you want to communicate with this vast audience—or even a small subset—you need to respect the conventions of HTML. Fortunately, FrontPage works within HTML's framework. To understand this process, let's look at how Web sites really work.

Finding the HTML Files at a URL

When a Web browser contacts a Web site, the browser is really making a request to the Web server for the HTML file at the site. The process begins on the browser's *URL line* (that's the line labeled *Location* on Netscape Navigator and *Address* in Microsoft Explorer). The URL entered must start with the protocol to be used (that's *http://* for Web documents) and then contain the exact location of the file. Sometimes, the URL includes a file name for this HTML file. In the following address, the URL includes a domain name (*itour.com*) and a file (*govt.html*):

```
http://www.itour.com/govt.html
```

Other URL's don't require a specific file name because the Web server software at the Web site will load an HTML file when the domain name is called. For example, in the following URL, the file **index.html** is loaded when a browser contacts the domain:

```
http://www.itour.com
```

You don't need to type in the name of the file **index.html** because of a simple rule. Web server software can display a default HTML file when browsers invoke the top-level directory for the domain. At the **itour.com** site, the Web server software specifies that the default page should be named **index.html**. As long as such a file is stored in the directory, the browser doesn't need to specify the file name. Figure 3.1 shows a listing of the files at this Web site. Both **govt.htmt** and **index.html** are stored in the root directory. (The software used for this illustration is WS_FTP, a shareware program that lets you see directories and transfer files to other computers on the Internet.)

CHAPTER 3—Web Site Building Blocks

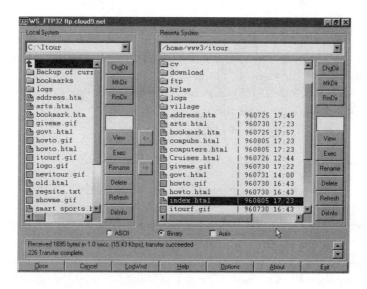

Figure 3.1 The listing of files at www.itour.com.

WARNING

Many Web sites put an extra burden on visitors by failing to properly name the page that should be displayed first at their site. This usually happens because the person creating the page doesn't know the correct name for this default file. The most common default names are **welcome.html** and **index.html**.

The same holds true of files in directories. On the Web server that hosts **itour.com**, there is a directory called **/cv**. Because this directory has another file named **index.html**, the following is a valid URL.

    http://www.itour.com/cv

Thanks to this simple convention, Web sites are usually organized around a main page, usually called the *home page*.

NOTE

Because it's so much easier for people to remember your main address, you'll want to treat the home page as a focal point for your site. All major categories should be accessible from this page, and secondary pages should have a link back to the home page.

49

Links: Local and Remote References

The concept of a home page works so well because every HTML file can have links to other files. Those other files can be located in the same directory or at other computers on the Internet. A link can even refer to a specific place in the same file.

The basic format of an HTML link is:

```
<a href="URL">text displayed by the browser</a>
```

The link consists of two separate HTML tags. All HTML tags begin and end with angle brackets (< and >). The first tag announces the beginning of an HTML code. The code for a link tag begins with a tag containing "a href," which is short for anchor hypertext. The characters appearing after the equal sign are the destination for the *link*, the file that will be displayed when the link is activated. Immediately following this instruction the closing angle bracket (>) appears, signaling that the tag is complete.

After the first tag, the words that appear on the Web page are entered. This is the visible link, and in most browsers it appears underlined and highlighted in blue, as shown in Figure 3.2. Following this text, a tag that closes the link must appear </a>: these closing tags are essential. If the closing tag did not appear, everything that followed the **href** tag would be perceived as a clickable link.

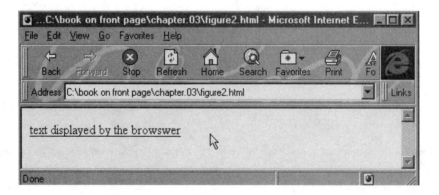

Figure 3.2 Microsoft Explorer displays a simple link.

It sounds easy to add links to HTML pages, and it is—until you start entering the URLs. The syntax of the URL must be precise. We've all vis-

CHAPTER 3—Web Site Building Blocks

ited pages where some of the links don't work. A number of different error messages appear, based on the type of mistake in the URL. When a browser requests a file from a valid domain that doesn't have the file in the directory specified, the server will send an error message reporting that the file couldn't be found.

Some link errors occur because the link points to a file that's stored somewhere else. When the error in the HTML link attempts to display a graphic that can't be found, the browser displays a "broken link" icon. Figure 3.3 shows what happens when Microsoft Internet Explorer encounters a link that doesn't work.

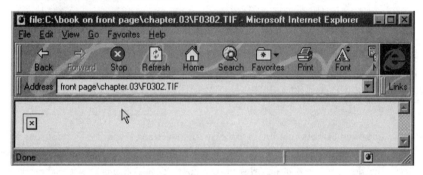

Figure 3.3 Microsoft Explorer showing it's "broken link" icon.

Each browser has its own way of handling the problem. Figure 3.4 shows how a missing graphic is represented in Netscape Navigator.

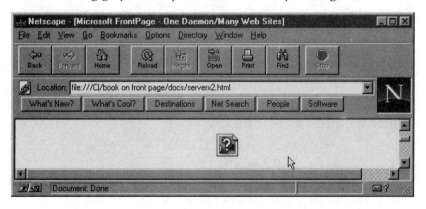

Figure 3.4 Netscape Navigator showing a "broken link."

51

To the person who clicks and sees an error, it doesn't matter if a link is remote or local, but it matters a lot to the Web browser. The main reasons why links don't work is that files are stored in the wrong place. The file may have been moved since the original link was written or the person who wrote the link didn't create the proper syntax for finding the file.

A remote link points to a different domain; a local reference points to files within the current domain. When you create remote references, you can refer to specific files at that domain as long as you include the complete path. When you create local references, you're referring to files within your Web's own directories and so you don't need the full path. You need only the name of folders that are stored in directories below the top-level directory.

Web sites can be kept organized with a directory structure that's identical to the directories used for storing files on your hard disk. The top-level directory is like a hard disk's root. Subdirectories below the root can be used for creating a structure.

NOTE

Local and remote references are easy to understand if you think of domains as hard disk directories. It's as if the World Wide Web was an enormous drive C:/ and all the domains were directories on the root. Most domains create elaborate structures of subdirectories branching off of their top-level directories.

The problem is compounded by the fact that most Web pages are not created on the system where they'll run. So the directory structure changes after the page is moved up to the Web server.

FrontPage solves this problem by creating a directory structure on your hard disk and tracking the links. When you move your Web pages to the server, FrontPage adjusts local references as the page moves. It can even verify remote links, helping to catch references to sites that were rearranged since you added the link.

Tags: Basic and Extended

The HTML pages displayed when a browser visits a Web site are a simple combination of the text you can read and tags. Although some of the text you read is contained in graphics, most of the text is formatted with

HTML tags. FrontPage inserts the tags based on selections you make from the program's menus and toolbars, but there are times when you may want to edit the tags directly. Understanding tags will also help you understand what you can and can't do with FrontPage.

The basic format of HTML codes starts with a tag that selects a formatting option, followed by the text that will appear on the page, and closed by a "slash" tag. For example, the following HTML code uses two different styles; it produces the page you see displayed in a browser in Figure 3.5.

```
<H1>An announcement</H2><p>We are pleased to announce the opening
of our new location.</P>
```

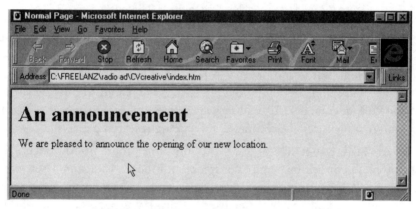

Figure 3.5 An example of the Head 1 and plain text tags.

You can also *nest* tags, formatting a section of text in between two existing tags. For example, to add emphasis to a few words on the same bit of HTML code, you would use the **<strong>** tag.

```
<H1>An announcement</H2><p>We are <strong>pleased to announce
</strong>the opening of our new location.</P>
```

The **<strong>** tag is similar to boldface. This example will display "pleased to announce" in boldface, as shown in Figure 3.6.

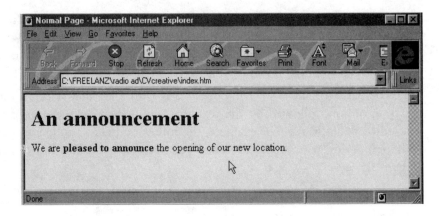

Figure 3.6 Adding an additional tag to the HTML code in Figure 3.5.

The HTML spec provides a long list of tags for formatting text and page layout. By combining the various tags, you can end up with a highly stylized design. But if you haven't worked with HTML before, it's important to keep in mind the limitations. HTML was created to provide structure for Web documents. After all, it was created by scientists and researchers who first envisioned a technique for sharing research papers.

HTML is not like a desktop publishing program. You do not have complete control over the appearance of a page. You cannot set margins or specify the point size of type. Instead, HTML provides a general framework, and the browser used to display a page controls the final appearance, as explained in Chapter 1. Fortunately, you won't need to learn all of HTML's rules. FrontPage keeps track of them and gives you the option of trying out different designs simply by choosing tools from the menus.

WARNING

HTML imposes so many limits that it is rarely a good idea to copy the design used in a printed document for a Web site. Be flexible as you create new pages, until you understand HTML's unique ways.

Once you understand the format for a tag, you can edit it directly using FrontPage's **View**, **HTML** command or by opening the HTML file with a word processor. However, specific rules govern the correct syntax for tags so it's best to not edit tags directly unless you are sure you know the correct syntax. You'll also find that FrontPage inserts tags that you didn't select. For example, you'll find several tags at the top of the HTML page created in Figure 3.6 with FrontPage using the HTML **View** command. These changes are shown in Figure 3.7.

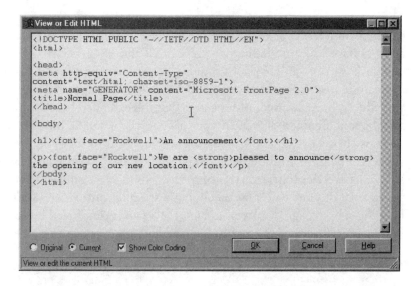

Figure 3.7 FrontPage inserts "meta" and "document" tags in all pages.

Extended Tags: Risky Business

Some of these tags are required for proper display of the page, such as the <HTML> tags. Others are purely optional. In Chapter 18 you'll learn some tricks that you can use with these optional meta tags.

Because browsers will ignore tags that they don't understand, HTML is evolving with new tags that can enhance page design. The extended tags produce exciting special effects on computers that have the latest software but will be ignored by other computers. FrontPage gives you easy access to all of these tags, but you need to be careful about how you use them. Remember that the HTML was designed so that all types of computers display the same page even if they didn't share the same resources.

WARNING

Many extended tags can produce beautiful effects on your system that cannot be duplicated on other systems. Avoid selecting a font when formatting text if you want others to see the same page you see.

The font format tags are one of the most problematic. Tags that add emphasis in a general way—such as headers, emphasis (including italics and boldface), and underlining—are part of the basic HTML spec and will display the same on all systems. Extended tags that increase or decrease text size almost always work since most computers (except the very oldest) have a variety of font sizes. But the extended tags that name a specific font are unpredictable if your page is on the public Internet. Only systems that have that font installed will be able to view the page. If you're working on an intranet where you know every user who visits the site will have the fonts you're using, then you can greatly enhance the appearance of your pages by specifying a specific font. Figure 3.8 shows how the simple page displayed in Figure 3.8 can be improved by specifying the fonts Rockwell, News Gothic, and Lucinda Handwriting.

Figure 3.8 Extended tags allow you to display fonts.

When this page is displayed by a browser that does not have the fonts installed, it will look like Figure 3.6. That's not a major problem, as long as you keep it in mind and, for example, don't refer to the "handwriting" in your announcement.

CHAPTER 3—Web Site Building Blocks

GRAPHIC FORMATS THAT COLOR THE WEB

HTML pages are the core of a Web site, but graphic images do more than add decoration. Because HTML has limited the special effects of text, many Web sites create highly stylized graphics. As you would expect, graphics are used to display product logo, photographs and diagrams. But they've also been used to dress up a page, adding spots of color and flair. Images are displayed by the HTML <IMG> tag. Browsers support two formats—GIF and JPEG.

WARNING

Graphic formats other than GIF and JPEG can be inserted into a page, but they will be displayed only if the browser displaying the page has installed a helper application or plug-in that can decode the image. The Web server must also have registered the graphic format.

A common use for graphics is to create a *clickable image*—when users click on the graphic, a link is activated. The technique is commonly used to call attention to an option that might be ignored if the link were displayed only with text. Chapter 6 explains the techniques you can use for inserting graphics. And Chapter 8 describes Image Composer, the software included on the FrontPage CD-ROM for creating and editing graphics.

Before you spend too much time working with graphics, you'll want to understand the differences between the two most common formats so that you choose the right format for the job. Table 3.1 summarizes the differences between the two types of files.

Table 3.1 Choosing the Right Graphic Format

Format	File Type	Best Uses
GIF	8-bit (256 colors)	Logos, icons, diagrams, decoration, drawings, and illustrations with fewer than 16 colors
JPEG	24-bit (16 million colors)	Photographs; drawings and illustrations with more than 16 colors

GIF: Fast and Flexible

The FrontPage CD-ROM comes with hundreds of GIF images. You can use them for anything from the background "wallpaper" to decorative art. Images stored as GIF (Graphics Interchange Format) files are by far the most common on the Web. The reason is that the format was designed specifically to be used by online systems (CompuServe deserves the credit for GIF). The files are compressed so that they require less time to download and the specification includes an error-checking protocol so that data losses that can occur with other graphics formats are minimal.

The GIF format also provides a few special features that have helped to define the unique graphic style of the Web. The most important, in my opinion, is the ability to set the background color making it possible to create a transparent effect. When you match the background color of the graphic with the background color of the page, the graphic seems to float on top of the page rather than display the more traditional boxy look of many publications. Figure 3.9 shows a page that includes several GIF images. The large logo for iWORLD uses white as a transparent background color to help it blend in with the rest of the page.

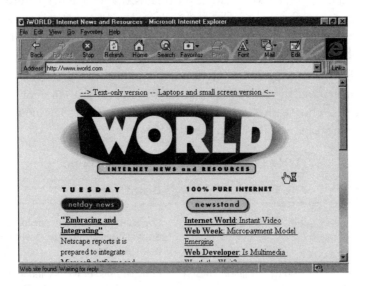

Figure 3.9 Transparent GIF files blend in with the background.

Less common, but more striking, is animation. An extension to the GIF spec, known as *GIF89a* makes it possible to string together a series of images in a single file. When the file is displayed by a browser, the illusion of motion is created: like a Saturday morning cartoon, GIF89a files create animation by playing several images quickly in sequence.

GIF is great for splashes of color and high impact, but it cannot be used for very complex or photo-realistic images. The format can display a palette of only 256 colors because it is an 8-bit format.

JPEG: For Quality and Realism

The JPEG format is all about quality. It was created by a group of photographers interested in preserving the integrity of their work and is the most commonly used format for displaying photographic images. JPEG stands for Joint Photographic Experts Group; JPEG file names are shortened to JPG to conform with the three-letter convention for file name suffixes used on UNIX and PCs.

JPEG's specialty is compressing files that have continuous tones, such as photography. The compression can provide reductions as great as 10 to 1. GIF provides a lower rate of compression—only about a 4 to 1 reduction—but JPEGs are usually much larger because they contain more data. The JPEG format is a 24-bit format, providing up to 16 million colors. As a result, a JPEG image will usually be a larger file size than a GIF image. And JPEG images take slightly longer to decode and display than GIF images after they are downloaded.

As long as you start with good quality photography, you can display excellent images in the JPEG format, but keep in mind that the JPEG compression algorithm is designed for subtle gradations of color. It falls in the category of "lossy" compression methods, meaning a (very, very) small amount of data is lost during the process of shrinking and unshrinking the file. The loss is virtually unnoticeable in most applications. If your images suffer a loss of quality between the original and on-screen display, the most likely culprit is a problem with the settings used for scanning the image. Figure 3.10 shows a photograph taken on the lunar surface during the Apollo 15 mission; NASA displays the image at its Web site as a JPG file.

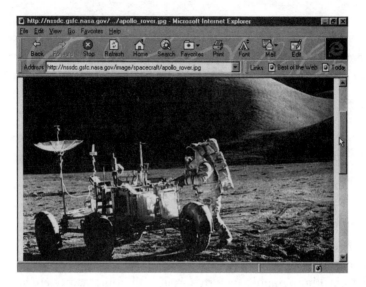

Figure 3.10 The JPEG format does an excellent job at displaying continuous tones.

JPEG does a poor job of displaying simpler images, such as line drawings. In general, don't use JPEG for images that have fewer than 16 colors or 16 shades of gray.

OTHER WAYS OF INTERACTING

This chapter has explored the traditional ways of building a Web site—if you can call something that's only a few years old, traditional. HTML formatting and images are the tools that were used to build the World Wide Web to well over 20 million pages.

The HTTP specification, however, is being extended with other ways of presenting information. Multimedia files can be as simple as a short sound clip or an interactive presentation. Scripts can be short question-and-answer sessions or software applications that rival traditional desktop programs.

In later chapters we'll explore how to exploit all these opportunities. But to understand how they fit in to the basic essence of a Web site, there are just a few points to understand.

Multimedia of All Kinds

Multimedia covers a broad range of topics. Strictly speaking, any type of data that is not static is multimedia. Moving images and audio are the broadest categories, but new developments are pushing the borders all the time.

Sound files at their simplest are simple audio clips, ranging from the sound files that play when Windows opens to recordings of speeches, which are available at some Web sites. There are a number of general-purpose sound formats. WAV, AU, and AIFF are common on the Web, and most browsers can play clips in these formats, as long as the system has multimedia support. They haven't been widely used because it takes so long to download clips of any meaningful length.

Newer technologies make it possible to play sound in a streaming fashion so that users don't need to wait for the entire file to download before the file begins to play. RealAudio is the most common of these formats. Most sound files take so long to download because they need to include data for the sound as it was recorded and as it plays back. One music file format, however, is more compact. The MIDI format (Musical Instrument Digital Interchange) records music in a structured format that represents tones as numbers. Thanks to the small file size, MIDI files are starting to be used as background music for Web sites.

Motion pictures can also be inserted into a Web site. AVI is the Windows Video for Windows format, MOV is the Macintosh QuickTime format, and MPEG is a fairly popular format for compressing motion picture clips. Browsers are beginning to add software for playing these files back; older browsers play movie files only if a plug-in application is installed.

You can insert any of these multimedia formats into a Web page using the FrontPage **Insert** command. FrontPage inserts the HTML code that's required to execute the link.

Scripts That Communicate

Users who visit a Web site can interact with a site only to a limited extent. They can display different files, but they can't send data back to the site unless a script is used. There are a number of different ways to add scripts to a site. The section, "The Rules of the Web," in Chapter 1 outlined the most popular.

Scripts are inserted into HTML pages as self-contained programs. When the page is displayed by a browser, the script is executed but only if the browser supports the language used by the script. For example, Active X is supported by Microsoft Explorer 3.x and Netscape Navigator 4.x. Earlier versions of these browsers and all other browsers can't run Active X scripts.

Scripts can be inserted into FrontPage Web pages using the **Insert**, **Script** command. You don't need to be a programmer to add scripts to your Web site. The FrontPage wizards makes it possible to create JavaScript or VBScript routines by choosing menu items; the wizard inserts the correct code in the page. And if you write scripts or have access to code written by a programmer, you can add them to your pages using FrontPage's menus. Chapter 16 explains the techniques at length.

PART II
BUILDING YOUR WEB SITE

CHAPTER 4

THE TWO FACES OF FRONTPAGE

FrontPage is far from being a simple program. It includes several distinct programs, along with several megabytes of clip art, a Web server and two distinctly different automated scripts: wizards and WebBots. Plus, if you have the FrontPage Bonus Pack, you also get Image Composer, a graphics editor. Each of these tools will be covered in the chapters that follow.

To get the most from these tools, you will want to be thoroughly familiar with two programs that form the heart of FrontPage: the FrontPage Explorer and the FrontPage Editor. All other tools can be opened from menu commands within these programs.

Just to make things more confusing than they need to be, Microsoft has used Explorer in one product name after another. In case you're starting to lose track of all the different Explorers, here's a brief rundown:

- Windows Explorer is the file-management utility that comes with Windows 95.

- Internet Explorer is the Web browser that Microsoft offers for free (it's included on the FrontPage Bonus Pack CD-ROM; if you didn't get it, you can download it from Microsoft's Web site at www.microsoft.com).

- FrontPage Explorer is the Web management software that loads first when you click on the Microsoft FrontPage icon.

In this chapter, we'll learn basic operational procedures for FrontPage Explorer and FrontPage Editor. You'll learn the interface, the configuration options, and the most essential commands in each of these distinct programs, and you'll see how they interoperate. All these features are fundamental to how you'll work with FrontPage and how you'll structure your Webs.

FRONTPAGE EXPLORER: THE BIG PICTURE

FrontPage Explorer is designed to be a kind of control center for your Web sites. The program's graphical display allows you to see how the files in your Web are related to each other. Without Explorer, a Web site is just a list of HTML, GIF, and other files. But when you look at a Web with FrontPage Explorer, you see a diagram that shows the links connecting files.

TIP Explorer offers features that aren't essential to the job of creating a Web site. In fact, you can use FrontPage without using the Editor at all. It offers so many helpful tools that it can make the job of managing a Web much easier.

FrontPage Explorer also offers a few other features that aren't as obvious as the Web diagram. Using Explorer you can:

- Import a Web site you created with another program into the FrontPage environment.
- Spell check the text on every page in a Web site with one command.
- Replace a word or phrase on every page in a Web site with just one command.
- Keep track of tasks that are incomplete on a To Do list.
- Confirm the validity of links between pages, graphics, and URLs.
- Move a site from your system to a public server without changing URLs from local file references to server references.
- Control access to your Web site with password protection.
- Perform file management, including renaming, deleting, and moving files or folders, both on your system and on the server.

It's worth keeping these features in mind because you can pass Explorer right by and never use any of these features. Explorer opens when you launch FrontPage, but after you open a Web site, the FrontPage Editor loads and you may forget about the Explorer.

After you look at these features and understand what they can do, you won't want to miss out. Some of these features—like the To Do list and spell checking across a Web site—will be covered in later chapters since they are useful only after you've created Webs and are revising your work. In the following sections, we'll look at the tools you'll want to master right from the beginning.

OPENING WEBS IN FRONTPAGE EXPLORER

When you open FrontPage Explorer, you have the option of choosing the Web site you're going to work with. The opening dialog box, shown in figure 4.1, lets you open the Web you worked on most recently, import a new Web, or create a new Web from scratch. (The first time you run Microsoft FrontPage, you will be prompted to open a tutorial Web.)

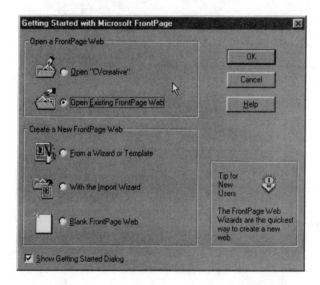

Figure 4.1 FrontPage Explorer's opening dialog box.

You can also choose an option to build a new Web, using FrontPage wizards and templates. This option offers a head start on your Web site. The wizard will prompt you to select a variety of features for a Web site and then generate the Web. Chapter 5 explores at length the process of building a Web with templates.

If you're building a new Web from scratch and don't want FrontPage to offer help, select the option **Blank FrontPage Web** from the Getting Started dialog box. You'll see the dialog box in Figure 4.2; selecting **Normal** will create a blank page for your new Web. (If the Getting Started dialog box is not open, you can achieve the same result by selecting **File, New, FrontPage Web**.)

Figure 4.2 Your choices in opening a new Web.

Explorer's Graphical Overview

The FrontPage Explorer screen provides the big picture on every Web site you manage. The left-hand side of the screen lists every URL in the Web, and the right-hand side displays a diagram of the Web where every link is represented by a line. See Figures 4.3a and 4.3b.

CHAPTER 4—The Two Faces of FrontPage

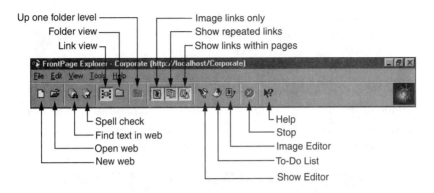

Figure 4.3a

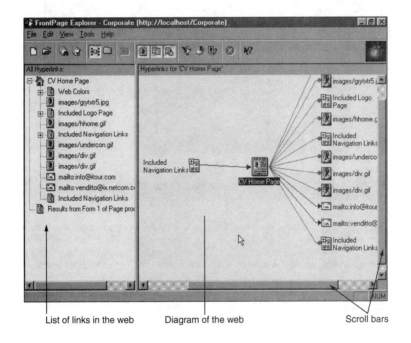

Figure 4.3b FrontPage Explorer lists a Web's URLs on the left and displays a diagram on the right.

This display can give you insight into how your Web works and may suggest ways you can improve it. It may look like a graphic program, but it's not. You can't drag the icons in the diagram; they're here only to show

how all the pages in your Web connect to other URLs. Every link, including links to files you create, links to pages on the World Wide Web, and even links to e-mail ("mailto" URLs), are displayed.

The opening view for a Web is the first page; usually, that's the **index.htm** file. When you select a different link from the list in the left window, the diagram on the right will change to show the links to this file; only files and URLs that link to this file will be seen. Figure 4.4 shows the same Web as in Figure 4.3 after a different link was selected.

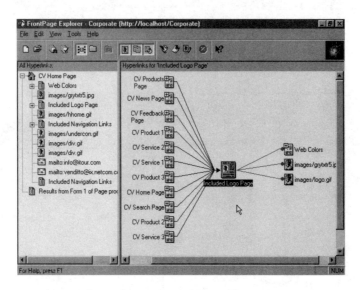

Figure 4.4 The Web diagram changes according to the link you select from the list.

TIP

A good way to review a Web is to move down the list of links to see how the diagram changes as each link is selected. If you want to encourage your audience to see all your Web, be sure there are plenty of links that connect pages and not just one link from the main page to secondary pages.

The size of the two windows in FrontPage Explorer can be adjusted for a better view. Drag the border in the center of the display to increase the size of one of the panes. If part of the display becomes hidden, you can use the scroll bars at the bottom and sides to move hidden sections into view.

FINE-TUNING YOUR WEB VIEW

You have a number of different options for changing the perspective on the Web. FrontPage Explorer lets you control these options with the toolbar icons that run along the top of the display. When you move your mouse slowly over the icons, a small window will open to describe the tool. You can also find a command for each of these tools listed on the drop-down menus.

Showing Links among Pages and URLs

To show all links to a URL, click on the URL's icon in the diagram view and right-click your mouse. A dialog box will open with the option, **Move to Center**, as shown in Figure 4.5. Select this option and the diagram will be redrawn, showing every link to this URL. You can accomplish the same effect by double-clicking on the URL's name in the list view.

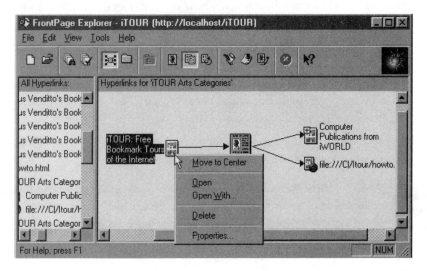

Figure 4.5 Right-click on a URL to select the option of making this URL the center of the Web view.

To view the file that is referenced by a URL, double-click on the icon in the graphic view or right-click on the icon and select **Open** from the menu that opens. HTML files will open in FrontPage Editor; graphic files will open in Image Composer.

Revealing Repeated Links

Often, you'll want to create more than one link between two files. For example, you'll want your main or home page to link with other important pages, but you'll want to provide a link back to the home page so that visitors to your site will be encouraged to see all of it.

You have two ways to display such multiple links between URLs in Explorer: you can either click on the **Repeated Hyperlinks** button or select the **View, Repeated Hyperlinks** menu command. The view will change to show a separate icon and line for every single link between two URLs. With this option turned off, only one line and icon would appear. For example, if your main page had two links to page 2, with the **Repeated Hyperlinks** option turned off, you would see only one link; turn the option on and the display will show the link twice, as shown in Figure 4.6.

For most of your work, you'll probably want to keep the option off because it can create the impression that you have more pages in your Web than really exist. In the Web shown in Figure 4.6, only two pages exist: Home Page and Page 2. But because there are two links from Home Page to Page 2, FrontPage Explorer shows two icons for Page 2.

You'll want to use this command after your Web is fairly well developed and you're reviewing the overall structure.

TIP
When the **View, Repeated Hyperlinks** option is turned on, your home page and other important pages should show many repeated links. If they don't, consider adding more links between your most important pages and supporting pages.

CHAPTER 4—The Two Faces of FrontPage

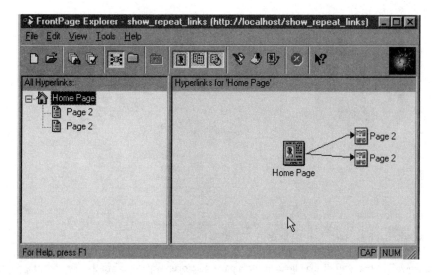

Figure 4.6 The Repeated Hyperlinks option shows an extra icon every time you have two links between URLs.

Showing Links inside Pages

Links inside a page go by many different names. Some software programs call them internal anchor links, and others call them intra-page links. In FrontPage Editor, they're known as Bookmarks, but when you're using FrontPage Explorer, they're called Hyperlinks Inside Pages. (Go figure!)

To show links that exist within a page, select the option **Hyperlinks Inside Pages** or select the command **View, Hyperlinks Inside Pages**. This option is similar to the **Repeated Hyperlinks** command in that it will display duplicate icons for a page. Figure 4.7 shows the same Web seen in Figure 4.6 with the **Hyperlinks Inside** option turned on. Because Home Page contains a link from one part of the file to another, the Explorer view adds a second icon for Home Page.

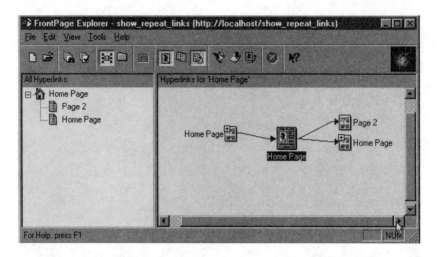

Figure 4.7 When you display links inside a page, Explorer will duplicate the icon for the page.

FOLDER VIEW VERSUS HYPERLINK VIEW

FrontPage Explorer has two faces of its own. You can view a Web as a graphic representation, with icons depicting every file and URL. This is known as the hyperlink view. Or you can view the Web as a list of files and URLs, similar to file management programs. This is known as the folder view.

Hyperlink view shows links between files and URLs, so it's useful for viewing the structure of a Web site. However, you can't do much with the Web's structure in hyperlink view. To fix problems, you need either to load a file in FrontPage Editor or to switch to the Explorer's folder view.

In folder view you can rename files, delete files, or move them from one folder to another.

Switching from Hyperlink to Folder View

To change the view so that names of files, rather than icons, are displayed, click on the **Folder View** tool or select the **View, Folder View** command from the menus. Figure 4.8 shows a Web using the **Folder View** option. To change it back to the graphic display, click on the **Hyperlink View** tool or select the **View, Hyperlink View** command.

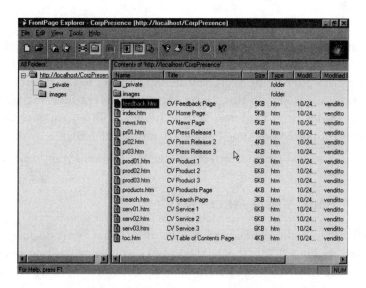

Figure 4.8 The folder view displays file names rather than icons.

Managing Server Folders with Explorer

FrontPage Explorer's folder view is essential for managing the structure of a Web. For example, to create a new directory on a Web site, you need to use the folder view. The more traditional way of managing folders on a Web server—FTP and Telnet programs—can cause problems for a FrontPage Web site because FrontPage manages the Web structure using index files that can be updated only by the combination of FrontPage Explorer and FrontPage server extensions.

A typical way to structure a Web site is to run a single Web site from a main domain (www.mycompany.com). Normally, the files in this domain would correspond with one of the Webs you create with FrontPage. When you publish your files, FrontPage will move the files from your hard disk Web to the server domain. But if you want to maintain a totally independent Web site, not connected to the Web pages at the main domain (for example, www.mycompany.com/expansion), you will want to create a new folder on the server for this new site (for example a folder named *expansion*). Then when a browser looks for the URL:

```
http://www.mycompany.com/expansion
```

the **index.htm** file in this folder will load. You can create and manage this Web on your local system with FrontPage, but before you use FrontPage Explorer to publish the Web, you should connect to the server and create the new folder. To do this, select the Web server's root and select **File, New, Folder** from Explorer. When the new folder icon appears on the server's root directory, type in a new name for the folder.

You can also rename, move, and delete folders on your local system.

Keeping Your View Accurate

You'll often make changes to a Web after it has been displayed in the FrontPage Editor. Whether you add links or change existing links, much of our work in FrontPage Editor will alter the structure of the Web. When you switch back to FrontPage Editor, the view of the Web will not reflect all your changes until you select the **Refresh** command from the menus or using the shortcut **F5**. Remember that you need to save your changes in FrontPage Editor before the changes will be reflected; fortunately, the **Refresh** command will remind you to save your work in FrontPage Editor if files are open.

The Secret Ingredients in a FrontPage Web

No matter what type of Web you create—even a simple blank Web using the Normal template—FrontPage generates a series of files and folders as soon as you start the new Web. These files and folders are unique to FrontPage. They're not needed for the page to display properly on a HTTP server, and most Web sites don't employ them. But FrontPage Explorer uses this method so that it can better manage your site and give you access to the server extensions.

WARNING

If you create and save a new Web page in FrontPage Editor, without using the Explorer, FrontPage will not be able to manage the links in the page or publish the page on a server. You'll need to perform those tasks on your own.

CHAPTER 4—The Two Faces of FrontPage

The first thing FrontPage does when you start a new Web is to create a new folder on your hard disk where it will store files in this Web. FrontPage stores all Webs in the same folder. Unless you selected a different name for the folder when you installed FrontPage, the new folders are nested inside the folder:

c:\FrontPage Webs

Look at the hard disk on a system where FrontPage was installed and in the root directory. You'll find this folder and a number of other folders inside. Every new Web will be identified with its own folder (unless you override the default and store it elsewhere). Figure 4.9 shows the directory structure for the FrontPage folder after a Web entitled "normal" was created.

Figure 4.9 Viewing the folders created by the smallest FrontPage Web, "normal."

Not only does FrontPage create a folder for each Web you build, but the software also creates additional folders nested inside the main Web folder. These separate folders are created to store images, scripts, and permissions files. Even when you create a Web that's just a single page (for example, if you select the "normal" template with just a single page and no

77

graphics), FrontPage will still create this hierarchy of folders so that it will be ready for the goodies you add as you go along.

A look inside the folders will reveal the typical elements of a Web (for example, the **index.htm** file, which is the opening page for most Web sites) and the other Web pages you've created. But you'll also find files that are unique to FrontPage. For example, **#haccess.ctl** is a text file that stores parameters about the Web, including access privileges for the Web and directories where other components of the Web will be stored. Dig down into the folders nestled inside these main folders and you'll find a variety of files that control specific FrontPage features. For example, in the folder named

_vti_pvt

you'll find files that provide information for specific FrontPage features. The File **_x_todo.html** maintains chores on your Explorer To Do list. The **service.cnf** file stores settings the server will need to know about your Web including the name of the default welcome page and text character set.

Don't ever edit these files. When FrontPage Explorer publishes your Web on a Web server, many of these files are read by the server and will have a big impact on how your Web pages work. And as you work on your own system, the FrontPage Personal Web Server will read these files to determine how to execute scripts and establish configuration settings. (The only time they won't be needed is if you move your Web site to a server that is not using FrontPage extensions.) To satisfy your curiosity and spare you from the possibility of damaging one of these by opening one, here's what's inside one of them.

```
# -FrontPage-
IndexIgnore #haccess.ctl */.??* *~ *# */HEADER* */README* */_vti*
<Limit GET POST>
order deny,allow
deny from all
allow from all
```

```
</Limit>
<Limit PUT>
order deny,allow
deny from all
</Limit>
AuthName default_realm
AuthUserFile c:/frontpage\ webs/content/_vti_pvt/service.pwd
AuthGroupFile c:/frontpage\ webs/content/_vti_pvt/service.grp
```

Most of the entries in the **#haccess.ctl** file point to other files where a list of authorized users is stored.

Sharing and Controlling Access to Webs

If you are connected to a network or you have setup accounts for several users on a system, you can use FrontPage Editor to control who has permissions to work on the Web. When FrontPage is installed, the person who runs the setup software becomes the administrator for all the Webs created on that system. When working on a network where several people share access to the Webs, there will be several types of permissions. You will be able to set permissions to the Webs on your system, but Webs stored on a network server may not be under your control. The person who set up the FrontPage Explorer software on that network directory will control access.

The administrator has the authority to give other users control over the Webs created. By default, the administrator is the only person who has access to the Webs, and all Webs share the same permissions.

You have the option of giving other users access to the all the work done in FrontPage or granting permission to only some of the Web pages. You'll want to take advantage of this option if you want to keep some of your work private while giving some of your co-workers the freedom to work on other Webs. To establish a set of blanket permissions applying to all Webs, open the Root Web and choose the permissions to users and computers on your network. If you want to set a unique set of permissions for a specific Web, you first open that Web and edit the permissions. When you begin the process of editing permissions in anything other than the Root Web, FrontPage will ask you to confirm that you're setting up unique privileges for the Web, as shown in Figure 4.10. The reminder is useful because it's easy to forget that just because you've give someone access to one Web, it won't affect their ability to work on other Webs, unless you set permissions in the Root Web.

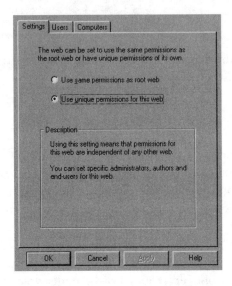

Figure 4.10 When users share a FrontPage system, you can control access to the Webs.

There are three types of permissions an administrator can control:

- Browsing rights control who can see the pages in the Web. By default, all users will have browsing rights as long as they have access to the system folders where the Webs are stored.
- Authoring rights establish who can browse and make changes to a Web. By default, the person who installed FrontPage and created a password for using the program is who has authoring rights.
- Administrator rights provide the authority to browse, make changes, and determine the access privileges of others on the network.

CHAPTER 4—The Two Faces of FrontPage

Keep in mind that your ability to control access to the Web is determined by the administrator of the network you're using. If FrontPage is installed on your own system, others will be able to use the privileges only if they have access to the files on your system. If your system is not connected to a network, you can add any user name that you want, but the user will need to be physically present at the system in order to access the files.

NOTE

Only someone who has administrator privileges can add or edit permissions. If the options in the Permissions dialog boxes are grayed out, you do not administrator privileges.

Follow these steps to grant others permission to access Webs.

1. Open FrontPage Explorer.
2. Open the Web you want to make available to others by selecting **File, Open FrontPage Webs** and choosing the Web from the dialog box that opens. If you want to provide the same access privileges for all Webs, choose **<Root Web>** as shown in Figure 4.11.

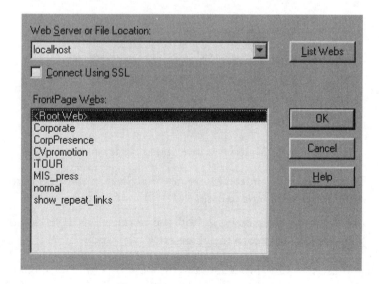

Figure 4.11 Selecting the Root Web.

81

3. Once the desired Web is open, select **Tools, Permissions** from the FrontPage Explorer menus. If you have not opened the Root Web, you'll see the message in Figure 4.10. Select the option **Use unique permissions for this Web**, and you'll be able to select which privileges are granted to specific users. (This dialog box does not appear when you open the Root Web.)

4. With the exception of this one tab, the Permissions dialog box provides the same choices for adding and editing privileges. There is a tab for managing users and another for managing computers, as shown Figure 4.12.

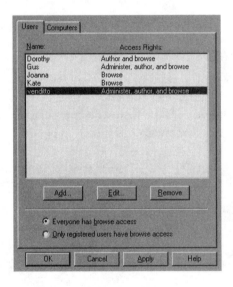

Figure 4.12 A list of users who have permissions to work on a Web.

5. To add a user, select the **Users** tab and click on the **Add** button. The Add Users dialog box will open.

6. Enter the name, password, and the permissions level for the user. Click on **OK** to record the changes.

You can use the same procedure to edit a user's permissions, change their password, or remove the permissions. When working on a local area network, you would normally set access privileges using a user's name. But you can also control access by specifying a computer's IP address. In step 4 above, if you select the **Computers** tab and click on the **Add** button, the dialog box in Figure 4.13 opens. Type in the IP address, choose the access level, and click on **OK** to confirm the settings.

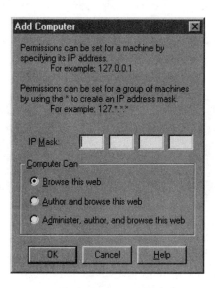

Figure 4.13 You can set access rights for a computer on your network.

Remember that the other computer will need to be able to access the FrontPage system. The network operator controls these permissions if you're running on a LAN. The technique can be used across the Internet if the other computer has a fixed IP address. If you allow another computer to access your system across the Internet, your system will need to be running server software to mange the connection, such as the FrontPage Personal Web Server (see the section on the Personal Web Server at the end of this chapter).

T I P

You can allow FrontPage users to have access to your system so that they can edit Webs on your hard disk. They'll need to know your system's network name or IP address, you'll need to be running a server, and you'll need to set permissions access so that they can connect.

Testing Your Net Connection

Whenever you experience connection problems or need to know the status of your system, FrontPage Explorer can test the connection. You'll be able to learn the IP address of the system you're running, your system's network host name, and the IP address of the server hosting your FrontPage session. It will also verify that your system is able to access TCP/IP networks using Winsock. If you have problems connecting to a network, be sure the Winsock box displays a Yes. See Figure 4.14.

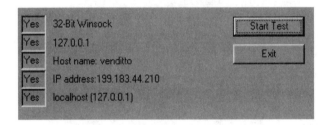

Figure 4.14 FrontPage Explorer's Network Test.

Before running the test, connect to your network. (If you use a modem connection, begin the dialing process.) On FrontPage Explorer's menu bar, select **Help, About Microsoft Explorer**. When the About dialog box opens, click on **Network Test**. In a few seconds, you'll see the test results.

Changing HTML, Graphics, and Multimedia Editors

FrontPage Explorer opens the FrontPage Editor when you select an HTML file. But it doesn't have to. If you happen to like another HTML editor or graphics editor, you can change the program that runs when you select one of these files.

Select **Tools, Options** from the FrontPage Explorer menu. The Options menu opens. First, select the type of file you want to edit with different software (for example, HTM); then click on the **Modify** button to select a different software program.

If you own the FrontPage CD-ROM Bonus Pack, FrontPage Image Composer was installed as your image editor. You can enter a different graphics program here for GIF and JPG files. If you didn't get the bonus pack, you'll want to select another graphics program on your system. This program will then open when you select the **Tools, Show Image Editor** command in FrontPage Explorer or FrontPage Editor.

You may also want to add a new type of file to the range of file types that you can edit in FrontPage, such as a multimedia authoring program you'll use for editing video or audio clips. Click on the **Add** button and then insert the file extension for the new file type (for example, MOV for QuickTime movies).

FRONTPAGE EDITOR: YOUR WEB PAGE TOOLBOX

If FrontPage Explorer is the control center for your Webs, FrontPage Editor is the factory floor where the real work gets done. From here on, the book is centered on the tools in FrontPage (with only a few minor side trips). So the rest of this chapter will give you only a general overview of FrontPage Editor. The following chapters dig in and explore all the features very closely.

Moving Between the Editor and Explorer

When you launch FrontPage, the Explorer view opens, and you are prompted for the Webs you want to work with, which were shown in Figure 4.1. When you're ready to begin working on a Web, Chapter 5 explains the many choices you have for creating new Webs, including blank pages, templates, and wizards.

Normally, you'll open a Web and go to FrontPage Editor using the technique that feels most comfortable.

- Double-click on the Web page you want to edit.
- Select **Tools, Show FrontPage Editor** from the FrontPage Explorer menu.
- Click on the **Show FrontPage Editor** toolbar icon.

The first option—double-clicking on a file—can save time because it will open a file. If you use the other two techniques, you need to use FrontPage Editor's **File** command to select the files you'll use.

WARNING

Every time you double-click on a URL in Explorer, the file is opened in the Editor. As a result, you may end up opening more pages than you realize.

You can open several files in FrontPage Editor. You can switch among them using the **Window** command. Every open file is listed on this menu.

FrontPage Editor's Graphic Preview

FrontPage Editor shares a similar interface to the Explorer. You'll find a range of icons on the toolbar that runs along the top of the window. If you move your mouse slowly over the icons, a small window will open to describe the tool. Each of these tools can also be found on the menu commands. See Figures 4.15a and 4.15b.

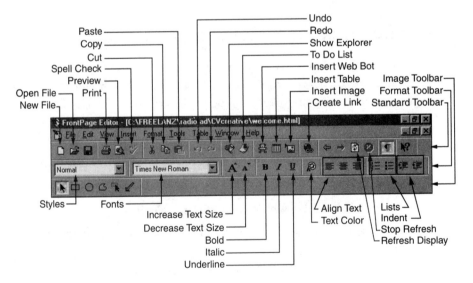

Figure 4.15a

CHAPTER 4—The Two Faces of FrontPage

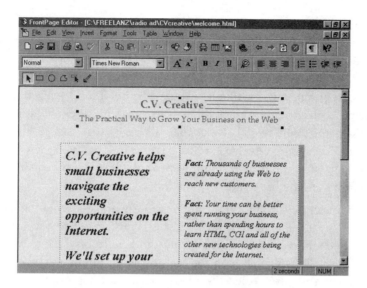

Figure 4.15 The FrontPage Editor window.

The FrontPage Editor toolbar expands to include graphic-editing icons if you double-click on a graphic or select the command **Tools, Show Image Composer**.

Web pages displayed in the FrontPage Editor—including HTML files and graphic files that link to the HTML page—appear in a rough simulation of a browser display. The simulation is close enough that you can make good design decisions, but some of the editing tools prevent you from getting an exact view of how the page will appear when it's viewed at a Web site. For example, tables are displayed with dotted-line borders in FrontPage Editor even if you have chosen a no-border option. You'll want to check your work frequently in a Web browser as you edit your pages. FrontPage Explorer includes an option for previewing a page in a browser, but you must have the software installed on your hard disk (the option supports the two leading browsers, Netscape Navigator and Microsoft Explorer, which is included on the FrontPage CD-ROM).

Tricks and Traps

In order to work at your best with FrontPage, you'll want to switch frequently among Explorer, Editor, and a browser. When working with graphics, you'll also want to open the Image Composer, with these other programs still active. That will require a good amount of RAM—at least 16 Megabytes. If you have that much or more memory in your system, you'll be able to check the appearance of your work quickly in a browser as you try out new techniques. You'll also be able to keep track of your overall Web's design in the Explorer view, making sure that you are adding links to the right files. For example, all pages that have a link from the home page should also have a link back to it; when you view the Web in Explorer with the option **View Repeated Hyperlinks**, you'll be able to confirm that you have added all the links you need.

You can switch among the applications with the key combination **Alt-Tab**. If you press the two keys quickly, you'll move to the last program you used. If you hold down **Alt** and tap briefly on **Tab**, a Windows 95 message will display an icon for each program running. The current program is highlighted. Keep the **Alt** key down and tap briefly on **Tab** again and you can select a different application. When you have selected the application you want to use, release the **Alt** key and you'll be able to work in that application.

If your system has fewer than 16 Megabytes, you'll be able to switch among applications, but you'll find that the system runs very slowly with all of these programs open. (Windows 95 will slow down when you switch because it will need to save some of the data in memory to a cache on your hard disk.) To avoid these slowdowns, you'll want to conserve memory. Close programs after you've finished using a specific command. Close HTML files in FrontPage Editor when you've finished editing them. Be sure to close the browser after you've performed a preview and close Image Composer after you've finished working on a graphic. (Be sure to save your final work!) Also, you can safely close the FrontPage Explorer while working in the FrontPage Editor. You can re-open Explorer and display the Web when you've finished editing it.

The most important thing to keep in mind is to save your work frequently. In fact, to view changes to a page in FrontPage Editor or to graphics in Images Composer, you must save your file before switching. Otherwise, when you switch to the browser for a preview or to Explorer for an overview, you'll be seeing the files before you updated them. And, whenever you view changes in the browser's preview, you need to select the browsers' option to **Reload** (in Netscape Navigator) or **Refresh** (in Microsoft Explorer).

CHAPTER 4—The Two Faces of FrontPage

PERSONAL WEB SERVER: AT WORK BEHIND THE SCENES

FrontPage requires the services of an HTTP server for a number of functions ranging from testing hyperlinks to executing WebBots you add to pages. If you're running FrontPage on a system with a Web server installed, you won't need additional software. For example, Windows NT systems come with a Web server; NT Workstation comes with a peer Web server, and NT Server comes with Microsoft Internet Information Server.

All other systems require the FrontPage Personal Web Server, a limited Web server that is installed as part of the FrontPage Bonus Pack setup. It provides a limited range of HTTP server functions; just about the only setting you can control is access privileges to the Web site. After it is installed, Personal Web Server will load whenever you launch FrontPage. Under normal circumstances, you don't need to concern yourself with it; it will just sit there quietly in the background as you work. See Figure 4.16. It should close by itself when you exit from FrontPage Explorer.

Figure 4.16 The Personal Web Server works quietly in the background.

89

You will "pass" it as you switch among applications, but it has no options to set and no features you can use. The FrontPage Editor and Explorer will call on its HTTP services when necessary.

TIP If you're short on RAM, you can close the Personal Web Server. You won't be able to test links or execute some of the WebBots, but you can re-open it when you need to do perform those tasks by running the file **fpserver.exe** in the FrontPage **\bin** directory.

Giving Others Access with the Web Server

The Personal Web Server is intended only to help you simulate a server environment so that you can adequately test a Web site you're developing. It's not intended to be used as a functioning server on the Web or local intranet, but it can. You can have someone else collaborate on developing your Web site if they have a copy of FrontPage on their system and you want them to be able to access files you're developing.

After you load Personal Web Server and connect to the Internet or network (you can use the Network Test in Personal Web Server), all you need to do is find out the IP address of your system. Then set up permissions in FrontPage Explorer so that when the other computers log in they'll be granted permission to work on the Web. Give the IP address to your colleague so that they can use FrontPage Explorer to open the Web at this IP address.

Setting Personal Web Server Permissions

In addition to setting up access to the FrontPage Webs from Explorer, the FrontPage Personal Web Server has its own set of permissions. The FrontPage Personal Web Server has an administrator program, which is shown in Figure 4.17. You can use it to enable or disable authoring on the server.

You can also add new administrators who can control authoring permission. You might want to disable authoring with the Personal Web Server Administrator if you share the system with others and want to prevent anyone else from tampering with the files while you're not there.

Chapter 4—The Two Faces of FrontPage

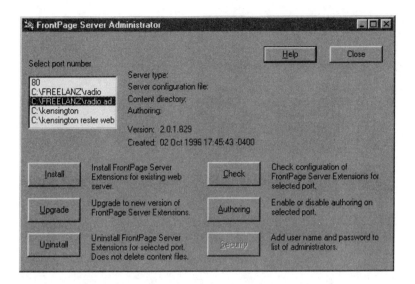

Figure 4.17 The administrator for the Personal Web Server.

NOTE

The Administrator program allows you to require that SSL security be used for all access to the Web.

Run the program using the Windows 95 **Run** command with this file name:

`fpsrvwin.exe`

This program is installed in the same directory where FrontPage Explorer is installed. The default directory is:

`C:\Program Files\Microsoft FrontPage\bin`

You can also use the Administrator program to upgrade the server if Microsoft releases a newer version.

Chapter 5
Fast Starts with Wizards and Templates

You don't need to learn all about HTML codes and spend hours poring over color choices to build an attractive Web. FrontPage wizards and templates can save hours of work by generating the files you can use for your Web site. You can devote your energies to adding the substance, rather than the style. These files are based on the work of professional designers who select fonts, colors, and graphics that work well together. Not only do you save time and labor, but your site will also have an artistic flair that you may not have been able to add by yourself.

That doesn't mean you're locked into a canned look that will be on the page of everyone else who owns FrontPage. You can make all the changes you want after you get your head-start. The only aspect that you must change is the text, replacing the boilerplate words with your own message, but you're free to replace all the graphics and design choices with your own so that it will have your own look.

Perhaps the greatest value of using a wizard or template is that you'll be exposed to some of the most innovative ways to create a Web. If you've spent any time developing Web pages from scratch, you're sure to be impressed with some of the techniques that the wizards employ.

In this chapter, we'll walkthrough several of the wizards and templates that come with FrontPage. You'll learn how to get up to speed quickly in building a Web site, including some tips on how to avoid problems down the road by naming your Web properly. You'll also learn how to select the wizards or templates that are most appropriate for your own work and how you can learn more about Web-authoring techniques from the wizards.

Finally, you'll learn how to move your Web from your hard disk up to the World Wide Web or the intranet server where it can be viewed by the rest of the world.

BUILD A WEB IN 60 SECONDS

Professional Web managers will scoff at the notion that you can create a quality Web site without putting in long days, but then again, they're paid for developing original sites. Some of the most popular Web sites have staffs of more than 100 people working full-time to generate the graphics and text. While you may not be able to match their work by yourself with just a copy of FrontPage and the wizards, you absolutely can create Web sites that are attractive and put your work in the best light. It takes just 60 seconds to run the wizard, but you can spend as long as you want customizing the pages. And you may well be working on them every day for many months to come, changing the text and adding new files and new pages. The value of using a wizard or template is to give you a head-start not to replace you as the designer of the pages. Good Web sites are constantly changing. If you think of a Web site as a physical plant, the wizard is a way of acquiring a modern office you can move right into rather than building on an empty lot.

Where WebBots Fit in

One of the most exciting technologies in FrontPage is the *WebBot*, which is a dynamic object that performs a specific function in a Web page like giving your Web site a search command for finding text in the Web pages. Don't confuse WebBots with wizards. A *wizard* will generate a new Web page or series of Web pages; a WebBot will add a function to an existing page. WebBots are covered at length in Chapter 13.

The Difference between a Wizard and a Template

Both wizards and templates allow you to create new pages with most of the design work already done, but it may not be clear which one is appropriate for a specific task. The difference between the two is a matter of degree.

Many wizards prompt you to make choices about the Web you want to create. It may ask you for the name of the company to be displayed, and it may give you a choice of design styles (conservative or flashy, for example). Then it will generate new files, incorporating your selections in the Web it creates. Figure 5.1 shows one of the prompts for the Discussion Web wizard.

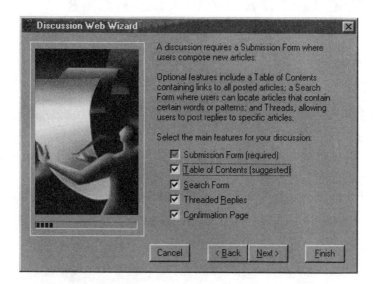

Figure 5.1 Selecting options for the Discussion Web wizard.

A template is less ambitious. It does not give you any control over the Web pages it will create for you; it will provide the same Web pages to every FrontPage user. Templates are available only in FrontPage Editor.

Clearly, the Explorers wizards give you more bang for your buck in starting a site quickly. But you will need to customize the Webs generated by either method since most of the text is displayed with generic terms rather than the text you'll want to display.

You can create your own wizards and templates, but there are clear differences here as well. You need to use Microsoft's FrontPage Software Developer's Kit to create a wizard. But you can save any Web page you design in FrontPage Editor as a template simply by clicking on a dialog box option when you are saving the page.

TIP A template can be a very powerful tool for creating a custom look that you use in all your Web pages. Once you build a page you like in FrontPage Explorer, you can repeat the basic design simply by saving it as a template.

WHIPPING UP NEW WEBS IN EXPLORER

The process of launching a new Web starts out with the same steps. Whether you want FrontPage to create a complicated structure that you can flesh out or you want to build everything from scratch, you use a FrontPage Explorer wizard. This section describes the steps you use to create a new Web site, pointing out a few tricks you'll want to use and some traps to avoid.

When you launch FrontPage by clicking its icon on the Windows 95 Start menu, you should see the Getting Started dialog box in Figure 5.2, displaying a variety of options for opening the Web you'll work on.

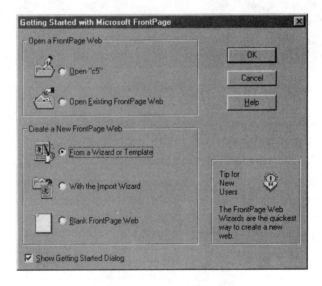

Figure 5.2 The Getting Started dialog box.

This dialog box will not appear if you or someone else who uses the system has clicked off the option **Show Getting Started Dialog** in the lower left-hand corner. You can get along without the Getting Started dialog box but it's worth using because it can clarify the options available to you. To turn on the Getting Started dialog in FrontPage Explorer, select **Tools, Options**. You'll see the Options dialog box, shown in Figure 5.3.

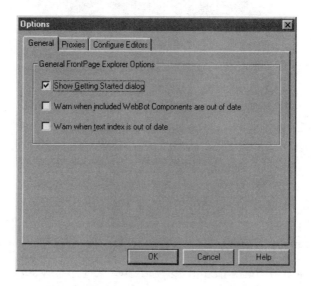

Figure 5.3 The Options dialog box.

Click on the box **Show Getting Started Dialog**. When a check mark appears in the box, click on **OK**. When the Getting Started dialog box appears, click on the option **Show Getting Started Dialog**. When this option is selected, the Getting Started dialog box opens every time you launch FrontPage and whenever you close a Web.

The Getting Started dialog box is valuable when you start with FrontPage and are creating new Webs frequently. After you've built up your work, you may find that it gets in the way and it's easier to select existing files from the File menus in Explorer and Editor.

If you prefer to work without the Getting Started dialog box, you will need to use the **File, New, FrontPage Web** command or the **File, Open FrontPage Web** command.

When you select the option on the Getting Started dialog box to create a new Web using a wizard or template, the window in Figure 5.4 opens.

Figure 5.4 FrontPage Explorer's options for new Webs with wizards.

If you're eager to start building your own Web pages and don't want any help from FrontPage's wizards, select **Blank Web**. If you're moving a Web site from another environment into FrontPage, see the section, "Import Web Wizard" later in this chapter for a full discussion of importing a Web.

TIP

If you're not sure that a Web wizard is right for you, you have nothing to lose by experimenting. You can stop the Web wizard process at any time by selecting **Cancel** on any of the dialog boxes. If FrontPage already stored some of the files on disk, you'll have the option of deleting those files when you cancel.

After you choose the wizard that FrontPage will run, you need to enter a name for the new Web.

Naming Your New Web

Naming a Web isn't nearly as simple as naming a file you'll use on your own system. A Web may consist of hundreds of individual files, and the

Chapter 5—Fast Starts with Wizards and Templates

name will link to other files and other sites. Your choice of a name can have a big impact on the success of your site, too, so it's worth spending a little effort on getting it right.

Immediately after you choose a wizard in FrontPage Explorer, the dialog box will ask for the server where you'll store the Web. If you're working on a standalone system, accept the default of **localhost**. If you have an active connection to other servers, you can select any of the available servers from a drop-down list. Keep in mind that the Web files will be created on the server you select; when you're working all by yourself, you'll want to create your Web pages on the local host and then move them to the server using the **Publish** command in Explorer when you're finished. But if you're working across a network, collaborating on a Web site, you can also store the files on a FrontPage Web located on a network drive.

If you do create the new pages on an HTTP server or a shared network drive, you'll need to have an active network connection to perform any work, and you won't have copies of the pages on your local system.

When naming the Web, think about the Web address you'll want your audience to enter in their browser. It should be memorable—both to the people who will visit your site and to you as you work on it. It's a good idea to give your Webs names that match the name of the folder where they'll be stored on the Web server. You'll be less likely to confuse the Web with a different Web. If you use this technique, keep in mind that the folder where you Web is stored forms the Web site's URL. When you're creating a Web that has it's own domain name (for example, www.mysite.com), you will want to publish the Web on the server's root. In this case, both Webs should be stored in folders called *mysite.com*.

When you create other Webs that will exist in a folder on the Root Web of a named domain, these sites can be reached with URLs that consist of the domain name and the folder name. For example, if you want your Web site to be reached with the URL

    http://www.mysite.com/info

then you will want your new Web to be called *info*. When you're ready to publish the Web site, you will move it from your system to a folder called *info* on the server *www.mysite.com*. It's not essential to use correct names from the start. You can rename folders with the FrontPage Explorer using the **Tools, Web Settings** command.

Don't use a name that's too elaborate; the name is restricted by the naming conventions of the server where you will move the Web. If you're working only with NT 4.0 or higher, you can use a long file name; however, on many UNIX servers, you're restricted to an eight-character file name. Remember that UNIX servers are also case-sensitive. If you capitalize the first letter of proper names and enter the rest as lowercase, you'll always need to refer to the Web this way. Unless you've got a photographic memory, you may want to reduce the possibility of confusion later by using only lowercase characters. Many servers do not allow file or folder names to include blank spaces, so it's a good idea to use an underscore character (the one to the right of the 0 key, with **Shift** depressed) instead of a space. Figure 5.5 shows the dialog box where you enter the name.

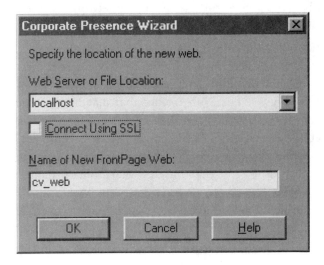

Figure 5.5 Naming a new Web.

This dialog box also gives you the option of configuring this Web as a series of "secure" documents. Check the box **Connect Using SSL** only if the server where you are storing this new Web requires that you use SSL (Secure Sockets Layer), a protocol that encrypts data as they move between a client and server over the Web.

NOTE SSL is used when a network administrator wants to protect the server from intruders; SSL confirms that the person opening the data transfer is who they claim to be before allowing the data transfer to begin and then it encrypts data as it moves across the Internet or internal network.

Public Internet Webhost services usually will not require SSL, although they may offer it as an option. If you're storing the files on your own system, do not select SSL.

Once you've give your new Web a name, FrontPage is ready to generate the Web, using the wizard you've selected. Some wizards will prompt you to choose among options, others will immediately begin to generate the Web's structure.

Choosing the Right Wizard

The Web wizard in FrontPage Explorer provides highly detailed Web designs so that you won't want to use them if you have very particular ideas about the designs you'll use on your Web pages. But even if you don't plan to use the Web wizards for work that you'll make public, you may learn a few techniques by running through the wizards and examining the pages that FrontPage creates. If you're a beginner, it's safe to say that the wizard will create a Web that's far more advanced than anything you would create on your own without putting in several days of labor.

TIP One of the more advanced techniques you'll learn from working with the wizards is the use of style sheets. FrontPage's Corporate Prescence wizard, for example, achieves very sophisticated results by sharing properties and text data in style sheets.

The Difference between Wizards in Explorer and Editor

The process of creating a Web with a wizard can begin in either the FrontPage Explorer or Editor. When you use a Web wizard in Explorer, you are building an entirely new Web that will consist of several HTML pages. It will not have any connection to another Web, but it will have a number of links between pages in the Web. When you use a wizard in the

Editor, you are adding a single page to an existing Web; text on the wizard will prompt you to add links between the wizard page and other pages in the open Web.

The Wizards of Explorer

The FrontPage CD-ROM is distributed with a set of wizards that show off FrontPage at its best. To fully appreciate each one, you need to try it out. But since trying out a new Web requires that you need to go through the process of naming it, you may want to read the following descriptions first to save yourself some time.

Corporate Presence Wizard

The Corporate Presence wizard is very elaborate. It creates a Web site with more than a dozen interlinked Web pages that you can fill with your own company's press releases, announcements, a table of contents that enable users to get an overview of the Web site, and even a feedback page that visitors can use to contact you. Figure 5.6 shows the home page, which provides a navigation bar that can link to other pages.

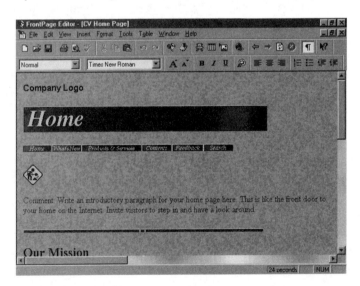

Figure 5.6 The Home page created by the Corporate Presence wizard.

During the wizard creation process, you can choose the types of information you want to include, such as a company mission statement and whether the site should have press releases. You will have a choice of four different graphic schemes (a plain scheme with virtually no graphics or color, a conservative scheme with blues and grays, a flashy scheme, or a cool scheme).

TIP

Be sure to look at the technique the Corporate Presence wizard uses for the navigation bar, which is stored in the private folder in the file **navbar.htm**. The navigation bar is inserted in other pages using the **WebBot Include** command.

Don't expect that you can use this wizard and publish your company's Web site in a short time. You'll need to spend hours replacing the text and graphics. The site assumes that you have a corporate logo and want to promote products at the Web site.

Anyone can build new wizards using Microsoft's FrontPage Software Developer Kit, so your copy of FrontPage may have been augmented with wizards that are not available to everyone else.

Customer Support Web

The Customer Support Web is not nearly as elaborate or impressive as the Corporate Presence Web. The pages are plain, very few graphics are included, and no style sheets are used. In fact, it's so simple that FrontPage does not even prompt you for optional settings. The Customer Support Web is something you are most likely to incorporate into an existing Web, such as the Corporate Presence Web. You'll probably want to have the main Web open when you run the wizard and select the option **Add to the Current Web**.

The most interesting technology you can learn from is the use of FTP (file transfer protocol) for making files available for downloading. To see this technique in action, select the **download.htm** file and display the Hyperlink Properties for the files that are being made available, as shown in Figure 5.7.

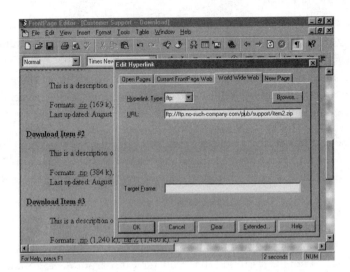

Figure 5.7 The Customer Support Web uses FTP for downloading software.

To give this Web the same look as others, you'll want to edit the Page Properties for each page and choose the option **Get Background and Colors from Page**, using the style sheet from your main Web.

Discussion Web Wizard

The Discussion Web wizard can save you hours of work if you want to add a message forum to a Web site. The wizard creates Web pages that give visitors to the site the chance to post messages that will be available for others to read and add their own comments. You can configure the discussion pages to be available only to selected users or open to everyone with access to the Web site. The Web pages you create will be most appropriate as additions to an existing Web, although the wizard allows you to configure this as a standalone Web site, too.

The wizard prompts you for many details about the discussion threads. You can choose the order in which messages are sorted (oldest first or newest first), and you can display message replies in frames next to the previous message, or without frames. If you select one of the options that uses frames, you'll also be guided through a second wizard that controls the settings of the frames, as shown in Figure 5.8.

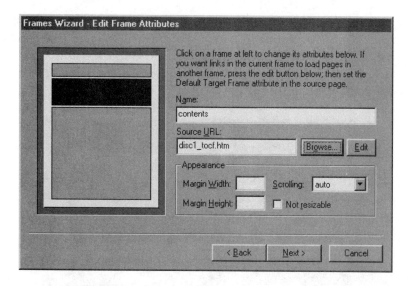

Figure 5.8 The Discussion Web wizard gives you control over the appearance of frames.

Don't expect to set up a Discussion Web and then walk away from it. A successful discussion group requires regular attention from a moderator. You'll need to monitor the discussion for the possibility of offensive postings (ranging from mildly abusive to outright obscene). Fortunately, as Web master, you'll have complete access to all the postings.

WARNING

Before you create a discussion Web, carefully consider the amount of space you'll be using on your Web server. Every time a visitor posts a comment, it will create a new file on the server.

Personal Web Wizard

Many people create personal Web pages to introduce themselves to others on the World Wide Web and to reveal a bit about their personal interests. The Personal Web is a very simple wizard that doesn't give you the chance to choose any preferences; the wizard creates a single main page without any graphics. The main advantage of using this wizard is that it will suggest possible topics for you to cover on your page, such as biographical information and your "hot list" of links to Web sites you like. The most interesting technique used by the Personal Web is the *bookmark*, a way to link to an area within the open page (other HTML programs call this an *internal link* or *anchor*). To see how this works, once you've used the Personal Web wizard, open the page in the FrontPage Editor and select the **Edit, Bookmark** command. As shown in Figure 5.9, you'll find that most of the links in this page are internal.

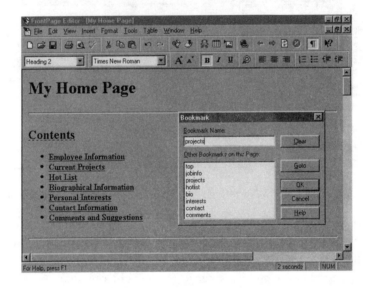

Figure 5.9 The Personal Web wizard uses bookmarks for most of its links.

Project Web Wizard

The Project Web wizard is designed to manage work groups where you want to share findings and papers. The design is very simple: very few graphics and no background color attributes are used. The Web does include several WebBots for managing the papers you would include over time. There is a search WebBot for finding other documents and a header WebBot that provides a consistent menu to the top of key pages.

Import Web Wizard

The Import Web wizard is used to bring an existing Web site into the FrontPage environment. You don't need to use this wizard to import a Web into FrontPage; you can create a new Web and then use the **Import** command in FrontPage Explorer or open the page in FrontPage Editor and then save it in the FrontPage Web. The advantage of using the Import wizard is that you are given the option of excluding some of the files in the existing Web, as shown in Figure 5.10.

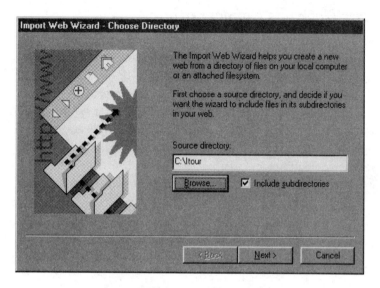

Figure 5.10 The Import Web wizard.

You may, for example, want to exclude log files or CGI scripts that won't be used in you Web now that you're moving it to FrontPage. The Import Web isn't comprehensive. It won't create a structure that you would normally want to use for a FrontPage Web. For example, if images were stored in the same directory as HTML files in the original Web, it will not move them to the \images folder normally used for FrontPage Webs. You will need to move them to the \images folder using FrontPage Explorer's folder view after the Import Web is finished. If you do re-organize your folders, be sure to move the files using the folder view in FrontPage Explorer rather than with a file manager, because FrontPage Explorer will adjust links within the Web pages to reflect the images' new locations.

If you're also planning to move your Web site from one server to a new server, you may need to rename the main page. Some servers require that the default page in a Web directory be named **welcome.html**. By default, FrontPage uses **index.htm** for its opening page (the default for

Microsoft NT Internet Information Server). If your opening page needs to be renamed, select it in FrontPage Explorer's folder view, right-click, and select the **Rename** command.

Fresh Start: Blank and Normal Wizards

The Blank and Normal wizards don't do much, but sometimes that's all you need. Both create the structure for a new Web, including folders for images and the index files that FrontPage will use to track the Web, but they add very little else. The Normal wizard creates a single blank page named **index.htm**—the default opening page for a FrontPage Web when FrontPage Personal Web Server is installed as your HTTP server. FrontPage may generate a different name if FrontPage has determined that your default server usually requires a different name for the default file in the server directory, such as **default.html** or **welcome.html**.

The Blank wizard doesn't create an opening page, it just creates the structure. If you need to name your opening page, select the Blank wizard or **welcome.html** or plan a different name for your pages.

JUMP STARTING NEW WEB PAGES

No matter which Explorer wizard you use to start your Web, you can create new pages quickly using templates that come with FrontPage Editor. The templates are HTML pages that provide a combination of formatting options appropriate to specific jobs. FrontPage Editor also has wizards, but these don't create new pages. Instead, they deliver specific features, like generating a database query that you can add to a form. These wizards will be explored in subsequent chapters as part of the discussion of a specific task where these are discussed. For example, the Database Connectivity wizard is discussed in Chapter 11.

Opening Up FrontPage Editor Templates

You'll want to use FrontPage Editor's templates and wizards only after you've already started a new Web in the Explorer. You can use the Editor's wizards to enhance a Web that you created with an Explorer wizard or to

Chapter 5—Fast Starts with Wizards and Templates

build up an empty Web. It's possible to bypass the FrontPage Explorer and create your Web from scratch in the Editor, but that's not a good idea. Over the long run, you'll waste time, putting in extra work to track the pages on your own and build the FrontPage folder structure. If you want to build your Web from scratch, just be sure you start the process with Explorer's Blank wizard.

You select FrontPage Editor templates from the same dialog box. With a Web started in FrontPage Explorer, open FrontPage Editor and select **File, New**. The dialog box shown in Figure 5.11 opens.

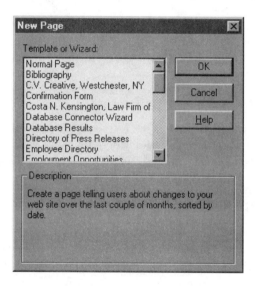

Figure 5.11 FrontPage Editor's File, New command lists templates and wizards.

The available templates cover a variety of common pages on the Web. Remember that they'll still need to be customized to fit your own needs. You may need to replace some of the graphics, but you will definitely need to replace most of the text.

Normal Page

The first choice for a FrontPage Editor template is the Normal page. It's essentially a clean slate, with no text, graphics, or formatting, but that doesn't mean it's an empty file. HTML files require a fair amount of coding in order to be a valid HTML file. If you select the **Normal** page, you can get an idea of what happens behind the scenes in an HTML file with the **View, HTML** command. Even when a brand new Normal page is empty, there is still a fair amount of HTML code in the background.

Once you've opened the Normal page template, you can add all the text, graphics, and formatting you want from the FrontPage Editor menus. The following chapters explore all of the options.

Bibliography

The Bibliography template will be a time-saver for students and academics preparing scholarly papers. It includes text in a form suitable for listing published credits in a bibliography. Very little formatting is used.

Feedback Confirmation

This form is provided mainly as a tool for use in building a discussion forum. Text within the page describes how you would use it reply to a message when using a FrontPage WebBot to create a discussion group.

Directory of Press Releases

This template would be appropriate on a corporate site where you want to organize a collection of press release documents. There's very little formatting. You'll need to edit the links as well as the text.

Employee Directory

This form doesn't have much formatting, but it provides a good amount of detail on how to structure a directory of employees. The template is set up to include several items that will prove overly optimistic in most organizations: in every person's listing there are links to an e-mail address, Web site, and photograph. Of course, you need to edit each of these links with the correct URL—if they exist!

Employment Opportunities

This template suggests a way to structure an online "positions open" page, as shown in Figure 5.12.

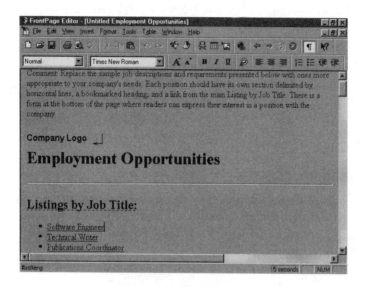

Figure 5.12 A template for an "open positions" page.

It provides links to an e-mail address (which you must edit) that the user would contact to apply, and it uses bookmarks (internal links) between a list of all jobs at the top of the page, and a detailed description farther down the page.

Feedback Form

The FeedBack form provides more help than most other templates. It includes a form that encourages visitors to your Web to give you feedback about your site. The template includes a series of form components, including a drop-down menu for asking visitors how they learned about the site.

Frequently Asked Questions

This template suggests questions you'll want to answer. Edit the list of questions at the top and then supply the answers below. The template uses bookmarks to link the questions with the answers.

Glossary of Terms

This template is similar to the layout of the Frequently Asked Questions template, except that it includes the letters of the alphabet linked to bookmarks that appear farther down in the file where you will provide terms and definitions.

HyperDocument Page

This template will be very instructive to anyone who hasn't used many links. It is designed to display the choices a Web site visitor has to review several documents. Instead of text links, the template uses buttons for displaying the choices.

Guest Book

The Guest Book template includes a simple form that allows visitors to a Web site to send you comments. The form uses the Save Results WebBot for processing the user's input.

Meeting Agenda

This page is very simple. It provides only text formatted in a way you might use to present an agenda. The greatest contribution that this template offers is that it uses the list format for the points to be discussed.

Product Description

This page can help you cover all the basics if your Web site describes a product. The template is organized into several sections devoted to specifications and benefits of the product. Bookmarks help speed users through the details.

Search Page

Use this page to add a search option to your Web site, as shown in Figure 5.13. The page is very simple, but it's powerful. It uses FrontPage's Search WebBot and requires no customization.

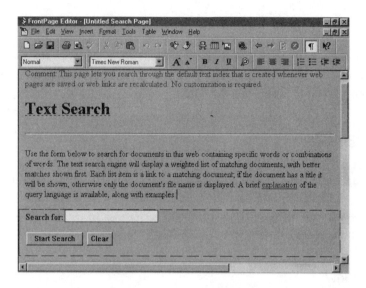

Figure 5.13 The Search Page template.

Save this page in your Web. If you add links to it, visitors to your site will be able to find any file where a specific word or phrase is mentioned. All you need to do is edit the text that's displayed.

Seminar Schedule

This page is a very simple text file that shows how you can list the events in a seminar or meeting.

Software Data Sheet

This template is similar to the Product Description template except that it inserts a graphic file as an example of how you could insert a screen image for a software product.

Survey Form

Every one of the WebBot components for generating a form is used in this template that's designed to gather information about visitors to your site. It includes checkboxes, radio buttons, and comment fields.

Table of Contents

Use this template for a very rudimentary introduction to the technique of building a table of contents. It shows text that can be linked to other pages. It will be useful only if you've never worked with links before.

User Registration

This template will be extremely valuable if you plan to set up a discussion group on a Web site. It uses a WebBot to create a registration entry for individuals, including user name, e-mail address, and password. The template also provides detailed instructions on how to use the form to keep a database of registered users at your Web site.

What's New

This template is merely a text file with a very minimal amount of formatting suggesting how you might organize a page that notes changes to your site.

PUBLISHING A NEW SITE

Beginning a Web site, using wizards and templates, is easy. Editing it with your own words, images, and styles is the hard part. The following chapters will describe hundreds of techniques you can use to create a dazzling, informative, and maybe even ground-breaking Web site.

Fortunately, the final job—the process of for moving the site from your hard disk to the public Web server—can be very easy. That doesn't mean it's *always* easy. If you have the correct access privileges to the server and you prepare properly, publishing your Web site will take just moments. The most common error is to publish it to the wrong place. If you work on just one Web site, that may not be a problem. But if you maintain more than one Web site, it's easy to publish the files on the wrong folder, even if you are working with just one server.

Step One: Prepare the Server

The directory of a Web server isn't much different from your hard disk. There are root directories and folders. The main difference is that the server administrator carefully limits access so that you can't create and rearrange folders at will. Normally, your Web site is a folder that's been identified as your Web site by the server administrator. If you have your own domain, this folder will appear in a browser and in FrontPage to be your domain (for example, www.mycompany.com), but it's actually a directory on the server's hard disk that's been set aside for your Web pages.

Before you move your Web pages up to the server, you'll want to create the correct folder. For example, if you plan to store this Web site in a folder off the domain name's root folder (for example, www.mysite.com/info), follow these steps.

1. Establish your Internet or network TCP/IP connection.
2. Open FrontPage Explorer, and select **View, Folder View**. You won't be able to identify the server's folder structure from the Hyperlink view.
3. Select **File, Open FrontPage Web**.
4. Select the server. You will probably need to log in with the name and password established by the network administrator (this will be different from the name and password used to protect Webs on the local host).
5. Once you've logged in, select the Root Web or main folder (e.g., http://www.mysite.com).
6. Select **File, New Folder**. FrontPage Explorer will add the entry NewFolder to the list of folders.
7. Select the **New Folder** icon and right-click the mouse button. A control menu will open as shown in Figure 5.14.

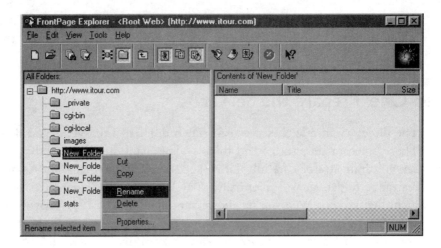

Figure 5.14 Renaming a folder on the server.

8. Type in the new name (for example, **sales**). Press **Enter**.

Now you'll want to publish your Web to this folder.

Step Two: Publish the Site

Once the folder is created, you'll be able to place the Web site in its new home. Select **File, Publish** from FrontPage Explorer's main menu. You'll see the dialog box in Figure 5.15.

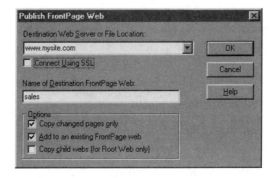

Figure 5.15 The Publishing Web site dialog box.

If you're still logged into the server, the correct server name should appear in the Destination Web Server box. Otherwise, select the server from the drop-down list box.

In the Name of Destination FrontPage Web, type in the folder where you want the Web site to be stored. Don't use slashes or any other punctuation. Check the option **Add to an existing FrontPage Web** only if you used FrontPage Explorer to publish a Web site at this location in the past.

When you update the Web site, you can use the **Publish** command with this same address, but you'll want to select the option **Copy changed pages only**.

After you've entered the correct information, click on the **OK** button, and FrontPage Explorer will transfer all the files in your Web up to the server. When it's finished, FrontPage will display a confirmation. You can now load a browser and visit your site. It should be available to everyone who has access to the network.

NOTE

When the main page in your Web site is named correctly (for example, **index.htm** on servers where this is the default page), a browser will need only the URL for your domain and this folder (example, `http:/www.mysite.com/info`).

Working with Child Webs

A child Web is a self-contained set of Web pages that is created within a Root Web. You have the option of maintaining Webs as children of the Root Web or as independent Webs that are not part of the Root Web. If you maintain Webs as child Webs of the Root, you won't need to create a new folder before you move the Web; FrontPage will do that automatically.

A child Web inherits the permission's structure of the root, so will want to create child Webs only when the new Web is closely related to the Root Web and plan to work on them together often.

Publishing to Sites without FrontPage

You don't absolutely have to be working with a Web server that runs the FrontPage extensions. If you're using a server without the extensions, your first course of action is to ask the server administrator to install them. They're free and can be downloaded directly from Microsoft's Web site at www.microsoft.com.

Your next course of action is to use the FrontPage Web Publishing wizard to upload the files to the server. You don't need to use this wizard, however, if you're comfortable using an FTP or Telnet program to copy the files to the server. The advantage of using the wizard is that it will compare versions of the files on your system and at the Web site and move only newer versions. When you use an FTP or Telnet program, you need to keep track of the versions of each file that needs to be moved.

When using any of these techniques, pay careful attention to the links that you've established between files in your Web. When FrontPage on your system communicates with FrontPage at the Web server, it can generate folders automatically and move files into the correct individual folders so that the links will be correct. When using an FTP or Telnet program, you'll need to create new folders at the Web site and make sure the links work on your own.

Naming Your Home Page

Ideally, when your file is published, you'll be able to load your main page simply by using the URL in a browser. But in order for this to happen, the main page must use a name that's specified in the HTTP server at the Web site. Normally, that name is **index.htm** on your system when FrontPage creates the file. But the name that must be used can be changed by the server administrator (for example, the name **welcome.html** is a popular alternative to **index.htm**). But if you publish the files to a server that doesn't use the extensions, you'll need to learn the correct name for this file from the server administrator and then make sure that your main page uses it. If not, a browser attempting to load your pages will need to include the name of your home page, in addition to the full URL, for example.

http://www.mycompany.com/index.htm

When FrontPage Extensions are installed on the server, you don't need to be concerned about this issue. FrontPage is able to ensure that the correct name is used so that your home file will load automatically.

CHAPTER 6

THE ESSENTIAL TOOLS FOR TEXT, GRAPHICS, AND LINKS

Web pages start out very simply. In essence, they're just a collection of words that you want others to see with formatting commands to make your message look attractive, a few graphics sprinkled around to illustrate your points, and links among your pages. Once you've got the basics down, you can go to town with multimedia clips, interactive forms, and scripts that execute in real-time. But even the most sophisticated pages still require the essential tools.

In this chapter you'll learn the techniques for inserting the basic elements of a Web page: text, links, and graphics. Each of these elements starts out as a simple addition to the page, but as you insert the elements you can choose from a wide range of options. Much of the style and impact in Web page design comes from choosing the options for these settings. When used properly, you can dramatically enhance your page. This chapter will help you develop the skills to make the most of these tools and to avoid common mistakes.

GETTING THE HANG OF IT: DRAG, DROP, AND PREVIEW

Whether you start out with wizards, templates, or a blank page in FrontPage Explorer, you develop your pages in FrontPage Editor. FrontPage Editor offers the same basic techniques for building and refining pages as word processors provide. Even if you never created a Web page, as long as you've used a word processor in Windows or on the Mac, you should soon feel right at home using FrontPage Editor tools.

- You can type words, highlight them with the mouse, and select a format from the menus.
- You can copy text from a different program, switch to FrontPage Editor, paste in the text, and then select a format command from the menus.
- You can first select a format command and then type.
- You can change the appearance of most elements by selecting the element and right-clicking. A control menu will open that allows you to select the type of property you want to change. For example, when you select a graphic, you can select the Image Properties dialog box.

FrontPage Editor is similar to most word processors, but it's most like Microsoft Word. FrontPage is produced by the same division of Microsoft that develops Microsoft Office and Word. The two programs share the same overall structure. FrontPage can also read your Word **.DOC** files, automatically converting the Word styles to HTML formats.

A brief tour of the menu commands is all you need to understand how much FrontPage Editor resembles a word processor. Table 6.1 shows many of the common word processing style functions and the menus where FrontPage Editor provides them.

Table 6.1 Basic FrontPage Editor Commands

Menu	Commands	Shortcut Key
File	Print	**Ctrl-P**
Edit	Cut	**Ctrl-X**
Edit	Copy	**Ctrl-C**
Edit	Paste	**Ctrl-V**
Edit	Find	**Ctrl-F**
Edit	Replace	**Ctrl-H**
Insert	Insert File	**Alt-I-F**
Format	Font	**Alt-F-P**
Format	Paragraph	**Alt-F-P**
Tools	Spelling	**F7**
Tools	Thesaurus	**Shift-F7**

CHAPTER 6—The Essential Tools for Text, Graphics, and Links

You'll become productive faster with FrontPage Editor if you start out by assuming that it's a word processor, even though there are key differences. Since your work will end up being published on a Web server rather than on paper, FrontPage Editor must conform to the HTML specification rather than the limits of the printed page. Don't assume that it's similar to a desktop publishing program; you can't control the appearance of a page as precisely in the HTML environment as you can with a desktop publishing program.

You may occasionally be surprised that FrontPage Editor's dialog boxes present an unfamiliar set of choices, but in time—and with the explanations here—you'll find that you can accomplish just about anything you want.

Avoiding Lost Files

One of the key differences between FrontPage Editor and a word processor is the way files in a Web site interact. The FrontPage Explorer will keep track of the links that you establish between files, as long as you don't try to work around it. Open documents with the FrontPage Explorer whenever possible. The FrontPage Editor File menu allows you to open any HTML file, but if you use this technique too often, you'll start to lose track of how the page fits into a Web site. For example, you could make the mistake of using the **File**, **Save As** command to store the file in a hard disk folder that is not part of the Web; the changes you make to this file will not be in the Web site. Use the FrontPage **Save** command when you're finished editing files that you want to keep in the Web with the same name. The **Save As** command (shown in Figure 6.1) can be used to generate new versions of a file—useful when you want to add a page to your Web that is similar to an existing page—just be sure that you rename it but keep it in the same Web.

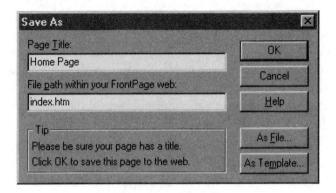

Figure 6.1 The FrontPage Save As command dialog box.

Fortunately, the **Save As** command helps you avoid the problem with a dialog box that's unique to FrontPage. The **Save As** command gives you the option of renaming the file but makes you to take an extra step if you want to store it outside the Web. You'll need to click on the **As File** button in Figure 6.1 to save the file outside the Web.

TIP
If you have saved a file outside the Web in error, you can bring it back into the fold using the **Import** command in FrontPage Explorer. When the file shares a name with an existing file, you'll need to delete the older version or rename one of the files.

And because pages in your Web are tracked by index files that can be used only by FrontPage Explorer, there are times when the pages you're using in FrontPage Editor will be out of synch with the rest of the Web. For example, if you import a file to the Web using FrontPage Explorer while you're working in the Editor, you'll need to use the Editor's **Refresh** button before the file will be recognized by some of Editor's dialog boxes.

Faster Than a Printout: Page Previews

Like a word processor, FrontPage gives you a general idea of how your final work will appear when its published on a Web server, but it's not perfect. The solution is to display your pages in a browser while you're working using the **File**, **Preview in Browser** command. The dialog box in Figure 6.2 will open.

CHAPTER 6—The Essential Tools for Text, Graphics, and Links

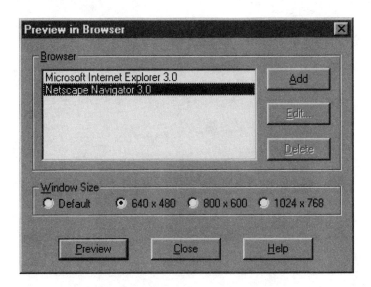

Figure 6.2 The Preview in Browser dialog box.

The dialog box will give you the option of viewing the current page in any browser that is installed on your system. In Figure 6.2, FrontPage was able to detect a copy of Netscape Navigator and Microsoft Internet Explorer. You can also can display the page in a choice of window sizes. You'll want to take advantage of these different resolutions for a thorough look at how your pages will be displayed because computers can use a variety of screen resolutions. The choices in the dialog box—640 by 480, 800 by 600, and 1025 by 768—are most common.

NOTE

When previewing pages in the browser, FrontPage does not actually change your screen resolution. Instead, FrontPage's preview simulates the affect of a different resolution by opening the browser window in a size large enough to approximate the display in the selected resolution.

When you select **Preview**, FrontPage Editor will load the browser and display the current page. Figure 6.3 shows a page in progress in FrontPage Editor with a preview in Netscape Navigator.

123

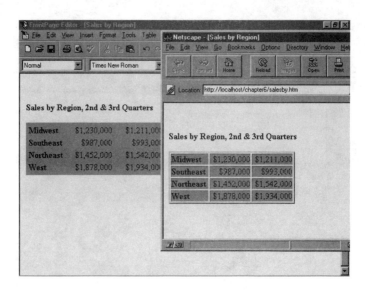

Figure 6.3 Previewing a page with Netscape Navigator.

A careful look at Figure 6.3 reveals the need for previewing. The table being constructed in FrontPage Editor at left appears different in Netscape Navigator. There are two reasons for the differences. First, the columns are squeezed together in the browser because the table width was set as a percentage of the available display. Second, FrontPage Editor allows table border colors to be set with options that Netscape Navigator does not support. These differences are minor and, to a very great extent, most pages will appear identical when displayed in FrontPage Editor and a browser. In this example, Microsoft Internet Explorer would have correctly displayed the table borders but would have also squeezed the columns. (You'll learn how to avoid this problem in Chapter 9.)

The browser can only display files stored on your hard disk—not in system memory—so before you can view the file, save it to disk. FrontPage Editor will prompt you to save the file if you run the **Preview in Browser** command with an unsaved file. But you need to remember to save files if you want to preview the page after you've made changes. Also, after the file is saved you must select the browser's **Reload** (in Netscape Navigator) or **Refresh** (in Internet Explorer) command so that the browser is reading the most recent version of the file.

CHAPTER 6—The Essential Tools for Text, Graphics, and Links

FrontPage Editor also lets you print hard copies of your pages (**File, Print**), and it provides a preview of the printed page (**File, Print Preview**). However, since publishing on a Web server is the ultimate destination of your pages, previewing a page in a browser will usually be more valuable to you than hard copy.

FORMATTING TEXT WITH STYLES

The biggest difference between a word processor and a Web authoring tool is in the way text is formatted. The HTML specification originally required that text formats conform to a system of numbered headings for emphasis. This system is starting to fade because browsers now support font specifications, but it's important to use the original system because some older browsers don't support fonts. You can still take advantage of the newer font specs. In fact, FrontPage Editor will require that you use them, while allowing you to dress up the page with fonts, too.

It does this by providing the basic HTML styles as the standard formatting option, but it also gives you the option of selecting fonts that you can add to a text. As a result, you're able to spice up your page to take advantage of the latest technology, but you don't run the risk of creating pages that are not compatible with older browsers.

HTML Text Styles

The traditional HTML styles are easy to find: the drop-down menu in upper left corner of the editing window lists all of them. By default, **Normal** is in effect until you select a different style by choosing from the drop-down list. Figure 6.4 shows the drop-down list and a text formatted in each of the basic text styles.

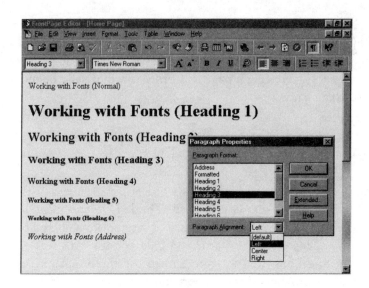

Figure 6.4 The basic HTML styles.

You can format text either by selecting the style and then typing or by highlighting some text you've already typed and then selecting the format. Don't bother to select only a single word or phrase—FrontPage will always format the entire paragraph. The basic HTML styles cannot be applied to just a single word or phrase; they are in effect for the entire paragraph (a *paragraph* is defined as the text that appears between carriage returns).

Changing Text Styles

After you format text with a style, you can change it to a different style quickly, or you can align the text differently using the **Paragraph Properties** command. Click anywhere in the paragraph or line you want to change and use one of two methods.

- Select **Format**, **Paragraph** on the main menu.
- Right-click with the mouse.

The Paragraph Properties dialog box shown in Figure 6.5 will open. You can select a different text style for the paragraph you selected or change the paragraph alignment from the default of left to centered or right-aligned.

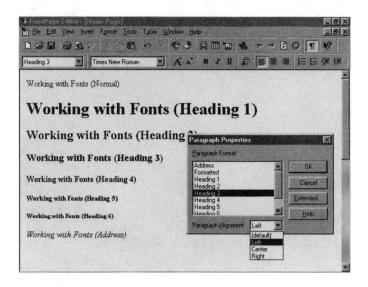

Figure 6.5 Changing Paragraph Properties.

You can change only a single paragraph or several paragraphs, depending on the amount of text you highlight before opening the dialog box. Remember that any HTML style selection will affect the entire paragraph, even if you've only selected a few characters within a paragraph. There is one exception to the rule. You can add emphasis to just a single word using the **Italics**, **Bold**, and **Underline** commands on the FrontPage Editor toolbar. FrontPage uses the HTML tags for emphasis, strong emphasis, and underlined when you use these options.

HTML List Styles

After you format text in any HTML style, FrontPage will return to the **Normal** style as soon as you hit a carriage return, with one exception. The list styles—bulleted list, directory list, menu list, and numbered list—will remain in the selected list style, formatting the text on the new line in the list format, until you press **Enter** twice. Then, the default style will return to **Normal**. Figure 6.6 shows the list styles.

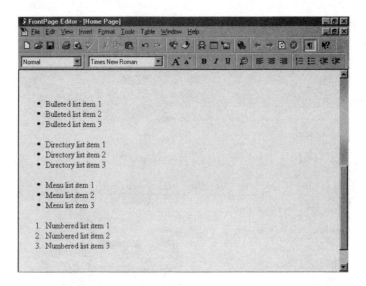

Figure 6.6 HTML list styles.

WARNING

HTML ignores extra carriage returns on a page. When you want to insert extra white space on a page, use the **Insert Break** command instead.

Three of the list styles in Figure 6.6 are identical—only the numbered list is different. In practice, only two lists styles are commonly used today, the bulleted list (usually called the unordered list) and the numbered list. In the early versions of the HTML specification, the other two list styles were supposed to be treated uniquely by browsers (directory lists should have been displayed as a columnar table, and menu lists should have appeared without bullets). But most browsers display them as if they were bulleted lists. As a result, they're considered to be on the road to oblivion.

Changing List Styles

Enhancements to the two major list styles—bulleted and numbered lists—that allow you to select the style of bullet or number used have become popular in HTML. Instead of selecting these enhancements from the drop-down list, you need to choose a list format and then edit the format.

The only way to edit the list properties is by placing the mouse cursor somewhere in the list, right-clicking the mouse, and selecting **List Properties** from the menu that opens. The dialog box, shown in Figure 6.7, will open.

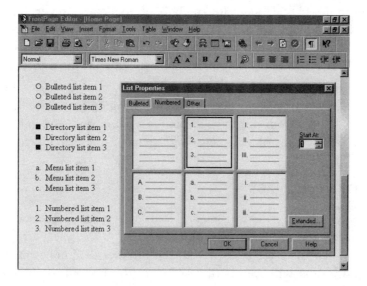

Figure 6.7 The List Properties dialog box.

You can change the basic format of the list to the **Bulleted** (unordered) or **Numbered** (ordered) format. And you can select options on how the list will be displayed.

- When you select the **Bulleted** tab, you can choose among solid squares, solid circles, hollow circles, or no bullet.

- When you select the **Numbered** tab, you can choose from decimal numbers, Roman numerals, capital letters, and lowercase letters.

The **Numbered** tab in the List Properties dialog box also gives you the option of selecting the first number to be used in the list. You would want to do this if you interrupted a list with text in a different format. FrontPage wouldn't be able to keep track of the numbers unless you select the number to begin the second part of the list.

Formatting Text with Fonts

The original HTML spec didn't make allowances for font formatting, but that's changing rapidly. Because many older browsers are still in use, you want to use HTML styles for the bulk of your text formats, but you can greatly improve your pages' appearance by adding text formats that can be displayed by most browsers. The older browsers will still display the HTML styles without your enhancements, but most of your audience will see the page the way you intend it to be seen.

You can have the greatest impact by changing font sizes. Rather than select a specific font size as you would in a word processor, in HTML you select from a range of increments or decrements for changing font size.

Selecting Font Sizes

When you change the text in an HTML page, you don't actually select a point size that can be measured in finite terms. You select a relative font size. When the page is displayed, the browser determines exactly how large the text will appear in relation to the normal font used by the browser.

To change a font size first highlight the text and then either select **Format**, **Font** from the menus or right-click with the mouse and select **Font Properties** from the menu that opens. Figure 6.8 shows the Font Properties dialog box.

CHAPTER 6—The Essential Tools for Text, Graphics, and Links

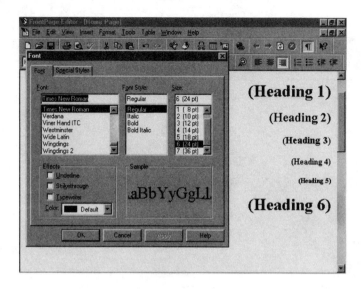

Figure 6.8 The Font Properties dialog box.

You select a new size from the list. On the Size list, FrontPage notes point sizes to give you a general idea of how large the type selection will be, but the font sizes are actually assigned on a scale of minus one to six. The point sizes noted for each size are only rough approximations. It might be easier to think of the font sizes as being comparable to the six different header sizes.

The use of font sizes is an extension to HTML that you can use without concern for compatibility. Most browsers can view the different font sizes without problem, and older browsers that can't will show the underlying style. Changing font styles can lead to a bit of confusion, though. In Figure 6.8, the text *Heading 6* is a Level 6 HTML header that should be smaller than every other header on the screen; but it was formatted with font size 6 so it appears the same size as Heading 1.

The advantage of using font sizes rather than header styles is that font sizes can control just a few words or letters. You can even use them for special effects or just to amuse yourself. The text in Figure 6.9, which started with capitalized letters in the normal style, was formatted with underline and different font sizes.

Figure 6.9 Fun with font sizes.

 You can quickly change font sizes by clicking on the **Increase Text Size** or **Decrease Text Size** buttons (those are the letters A with up and down arrows).

Selecting Fonts

FrontPage Editor gives you plenty of leeway in selecting fonts—more than enough rope to get yourself into trouble. While you can select any font that you have your own system in designing and displaying the page on your system, a browser will be able to display your page only if the font is installed on its system. You can safely select **Times Roman** because just about every computer surfing the web has some type of Times or Roman font. But few other fonts are as pervasive.

Fonts will be most useful when you're working on a relatively small or restricted network and you're confident everyone has a similar system. For example, if your Web server is on a corporate network and everyone who connects to the network runs Windows 95, then you can safely use the fonts Arial and Courier, which are standard with Windows 95. You can't make that assumption on the public Internet, however.

CHAPTER 6—The Essential Tools for Text, Graphics, and Links

There's no great loss if you want to make the bet that many of the people who visit your page will have a particular font. If their browser can't display the font, it will appear in the underlying HTML style. The danger is that you'll base your design on an effect that is invisible.

By now you're probably wondering why so many of the Web sites you see contain splashy text formatted in all types of exotic fonts. The fact is those are actually graphic files. By using a graphic program's text tool you can create any type of font special effect possible. The files are then inserted into Web pages as GIF graphics rather than as text.

Now that you've heard the warning, you can format any text in a page by highlighting the words and selecting **Format**, **Fonts**. You'll see the same dialog box, shown in Figure 6.8, that you use to control font sizes.

Removing a Font Format

It can often be difficult to change a font format in FrontPage: you may not be sure which formatting command created the effect (was it an HTML style or a font format?). You can quickly remove a font size or font selection with the **Remove Format** command. First, highlight the text you want changed and then select **Format**, **Remove Format**. It won't strip away an HTML style, but it will remove other formatting options.

ADDING GRAPHICS TO A PAGE

Creating graphic images requires artistic talent. But fortunately, you don't need to have any in order to dress up your pages with beautiful, world-class imagery. The FrontPage CD-ROM provides hundreds of graphic images that you can freely copy into your Web pages (they're distributed on a royalty-free basis).

Many of the images on the FrontPage CD-ROM are in Image Composer's MIC format, rather than in GIF or JPG, the standard formats used in Web sites. You need to open the images with Image Composer first and then copy them to your Web pages. But several dozen clip-art images are copied to your hard disk in the GIF format during the FrontPage installation (unless you selected the minimal installation option). If you want to use these images and they haven't been installed, you can run the FrontPage setup again. If they are installed, you should be able to see a list by selecting **Insert**, **Image**, **Clip Art**.

Chapter 8 covers the techniques you can use to build, edit, and perfect your graphics. The following section will explain the basic technique for inserting graphics into a page.

You can add graphics to a Web page in either of two ways.

- Select **Insert**, **Image** from the menus.
- Open a graphic in another application, copy it, switch to FrontPage Editor, and paste it.

After you have inserted an image, when you save the Web page, FrontPage will ask you to confirm the name of the file (giving you an opportunity to rename it), and then it will copy the graphic file to your Web's images directory. If you inserted a file that isn't in the GIF or JPG format, FrontPage will convert the file to JPG when it copies it to the Web.

Images that have been inserted into a page can be moved by dragging and dropping.

Inserting Clip Art in a Page

The **Insert Images** command gives you the option of selecting images on any directory on your system including clip art that was installed with FrontPage, shown in Figure 6.10.

CHAPTER 6—The Essential Tools for Text, Graphics, and Links

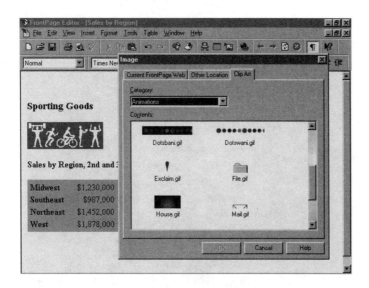

Figure 6.10 Inserting animated graphics using FrontPage clip art.

The **Clip Art** tab in the Image dialog box gives you a choice of several different types of clip art from a drop-down menu. The images span several common categories for decorative jobs, like banners, and backgrounds. One category in particular, however, is special. The Animations clip art consists of GIF files in the GIF 89a format that display moving images. BALL.GIF, for example, is a bouncing ball (it never stops!). SCISSORS.GIF actually snips away all by itself.

NOTE

Animated GIFs will not move when displayed in FrontPage Editor. Once you save the Editor file and load it in a browser, the animation will play.

Alternative Image Settings

After an image is inserted into a page, you can control how it will display with the Image Properties dialog box. You open the dialog box, shown in Figure 6.11, by selecting an image and then right-clicking.

135

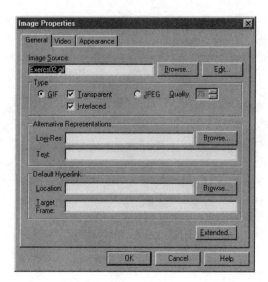

Figure 6.11 The Image Properties dialog box.

The most important attributes are the two settings for Alternate Representations. These attributes can help overcome the frustration visitors to your site will experience as they wait for large graphic files to download. You can enter text or an image that will appear as the larger graphic is downloading.

Low-Res image should be a graphic that provides a preview of the file you enter in the image source field. You can specify any image for the Low-Res file but normally you would want to use a version of the file that's smaller either because it was scanned at a lower resolution or because it uses a smaller color palette. For example, you might use a black-and-white image for the Low-Res file and a full-color image for the Image Source.

WARNING

There's no guarantee that the image you select for Low-Res will be smaller than the image source. It's up to you to be sure you've select a smaller file.

The Low-Res version will disappear from the browser display as soon as the image source file is downloaded. This setting is optional and, in fact, is not widely used. Instead, most Web sites use text instead of an image: it loads faster than any image and doesn't overburden your connection with an image that will disappear seconds after it is transferred.

Controlling a Graphic's Size

Graphic files don't need to appear at full size in a Web page. You can set the dimensions that the graphic image will occupy on a page by selecting the **Appearance** tab when editing Image Properties. See Figure 6.12.

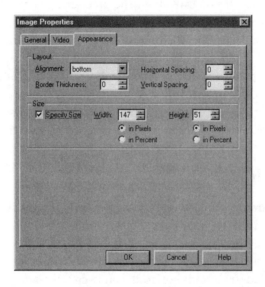

Figure 6.12 Controlling an image's size and alignment.

This setting is optional, but it can speed up the display of a Web page if the graphic file is large. The size setting is normally used with JPG photographs, which are large. Normally, the browser needs to determine the dimensions for an image's size; when the dimensions are established in the Web page, the browser has less work to do. You can take advantage of this performance boost simply by checking the box **Specify Size**.

The Size setting can also be used to adjust the size of an image to work better in your design. In effect, the selections you make under Size create an invisible, virtual window. The browser will fit the image into the border and if you set a border larger or smaller than the actual dimensions of the image, the browser will increase or decrease the size of the image to make it fit. You can set the image border using percentages or pixels.

WARNING
Be careful when working with percentages in setting an image size. If you use a different percentage for height and width, the image will look like it's been stretched out of shape by a fun house mirror! Unless you want to distort the image, use the same percentage for both height and width.

The Size section of this dialog box will display the dimension of the image in pixels. If you care about the precise appearance of your graphics on a page, pay attention to this number when inserting images. It can help you gain perspective on the proportion of your page that will be devoted to graphics. Keep in mind that your entire monitor display is probably 640 by 480 pixels (or 800 by 600 pixels or 1024 by 768). Thus an image that's 320 by 420 pixels will seem huge on a 640 by 480 display—it will be half of the entire display. An image that's 160 by 240 will fill about a quarter screen.

Aligning an Image

The **Appearance** tab in Image Properties can also be used to establish the position of an image in a page. There is a long list of choices that are all mixed in together, but you have fairly limited control over how the image will be aligned. Only one alignment option can be chosen even though this setting controls both horizontal and vertical planes.

You can align the image to the left or right of the available horizontal space, similar to the way type is aligned to the left or right margin.

You can also align it on the vertical scale, lining the image with the top of the baseline, at the baseline, or at the top or bottom of the vertical line. Figure 6.13 shows two of these alignments. The image at top is aligned to the top of the baseline (note that the image lines up with the top of the header). The image in the bottom half of this screen is aligned with the baseline.

CHAPTER 6—The Essential Tools for Text, Graphics, and Links

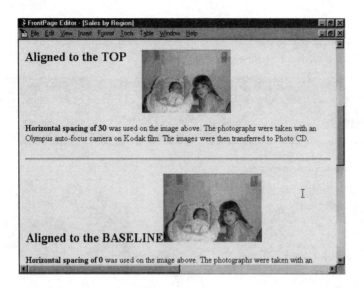

Figure 6.13 Two of the choices for layout alignment of an image.

The spacing settings in the layout section lets you establish "padding" around an image (designers call this "adding white space"). This option establishes an invisible border that will wrap around the image, setting the image aside from all other objects; you can also establish spacing on just the horizontal or just the vertical baselines. The setting controls the number of pixels to be used between the image and the nearest object.

TIP

You need to use a fairly high number for the spacing option to have a noticeable effect. The setting controls the number of pixels and the number of pixels in a monitor display ranges from 480 to 1024. The number 20 is a good starting point.

The spacing setting is often used when an image appears next to text. In Figure 6.13, the image at top has horizontal spacing of 30. The image at bottom is set with the default of 0 spacing.

Image Borders

Image borders are not widely used, but they can add an interesting effect to a page. You set border thickness on the **Appearance** tab of the Image

139

Properties dialog box. The number you enter will be used to draw a black line around the image; the setting is measured in pixels. Figure 6.14 shows an image with a border thickness of 6, at left, and no border, at right.

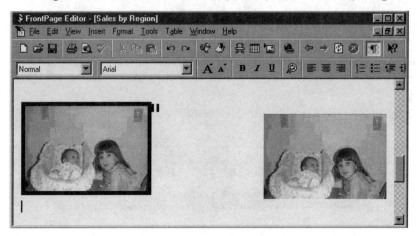

Figure 6.14 At left, an image with a border; at right, no border.

ADDING LINKS TO A PAGE

You can add links between any text or graphics using the **Hyperlinks** command on the Insert menu (as explained earlier, Microsoft FrontPage uses the term *hyperlink* even though the rest of the world uses the term *link*; this book will consistently use the term *link* except when referring to a menu or dialog box item in the program).

Links can connect pages at your Web site, pages on other servers, and specific areas of text on the current page.

Clickable Graphics Versus Image Maps

FrontPage allows you to attach a link to any graphic image using the same technique you use for adding a link to text. Select the graphic you want to make "clickable" and then select the **Insert Hyperlink** tool. You can add bookmarks, links to other pages in the Web, and links to externals URLs.

These links are generated as "client-side" image maps, meaning that the Web server does not need to record the link in a configuration file, as required by earlier generations of browsers.

When you want to select only a small area of an image as clickable, however, the procedure is different. You need to use image editing tools in the Editor, and FrontPage must invoke a WebBot that requires interaction with the FrontPage Extensions on the HTTP server. Note that graphic image maps will not work if you publish your pages on a server that is not running the FrontPage server extensions; the topic is discussed fully in Chapter 8 in the section entitled "Creating Clickable Image Maps."

Bookmarks: Linking Inside a Page

Bookmarks make sense mostly on long pages. They're most widely used on pages that are organized into categories, like an FAQ (frequently asked questions) page, which has a summary of all the questions at the top with the answers below. A bookmark can be used to link from one place in a page to somewhere else in the file. But it can also be used to display a specific area from a link from outside the page.

You must create the bookmark before you can link to it. The process is very simple. Highlight the text that you want to be the target of the link (for example, the answer to a frequently asked question). Then, select **Edit, Bookmark**. As shown in Figure 6.15, the Bookmark dialog box will open and enter the selected text as the name for this bookmark.

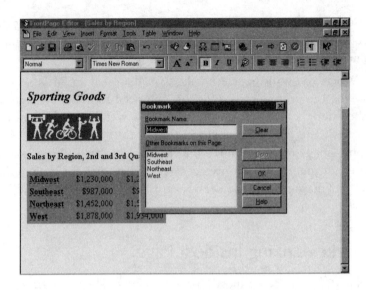

Figure 6.15 Creating a new bookmark.

You can change the name if you wish. Select **OK** and FrontPage will store a bookmark for this location. The text you've selected will now be underlined by a dotted blue line whenever the page is displayed in FrontPage Editor. Any bookmarks that are no longer needed can be cleared by opening the bookmark, selecting the name, and clicking on the **Clear** button.

Once you've saved a bookmark you can create links to it. First, highlight the place where you want the link to originate from. Then, select **Insert**, **Hyperlink**. On the **Open Pages** tab, select the current page and click on the drop-down menu for Bookmark, as shown in Figure 6.16.

CHAPTER 6—The Essential Tools for Text, Graphics, and Links

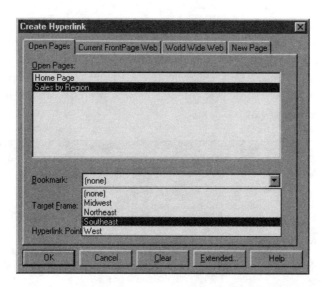

Figure 6.16 Inserting a link to a bookmark.

Select **OK** and the link will be established. The linked text will now be underlined by a solid blue line.

Linking to Other Pages in a Web

When you add links to other pages in your Web, you can create the link to the page or to a bookmark within the page. If you want to link to a bookmark, you must record the bookmark before you begin the process of adding the link.

Adding a link from one page in a Web to another is as simple as highlighting the text where the link will appear and selecting **Insert**, **Hyperlink**. The Create Hyperlink dialog box shown in Figure 6.16 opens. If the page you want to link with is currently open in FrontPage Editor, you can select it from the dialog box that opens. If the file is in your current Web but you haven't opened it for your current work session, you can select it from the **Current FrontPage Web** tab.

FrontPage doesn't limit you to existing files when adding links. You can decide to create a new page that will be the target for your link as you work. Select the **New Page** tab on the Create Hyperlink dialog box, and

FrontPage will not only allow you to build a link to a nonexistent page, but it will also help you start to build this new page by inserting a file name into the Page Title dialog box (using the linked text as a guide). In Figure 6.17, **Insert Link** was selected with the text "photographs." When the New Page dialog box opened, it was prepared to create a new file named **photogra.htm**.

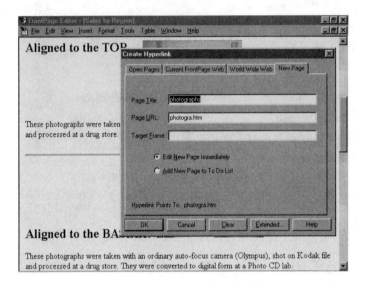

Figure 6.17 Adding a link to a file you haven't created yet.

NOTE

The ability to build a link to a file before you've created the file and then track this new link is one of FrontPage's major conveniences. If you ever wonder whether FrontPage is the best Web authoring tool for you, keep this in mind. It's an enormous aid to development.

This dialog box will give you the option of beginning to work on the file immediately or to add it to your To-Do list. The page will remain on the list until you edit the file at least once. You can open the To-Do list from the Tools menu on FrontPage Explorer or Editor any time your Web is open.

Linking to Other Web Sites and URLs

You add links to other Web sites or other URLs from the **World Wide Web** tab of the Insert Hyperlink dialog box. First, highlight the text where you want the link to appear, then choose **Insert Hyperlink** and select the **World Wide Web** tab.

If you don't know the exact address or aren't sure (who can remember all of those ridiculously long addresses?), click on the **Browse** button. FrontPage will launch a Web browser if one is installed on your system. Navigate to the site you want to use for the link and then, when your browser's Location box displays the correct URL, switch back to FrontPage. The URL of the site you're currently displaying in the browser will appear in the URL line of the dialog box, shown in Figure 6.18. Select **OK**, and FrontPage will add a link to this address to your page.

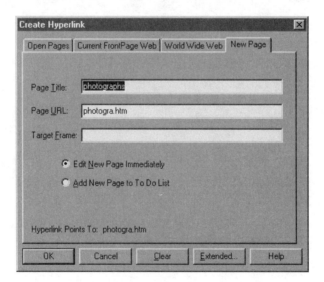

Figure 6.18 Adding a link to a Web URL.

You can also use this dialog box to other Internet addresses. Click on the Hyperlink type drop-down list to select among the following URL types:

- E-mail addresses (mailto)
- Secure Web sites (https)

- FTP sites (ftp)
- Gopher servers (gopher)
- Newsgroups (news)
- Telnet servers (telnet)
- WAIS databases (WAIS)
- Files on your system or local area network (file)

After you select the URL type, you'll need to add the specific address. You can use your browser to locate HTTP, FTP, newsgroups, and gopher servers addresses.

CHAPTER 7

ADDING COLOR TO YOUR WEB

Color is best applied to a Web site all at once, after a significant portion of the Web has been created. Trying to add color piece by piece is a sure-fire way to create an esthetic nightmare. Not only does FrontPage have a few tools you can use to apply colors and graphics consistently throughout a Web site, it also helps you avoid the problem of mismatched colors by providing palettes of colors you can use consistently throughout the Web site.

This chapter will show you how to apply color to page backgrounds, text, and links. We'll start by showing the techniques for applying these to all pages in a Web site and then explore how you can add color one spot at a time.

COLORS AROUND THE WEB

The World Wide Web has become a very colorful place thanks to the HTML spec's ability to colorize many elements in a page. You can select a color for the background of a page and select a color that will be applied equally to all of the text. You can also set up colors that apply only to the three different types of links: one color for the links that a browser has not yet displayed (the plain **LINK** tag), another for links after the browser has visited the URL (the **VLINK** tag), and a third for the link as it's being selected (**ALINK**).

On top of those five color selections, you can choose a different color for any specific text on a page. And you can choose a GIF or JPG image to be displayed as the background of a page. That's all separate from the color graphic files you can insert anywhere in a page.

How Colors are Conveyed on the Web

Most computers sold since 1994 come with 24-bit color so they can easily display HTML colors. Computers that aren't able to display color or display less than 24-bit color (usually that's 8-bit graphics displaying up to 256 colors) will attempt to re-create an approximation of the color by mixing two of the 256 colors or grayscales available on the system. This process is known as *dithering* and can make beautiful, smooth graphics look like ugly, cheap copies of an original. If you're using a computer with 256 colors, you can still add color using the full 24-bit spectrum, but you won't see the pages the same way most of your audience will. If you're creating pages that will be seen only on a corporate network and most of the computers still have older displays, this may not be a problem.

To check the color palette on your system, open the Windows 95 or NT control panel and click on the **Display** icon. Click on the tab for **Settings**; you'll see the window in Figure 7.1.

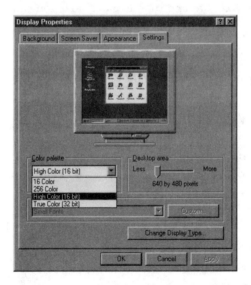

Figure 7.1 The Control Panel's display settings.

A color palette of 16-bit (High Color) or 24-bit (True Color) indicates that you should have excellent color reproduction. A palette of 256 or 16 colors means your display will need to dither many of the colors your sys-

CHAPTER 7—Adding Color to Your Web

tem encounters on the World Wide Web. It may be possible to select a higher value, but normally, Windows 95 is set up for the highest color palette capable in the graphics card; on some systems you can increase the palette if you select a lower setting for the Desktop Area (for example, from 800 by 600 pixels to 640 by 480 pixels). In most cases, however, the only solution is a new video graphics card or additional video memory for the graphics card.

If your system is capable of true color and you're using graphics heavily as you design your Web site, you should be sure to test the pages on a system that's capable of only 256 colors. You need to confirm that the lower level of color doesn't interfere with the message you're trying to convey. Don't expect the site to look just as good with fewer colors (there's nothing you can do to provide the same esthetic quality on a less capable system), but you want to make sure that you haven't used subtle color differences to such a great extent that graphics don't work at all. Remember that when you use a wide range of colors, less capable systems will dither in reproducing your graphics and font colors; two colors that appear dramatically different on a true color system may seem virtually the same on an 8-bit color system.

HTML Color Tags

It wouldn't be practical for Web pages to describe colors the way people do. Terms like "fire-engine red" and "bluish-greenish" don't cut it with computers. HTML, in an extension that Netscape created, specifies colors using the RGB (red, green, blue) scale. Each color is represented on a scale of 0 to 255, matching the way color monitors formulate colors using the blue, red, and green color guns in all desktop monitors (laptops use a different technique). The 256 different choices available for each of the three colors can be mixed in any combination to form a total of 16 million colors (also known as 24-bit color).

You won't normally need to be concerned about the values for HTML color tags since FrontPage allows you to assign colors by choosing from a palette of choices. But you will encounter them occasionally when you view the HTML code in a page.

An HTML color tag specifics a number in the RGB palette that's basically unintelligible to mere mortals since the numbers must be in the hexadecimal scale where numbers from 10 to 15 are represented by letters of the alphabet (the letter *F* equals 15). Each color is presented by two numbers: two numbers for the red value, two for green, and so on. For example, the following HTML tag displays lime green:

```
<font color = "#00FF00">
```

This one isn't too difficult to understand, since FF is the highest value; it's pure green.

But the numbers can be very complicated when colors are mixed. This HTML tag displays a bluish green.

```
<font color = "00FFC8">
```

You can count this as one more reason why using FrontPage is a far better choice for creating Web pages than a word processor.

A Master Scheme for Your Webs

With all the choices for colors and the different elements to be colored, it's easy to create an absolute nightmare in a Web site. Unless you've got the skills of a van Gogh (and you're willing to live with the abuse he suffered for his art), you'll want to apply colors in a rational manner so your tints don't clash.

WARNING

Not only can poor color choices result in unappealing pages, but some combinations of color can also render text illegible. Try using olive type on a green background sometime; the two colors blend together so well that the type disappears.

FrontPage has an easy solution: create a color scheme that works well and use it for all the pages in a Web site. FrontPage allows you to have the color settings in a page drawn from another page. Not only will this technique spare you the work of trying to remember all the color choices you made as you start a new page, but it also allows you to redo your site with

Chapter 7—Adding Color to Your Web

new colors by updating just one page, not the dozens of other pages that may link to it.

Creating a Color Scheme You Can Reuse

You can start a reusable color scheme with any Web page. To start out with a fresh page that you'll use for your colors, first open a Web in FrontPage Explorer and open a blank page.

You can set the color scheme for any page using the Page Properties menu on the File menu. Or you can also open this same menu, shown in Figure 7.2, by clicking on any blank area of a page and right-clicking.

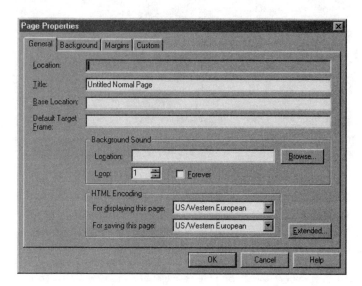

Figure 7.2 The Page Properties dialog box.

Now, you must go through the process of selecting colors for every element in the page (as explained in the following sections).

You'll want to give this page a name that suggests its purpose, like "Extravagant use of color for shocking customers" or "Understated tones for soothing the corporate board." FrontPage allows you to use long names for the Title, so you may as well use something descriptive (the names won't be viewed by anyone other than people who have permissions to edit the Web in FrontPage).

After the file is stored in your Web, you will be able to apply this page's color schemes to any other page by selecting **Page Properties** from the new pages. With the new page open, click on the **Background** tab, shown in Figure 7.3, and click on the **Get Background and Colors from Page** option.

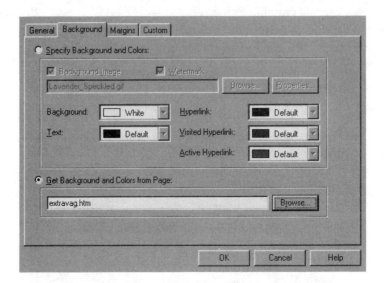

Figure 7.3 Getting background colors from your master scheme.

Select the **Browse** button and FrontPage will show you a list of the files in your current Web. Select the file where you stored your color scheme.

TIP

To make this color scheme available to other Webs, you'll want to open that Web and then import the color scheme page into the new Web. To make the color scheme available to every Web you create, save it as a template.

THE ELEMENTS YOU CAN COLOR

The Page Properties dialog box specifies some of the page elements you can color, but not all of them. The following steps will guide you through all the color choices available in FrontPage.

Selecting Background Images

The color choice with the biggest impact on a page is the background. Like the walls in a room, everything else will either blend in with it—or *clash*! You'll want to select the background before you do anything else.

For a background you can use either a solid color or a file in the GIF or JPEG format. The advantage of using a graphic file for the background image is that it provides an interesting texture, but it can also be practical to repeat a corporate logo. You can create your own graphic to be used as wallpaper in Image Composer or any other graphics program that can produce GIFs or JPEGs.

Follow these steps to add a background image.

1. Select **Page Properties** on the File menu (or right-click anywhere on the background).
2. When the Page Properties menu, shown in Figure 7.3, opens, click on the option **Specify Background and Colors**.
3. To configure the background image as a watermark, select **Watermark**. When an image is a *watermark*, it will not scroll with the image, instead it will always remain in place while the text and graphics scroll. Most background images on the Web are not watermarks and some browsers do not support this feature.
4. If you want to use a graphics editor for preparing the image, click on the **Properties** button.
5. To select an image, click on the **Browse** button. A dialog box will open showing files in the current Web.
6. To select one of the sample images that comes with FrontPage, select the **Clip Art** tab.
7. When the **Clip Art** tab opens, select the down arrow next to Category. Select **Backgrounds** from the list. See Figure 7.4. A sample of GIF files suitable to use as backgrounds will be displayed.

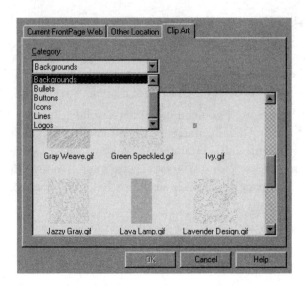

Figure 7.4 Selecting Background clip art.

8. Select one of these images and click on **OK** twice. The image will now be displayed as the background.

When you save the file, FrontPage will ask you if the background image you selected should be saved with the Web. Be sure to say **Yes** so that FrontPage will copy the file from its original folder to your Web folders. If your system is prone to occasional crashes, you may want to save the file immediately after you've chosen the background you plan to keep since saving the file begins the process of importing the graphic image to the Web.

NOTE

When using the **Watermark** option, preview it in Internet Explorer to see it work properly. FrontPage Editor will scroll the background even if you choose the **Watermark** option. Also, Netscape Navigator versions 3.0 and earlier do not support the **Watermark** option.

Selecting Background, Text, and Link Colors

You don't need to select a graphic image to add color to a background. You can choose a color that will display uniformly behind the page instead (you can't have both!). At the same time, you can also change the color for text, and links from their default.

Choosing these colors is easy if you select the color choices in the palette that FrontPage displays. But it gets tricky if you want to create your own custom colors. First, let's see how to select a color from the standard choices, then, if you're not satisfied, consider the custom color choices.

You begin the process of selecting background, text, and link colors from the Page Properties dialog box on the File menu, shown in Figure 7.2. When the dialog box opens, select the **Background** tab, shown in Figure 7.3.

In order to change any of the colors, you must first select the button **Specify Background and Colors**. You can change all the colors or leave some at their default values. Table 7.1 shows the items you can change and the default colors.

Table 7.1 Elements You Can Color and the Default Value

Element	Description	Default Color
Background	Page behind all elements	White
Text	All words, in all text and list styles	Black
Hyperlink	Text in links not yet selected by a browser	Blue
Visited hyperlink	Text in links after selected by a browser	Purple
Active hyperlink	Text in links currently selected by a browser	Red

You select the new color for any item by selecting the drop-down menu next to the default color. Figure 7.5 shows the list of colors as **Hyperlink** is selected.

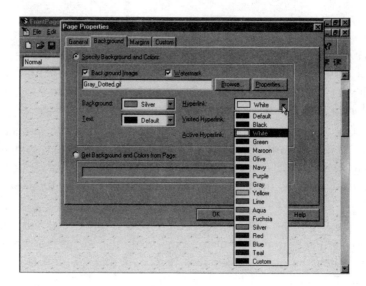

Figure 7.5 Changing the color used to display the text in links.

Selecting the right color can be tricky—as you move your mouse away from the desired color in the direction of the **OK** button, you can easily highlight the wrong color. Be sure the right color appears in the Color choice box before you select **OK**. If not, reopen the list and try again. When you're sure of your color choice, click on **OK** and the current page will be redrawn with your color selections.

WARNING

As a general rule, avoid using dark colors for the background color unless you're trying to create a striking effect. If you do use strong backgrounds, be sure the text is legible. Normal text may be impossible to read when you use a dark background. A possible solution is to display all text in larger than normal size.

Adding Color Highlights to Text

The color setting for text on the Page Properties dialog box affects every instance of text on a page. Because black text is so much more legible than any other color, you may want to leave the text color to its default.

Chapter 7—Adding Color to Your Web

A better way to create colorful impact is to change the color of just a small patch of text. These spots of color can create emphasis for a specific area of the page or be used for accent. It can be especially effective when used to match a graphic.

To color any text selection, first highlight the words you want to color, and then select **Format**, **Font** (or click the right-mouse button and select **Font Properties**). In the Effects section of the dialog box, click on the **Color** drop-down menu, shown in Figure 7.6.

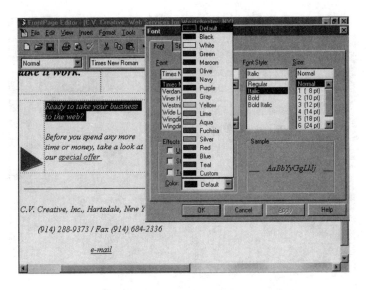

Figure 7.6 Changing the color of highlighted text.

Select a color from the list and move your cursor away. Be sure you've highlighted the correct color before you click on **OK**. The text will change to the new color immediately. You can repeat the process over and over again throughout the page.

NOTE

Unfortunately, there's no easy way to select colors for a specific type of text, like all Header 1 styles. You can change colors for every word on the page with the **Background** command or color just a highlighted selection.

157

Custom Colors

The list of color choices in the Page Properties and Font Properties dialog box lists only 16 colors, but as we saw earlier, FrontPage and Web browsers are capable of displaying more than 16 million shades.

You can try your hand at mixing colors for the page or fonts by choosing the option **Custom** any time the color choice list is open. The Color selection dialog box will open, as shown in Figure 7.7.

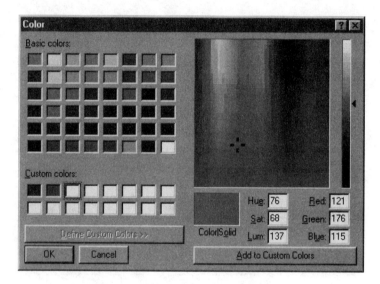

Figure 7.7 Choosing a custom color.

If you've used Microsoft Windows' Control Panel to set colors for your Windows display, you'll be familiar with this dialog box. It allows you to select colors using one of three different techniques.

- You can highlight a color from the spectrum of colors at the right. If you use this method, you first pick the amount of luminescence (from black to white) from the thin bar at the far right and then select the color in the large rectangle.

- You can mix colors by entering values for red, green, and blue ranging from 0 to 255 for each.

- You can set the amount of hue, saturation, and luminescence on a scale of 0 to 240.

The current color selection is displayed in the Color/Solid box. When you've selected a color you want to retain, select the **Add to Custom Colors** button. The current color will appear in the next open box under Custom Colors.

NOTE If your system is capable of displaying all colors, your colors will always appear as solid; on systems not capable of displaying all colors, you'll see a dithered version above Color and the closest pure color match above Solid.

To record your new custom colors, click on **OK**. The color you selected under Custom Colors will appear in the Colors dialog box. Click on **Apply** and the highlighted text will change. To use this color again for another font selection, you'll need to select **Custom** to reopen the menu and choose one of the boxes under Custom Colors.

As you pick a color using one method, the other two scales are updated to reflect your color choice, so if you want to gain a perspective on the other techniques, pay attention to how the selections change in the other boxes.

The custom colors you save can be used when changing the colors of backgrounds, text, or horizontal rules in this same page.

Reusing Someone Else's Color Scheme

If you don't want to go through the color selection process, you can use any HTML page that has a selection of color properties that you want to emulate. To do this, be sure to import the page to your Web using the FrontPage Explorer (don't simply open the page with FrontPage Editor) so that the indexes for your Web will be properly maintained.

TIP Several of the FrontPage Explorer wizards for new Webs come with professionally designed color schemes that you can copy for your own Web (don't worry, you're not stealing anything; a color scheme can't be copyrighted). Run the Corporate Presence Wizard and import the Web Colors page into your own Web.

Once the file that contains your color choices are in the Web, open the Page Properties dialog box on the File menu, select the **Backgrounds** tab and choose the option **Get Background and Colors from Page**.

Adding Color to Horizontal Lines

Horizontal lines can be used to organize a page into logical sections, and they can also be used for decorative value. You insert one with the command **Insert, Horizontal Line**. After the line has been added to the page, you can change the color from the default of black. Select the line, right-click, and open the Horizontal Line Properties dialog box, shown in Figure 7.8.

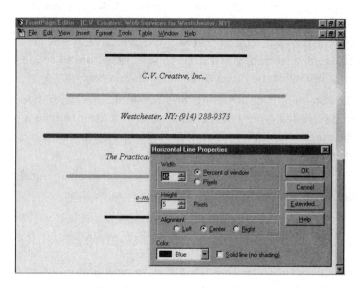

Figure 7.8 Changing the properties of a horizontal line.

The color selection process for a horizontal line is the same as for fonts, backgrounds, and links. You either select one of the 16 color choices or select a custom color.

If you're using the horizontal line to add a touch of color, you will probably want to experiment with the line's other properties: height and width. The default for a horizontal line is a thin 2-pixel height that stretches across 100% of the page. This type of line is practical when you're separating a document into major categories. But what about using the line simply as a decorative element? Try a thickness of 9 pixels and a width of 10%. Figure 7.9 shows a few different combinations of height and weight for horizontal lines. In the display, the properties for each line appear below the line.

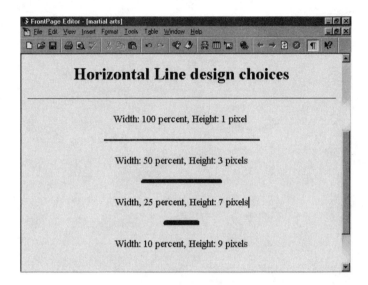

Figure 7.9 Sample height and weight choices for horizontal lines.

You have a choice of setting the width of the line in either pixels or percent. Since you have no way of knowing what size window a browser will use in displaying your pages, percent is usually the better choice. The browser will keep the line in proportion to the rest of the page. Use a pixel setting when you're trying to match the line's width with a graphic.

To create truly unique horizontal rules, experiment with GIF images. The **Insert**, **Horizontal Line** command generates HTML tags and has only a few options: alignment, color, height, and width. A GIF image can contain patterns and a variety of colors and have an unusual shape (rounded corners, for example). FrontPage installs several GIF images specifically designed for use as a horizontal rule in the clip art folder entitled "lines." See the section in Chapter 6 entitled "Adding Graphics to a Page" for a full discussion of the techniques used in inserting clip art.

CHAPTER 8

FINE-TUNING IMAGE PROPERTIES

Graphics add enormous impact to Web pages. They can illustrate a point, reinforce a corporate image, or just add interest so visitors stay at your site a little longer. For most Web sites, graphics are far more than decorations. They convey essential information that couldn't be presented any other way.

Fortunately, you don't need to be a professional designer to create the polished look that you'll want for your Web site. In this chapter, we'll look at the most important design techniques for integrating the graphics throughout your Web site. You'll learn how to create image maps, so that one image can be divided into areas that link to different URLs. You'll learn how to convert an image to a transparent format so it blends in well with a page.

You can spend days tinkering with the graphics, but this chapter will emphasize the most important skills you need to have in successfully integrating graphics into a site. It shouldn't take you more than a few minutes before you're able to compose original graphics that you'll be proud to post at your site.

These skills include cropping graphics you acquire so they'll fit on your page, making an image transparent so it will blend into your page's background, and creating colorful text-based graphics that can be used as logos. You can spend days developing your graphic design skills and perfecting your images. But you can also create perfectly good graphics in only a few hours.

ADDING IMAGE EFFECTS IN FRONTPAGE EXPLORER

FrontPage Explorer is a Web authoring tool, but it allows you to perform several chores normally found only in graphics editors. When you insert a graphic image to a Web page, the graphic file does not actually become part of the page. A link from the HTML file to the graphic file will be established. FrontPage normally stores graphic files in an **\images** folder within each Web, although you can choose to store the file in any folder.

But FrontPage provides two functions for helping to integrate graphic files into Web pages. You can:

- Create a transparent background for GIF images so they blend well into the rest of a page.
- Create image maps that divide a graphic into distinct sections with unique links.

The following sections explains both techniques at length.

Blending Images: Transparent GIFs

Making an image work well in a page is much easier when you can have the background color of an image turn transparent. Once the background is transparent, the colors around the edges of the graphic will seem to disappear, and the image will blend right into the page, instead of sitting in a box. Figure 8.1 shows the same image. At left the image is in its original form. At right, the background is transparent.

Figure 8.1 An image before and after it was made transparent.

CHAPTER 8—Fine-Tuning Image Properties

You can select any color in an image as the transparent color, but normally backgrounds are used so that the image can blend in. You can convert a color to transparent in many image editors, but you can also do it in FrontPage Editor at the same time you're placing an image on the page. Only GIF images can be made transparent, but if you want to convert a JPG file, FrontPage Editor will prompt you to save the image in GIF format when you select the **Transparent** tool. The following section will guide you through the process of inserting an image into a page, sizing it, and changing the background color.

Step-by-Step: Inserting a Transparent Image

In this example, we used the **runner.mic** image that comes with the stock photography included on the FrontPage CD-ROM Bonus Pack, but you can use any GIF or JPG. (The original image was in Microsoft Image Composer's MIC format; it was opened in Image Composer and saved as a GIF image.)

The background image used for the page is the **Gray Weave.gif** file that is installed by FrontPage in the background images folder.

1. Open the page where you want your graphic to appear in FrontPage Editor. Figure 8.2 shows our target page.

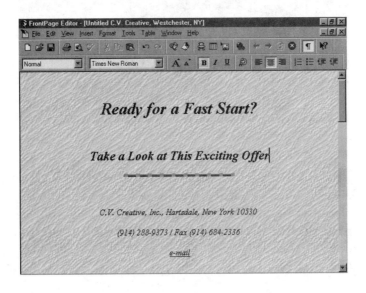

Figure 8.2 A Web page before the graphic is added.

2. Position your cursor at the exact spot on the page where you want the image to appear. In our sample page, we're inserting it in between two words on the top line.

3. Select **Insert**, **Image** from the FrontPage Editor menu. Locate the file you'll use. To search for an image you have not used in this Web before, select the **Other Location** tab. Double-click on the file name when it appears in the dialog box. The image will be inserted in your page at full size. Figure 8.3 shows the **runner.gif** image after it was inserted into the page. However, note that as soon as the image is inserted into the page, FrontPage Editor adds another toolbar at the top of the display with image editing tools. Since it's a large image, the entire graphic cannot fit into the current window but we can adjust the size using the Image Properties dialog box.

Figure 8.3 The image after it was inserted into the page.

4. Click on the image and then right-click the mouse or select **Edit**, **Image Properties**. When the Image Properties dialog box opens, select the **Appearance** tab. Since this image is very large, we'll want to reduce it by a significant amount. After trial and error, this image seems to work well at 25%. To change the size of this image, click on the **Select Size** button and the **Percent** option for both height and

width. Enter the number 25 for both height and width. Figure 8.4 shows the dialog box after the changes were made.

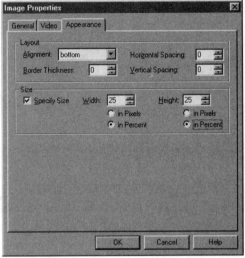

Figure 8.4 Changing an image's size.

5. Click on **OK** and the image will be redrawn at a smaller size. If the image is too large or small, repeat step 4 until you're satisfied.

6. Now we can use the **Make Transparent** tool, which appears on the image editing toolbar, to adjust the color of the background. If you're not sure which tool to select, FrontPage will identify the tools: hold your mouse over the icon and within a second, a small window will open showing the tool name. Click on the **pencil** tool at the far right end of the image editing toolbar and move your mouse to the image.

7. When the mouse pointer is resting on the image, it will change to a pencil eraser, as shown in Figure 8.5. The mouse pointer will not change into the pencil icon when you're pointing at text or blank areas of the page; you can confirm that you've selected the right tool by noting the icon on the toolbar; it will appear depressed when it's active.

Figure 8.5 Using the Make Transparent tool.

8. The **Make Transparent** tool can make transparent any color you select in an image. Normally, the selection of the right color is easy since the background color occupies a fairly large section of an image; it doesn't matter where you select the color in the image. The tool will convert every pixel where the color appears in this image to transparent. To select the correct color, be sure that the small arrow is resting on the desired color. Once the arrow is resting on the correct color, click the left mouse button. The background will disappear, as shown in Figure 8.6.

9. If you selected the wrong color, click on the **Undo** icon (the curving arrow that points to the left) or select **Edit**, **Undo**. Repeat steps 6 through 8.

The **Make Transparent** tool is so easy to use you'll want to use it on almost any GIF graphic you use in a page.

Figure 8.6 The image after using the Make Transparent tool.

Just about the only situations where you wouldn't want to use it are if the image is carefully designed to occupy every bit of its space and if the image doesn't have a single background color. (You can select only one color to become transparent. That's not a limit of FrontPage; that's a limit of the GIF 89a specification that says how transparent colors are defined.) In practice, you'll find that the effectiveness of many of the GIF images you use can be improved with the **Make Transparent** tool.

CREATING CLICKABLE IMAGE MAPS

Transforming an ordinary image into a clickable image is just as easy to do as making an image transparent. And it can be just as effective in adding impact to a page. In Figure 8.6, turning the runner into a clickable image can help capture the impulse of visitors to take that fast start if the image is linked to the information. Images can be linked in two ways.

- A simple link can be added to a graphic file using the **Insert Hyperlink** command. The entire image is linked to the same URL. These links are known as *client-side image maps*.
- An image map can be associated with the graphic file, containing detailed information about shapes in the image, linking different URLs to different shapes.

The process of creating a simple link between an image and a URL is no different from adding a link to text. You highlight the image and then select **Insert**, **Hyperlink**. The types of links you can add were discussed at length in Chapter 6.

TIP

Image maps are often used to create menu bars to guide users around a site. Each area of the graphic links to a specific page on your Web site, helping to create categories that visitors can choose among.

The process of creating an image map is a little more involved since you need to define a hot spot inside the image before you add the link.

Preparing to Add Hot Spots to an Image

When you highlight an area inside an image, FrontPage records it as a hot spot. The coordinates that define the hot spot are known as image maps. HTTP servers without FrontPage Server Extensions can process links to image maps only if an image map is stored on the server, and the link is recorded in a configuration file on the server. Before you add a hot spot to an image you should be aware of a limitation that it will impose on your Web page. The image maps that FrontPage adds require the use of a FrontPage WebBot that can be executed only by a server running the FrontPage server extensions. If you're publishing pages on a server that does not have the FrontPage extensions installed, you will need to change the setting for Image Maps in Explorer under Tools, Web Settings, Advanced. Refer to the section "Moving Files to Servers without FrontPage Extensions" in Chapter 18 for more information.

Standard HTML Web pages establish image maps by referring to an image map file that's stored on the server. FrontPage generates HTML code that calls a WebBot to execute the image map. Following is a sample of the HTML code inserted by FrontPage. FrontPage begins tags for WebBots with an exclamation point so that browsers will ignore the tags; it will be processed by the server using FrontPage extensions.

```
<!–webbot bot="ImageMap" rectangle=" (198,30) (369, 147)
index.html" src="bar.gif" border="0" width="640"
height="180" startspan –> <MAP NAME = "FrontPageMap"> <AREA
SHAPE="RECT" COORDS="198, 30, 369, 147" HREF =
"index.html"></MAP><a href=
"_vti_bin/shtml.exe/sports.htm/map"> <img src="bar.gif"
width="640" ismap usemap = "#FrontPageMap"
height="180" border="0"></a><!–webbot bot="ImageMap" endspan
i-checksum="45437" –>
```

Protecting Original Files

When you bring an image into a FrontPage Web, it's a good idea to retain an original version of the file on another folder on your hard disk or a different disk drive. If you resize the image, FrontPage Editor will save a reduced version of the file on the folders inside your Web.

FrontPage saves the file in a smaller size to offer the benefit of having the image transfer faster when your Web site is published and a browser downloads the version. But you may need to use the file in its original dimensions for other work, so be sure you don't delete the original.

Normally, FrontPage will not remove it from your system if you use the Import file in Explorer to bring the image into a Web or if you select it from a different folder using the **Image**, **Insert** command. But it's something you should keep in mind so that you don't assume that the original file isn't worth keeping any more: it is.

Step-by-Step: Creating an Image Map

In FrontPage, the area of an image that maps to a link is called a *hot spot*. You add hot spots to an image when you want only part of the image to link to a URL.

FrontPage allows you to define the hot spot using a **circle**, **rectangle**, or **polygon** tool. The tools for each appear on the same image editing toolbar that opens when you use the **Make Transparent** tool. Anytime you click on an image in a FrontPage Explorer, this tool will open.

In the following example, we'll import a JPG image and add different links to three distinct areas within the image. For our sample, we're using a JPG image that was created in Microsoft Image Composer using stock photographs on the FrontPage CD-ROM Bonus Pack. Three different photographs were inserted on top of a rectangle, and the image was saved as a single JPG image, as shown in Figure 8.7.

Figure 8.7 After an image is inserted, click on it to open the image editing toolbar.

1. Insert the graphic file using the **Insert**, **Image** command. After the image is inserted, click on it. The image editing toolbar will open, as shown in Figure 8.7.

2. You have a choice of three tools to use in defining the hot spot: a square, a circle, and a polygon.

3. To define a square, click on the **square** icon; the icon is highlighted. Move the mouse pointer toward the image. As soon as the pointer is inside the image's borders, the pointer will change to a pencil. Click

CHAPTER 8—Fine-Tuning Image Properties

in the spot that you want to define as the upper-left corner. FrontPage will begin to draw the square. Move the mouse pointer to the spot you want to define as the lower right corner. FrontPage will surround the area with a rectangle and display the Create Hyperlink dialog box, as shown in Figure 8.8. If you prefer, you can define the rectangle in the reverse order, beginning with the lower right corner and finishing at the top left.

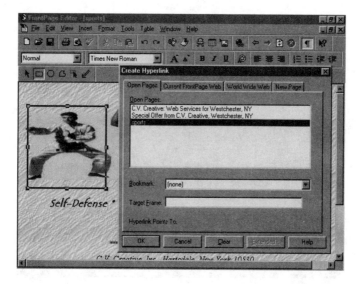

Figure 8.8 After a hot spot is defined you can select the URL for the link.

4. To define a circular hot spot, click on the **circle** tool. The pointer is highlighted. Move the mouse pointer toward the image; as soon as the pointer is inside the image's borders, the pointer will change to a pencil. Move the pencil to the point you want to define as the center of the circle. FrontPage begins to draw a circle; move the pointer until the circle encloses the area you want to define as the hot spot. Click again, and the hot spot is defined. The Create Hyperlink dialog box will open.

5. A polygon can be an irregular shape. You define the shape by clicking at each corner. Start by selecting the **polygon** tool; the icon is highlighted. Move the mouse pointer toward the image; as soon as the pointer is inside the image's borders, the pointer will change to a pen-

cil. Click the first point for the polygon. When you move the mouse pointer, FrontPage will indicate the corner with a square and it will draw a line toward the next point. Click and FrontPage will draw the line and begin to draw the next line in any direction you indicate. You can continue until you've defined the complete shape. Figure 8.9 shows how the **polygon** tool can be used to outline active human figures.

Figure 8.9 The polygon tool was used to create hot spots surrounding the two figures at right.

In creating hot spots within an image, you're limited only to the area defined by the image and by hot spots you've already created. In the illustration shown in Figures 8.7–8.9, the sample image is a transparent GIF so while it may seem that the background of the page is being selected as an image map, the image maps are defined only within the borders of the graphic file that was inserted. A background image cannot be connected to a link.

As soon as you define a hot spot, the Create Hyperlink dialog box opens with the same choices for adding links you have with text. You can choose a file within your current Web, a file on your system, or a remote URL or you can begin a new page. If you select the World Wide Web dialog box and click on **Browser**, the Web browser on your system will load, and you can navigate to a URL and have it inserted as the link. If you choose to create a new page, you'll have the option of working on it immediately or assigning it to the To-Do list.

Editing Hot Spots

After you've completed the process of creating a hot spot and assigning a link, you can change the links with the **Select** tool on the image editing toolbar. To display the image editing toolbar, click on the image.

- To remove a hot spot, click on the **Select** tool, point to the hot spot you want to remove, and press the **Delete** key.
- To change the shape or size of a hot spot, click on the **Select** tool and select the hot spot. Then, click on the corner you want to edit and drag it to the new location.

TIP Avoid the temptation to define very small hot spots. Visitors to your Web site will need to be able to select the area from a browser. If the spot is too small, they may not realize it's a hot spot.

You can also change the link at a hot spot. Select the area you want to change and right-click or select **Edit**, **Image Hotspot Properties**. The Create Hyperlink dialog box will open, and you can select a different link for the area.

WARNING Be careful when editing a hot spot. It's very easy to move the entire outline for the hot spot without realizing what you've done.

DESIGNING WITH TEXT

We normally think of word processors and desktop publishing programs as the proper tools to use for presenting text. And because FrontPage Editor has many text editing tools, it's natural to think of it as a good way to design text.

Unfortunately, the reality of today's Internet standards limits the effectiveness of any Web authoring tool in presenting text. Remember that fonts can be displayed in Web pages only when the browser's system has the fonts already installed. If you specify a font in your pages using FrontPage, you have no way of knowing if the page is being viewed properly.

In order to add accent to words, you'll need to use a graphics editing program. You don't need talent. In many cases, all you need to do is use the **text** tool to type in the words and then format them in the right font, size, and color. Finally, store it as a GIF file that can be inserted into your Web pages. You can add the borders, shadings, and other artistic effects, if you want. But even if you're just saving a specific word, you'll create a more effective page if you use a graphics program to create the text in a decorative font. For example, Figure 8.10 is composed entirely of GIF images.

Figure 8.10 Text often needs to be displayed as a GIF image rather than as text.

The most important consideration is to keep the dimensions of the graphics file small. Remember that you're working in a 640 by 480 pixel display; a graphic that is 320 by 240 will occupy a quarter of the display. A small area of text usually occupies a tiny fraction of the display and has dimensions of 100 by 50 or less. If you create files that are too large, not only will they waste disk space and take longer to download than is necessary, they'll also occupy too much screen real estate. Graphics files created for text messages should be only as large as the text being displayed. All white space should be cropped out.

Designing with Fonts on Intranets

Of course, the one exception to this rule is when you're pages will be published only on a network and you're confident that everyone who views the page will have the necessary fonts. Any system that has Windows 95, Windows NT, or Windows 3.1 installed will have TrueType fonts in Times New Roman, Arial, and Courier, so if you're organization is completely standardized on Windows, you can be confident that text you format in these fonts will display correctly. If the entire organization is also standardized on a word processor, you can also use the fonts that come as a default installation option.

WARNING

FrontPage installs more than a half dozen new fonts on your system as part of the setup for Image Composer. Unless you're able to have these fonts installed on other systems throughout your intranet, use them when designing graphics files with Image Composer, not with FrontPage Editor Web pages.

In all other situations, you'll want to create graphics files in order to gain more impact for text that you can using HTML styles.

CHOOSING THE BEST IMAGE EDITOR

The ability to create and edit graphics is so important for developing a successful site on the public World Wide Web or a private intranet that Microsoft includes Image Composer, a graphics editor, on the FrontPage CD-ROM Bonus Pack. If you've been using a graphics program like CorelDraw, PaintShop Pro, or PhotoShop and you're satisfied, you don't need to switch to Image Composer to create attractive graphics, although the discussion in the following chapters may convince you that it's better for you.

TIP To find links to Web sites that offer free clip art, go to a search engine and enter the search term (what else?) **free clip art**. More than 100,000 links showed up when we tried this at InfoSeek (www.infoseek.com). One site that does nothing but provide links to clip art is www.clipart.com. And if you're prepared to pay for professional photography, visit www.metatools.com.

The essential feature you want to have in a graphics program for a Web editor is the ability to store files in GIF and JPG format. You'll also want to be sure your system has the fonts you'll need to create graphics that incorporate text with the look you want to convey. For example, if your corporation uses a specific font for its corporate logo, you'll want to obtain the file to use with the graphics software. Windows 95 and NT support TrueType fonts, and any graphics design program you run will be able to access a TrueType font.

Selecting Your Own Image Editor

No matter which program you use for graphics work, you can open the program from the Tools menu in both FrontPage Explorer and Editor. If you don't want to use FrontPage Image Composer, you can substitute a different program with another program that's installed on your system.

To change the FrontPage default setting for your graphics image editor, open FrontPage Explorer, and select **Tools**, **Options**. When the Options dialog box opens, select the **Configure Editors** tab. Highlight the graphic format (for example, **JPG** or **GIF**) and then select **Modify**. The screen will look like Figure 8.11.

CHAPTER 8—Fine-Tuning Image Properties

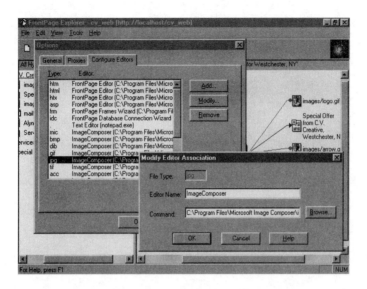

Figure 8.11 Selecting a different image editor.

Select **Browse** to search through your system for the software you want to use as your image editor. You may want to have one image editor for GIF files and another for JPG.

CHAPTER 9

CREATING AND PERFECTING GRAPHICS WITH IMAGE COMPOSER

Dozens of graphics editing programs can be used to build the images you add to a Web site. The FrontPage Bonus Pack CD-ROM provides one of the best on the market.

This chapter will explore Image Composer, guiding you through the process of creating, enhancing, and saving graphics files. Image Composer uses a vocabulary all its own, which you'll need to learn to use the product. In this chapter, you'll learn about sprites, composition guides, groups, and many other concepts unique to this software. You'll learn the interface for Image Composer and how to use the tools for creating images and enhancing them.

Image Composer is an enormously powerful program, and it will require many hours of experience before you can begin to master all its features. This chapter is designed to guide you through the software starting with the most important features needed for Web page design. Over time, you may find that you're using Image Composer for a wide variety of graphic applications, totally independent of your work with FrontPage.

OVERVIEW OF IMAGE COMPOSER

Image Composer is a full-featured graphics editing program that allows you to edit existing graphics or create new files. It has a wide range of tools for creating shapes, formatting text, and tinting images. You can create special effects with patterns and gradients. You can rotate images or text. And you can very easily combine images from different sources. For example, you can scan images directly into an Image Composer file using any device that installs to Windows with TWAIN drivers, and you can open graphics you obtain from clip-art CD-ROMs or online image libraries. The FrontPage CD-ROM comes with over 600 photographs in the Image Composer MIC format, but you can import files from other formats, too. A few professional graphics houses have begun to provide images in the MIC format; for example, MetaTools, which sells high-quality photographic images in the MIC format through its Web site at www.metatools.com. (Ten sample images are on the CD-ROM with this book.)

NOTE Image Composer supports the Photoshop plug-in API, so you can use graphics filters like Kai's PowerTools and other plug-in programs while you're working with Image Composer, even if you don't have a copy of Adobe Photoshop.

The name, Image Composer, actually suggests how you use the product. You use the software to compose an image from a variety of smaller elements. The workspace is like a big desk where you can assemble many different images.

Some of the tools help you organize these different elements, and others are used for changing the appearance of a single element. When working with existing graphics, you'll use the Image Composer tools to make the slight adjustments that may make a world of difference in creating the best-looking appearance for your graphics. FrontPage Editor will automatically convert files from several popular graphics formats—such as TIF, Windows MetaFile, Targa, Windows BMP and TIF—into the GIF and JPG formats that are most common on the Web when you use the **Insert Image** command. But if you take just a minute to first open the file in Image Composer, you'll be able to make changes that can adapt the image to your Web site. For example, you may want to add a few words as a caption before you store the file in the correct format. Or you may want to crop the file so that only the most important areas of the image are displayed.

Your work in Image Composer doesn't need to stop with FrontPage. Any images you save with Image Composer can be used in other applications, like word processing programs and presentation graphics. The program saves files in several formats used by graphics editors, including Windows BMP, TIF, Targa, and Adobe Photoshop's PSD format. For example, you may want to store one version of the file in GIF for use in your Web pages, another version in TIF for use in a printed document that you'll create with PageMaker, and another version in BMP for importing into PowerPoint. Image Composer will allow you to use most of the options available in each of the graphic formats, so if the format offers compression (as JPEG does) or color to grayscale conversion (as TIF and GIF do), then you'll be able to convert the files in Image Composer.

Loading Image Composer

Image Composer will load whenever you double-click on a JPG or GIF file in Web display from FrontPage Explorer or select the **Tools, Show Image Editor** command in either Explorer or Editor. FrontPage does not install an icon for Image Composer as a way of discouraging you from creating images outside of a Web. If you store images out of a Web, the FrontPage index files won't know about the file, and you make it more difficult to manage the links inside a Web.

TIP

To create an icon for Image Composer on your Windows desktop, select **Settings, Taskbar** from the Windows Start menu. Select **Add** and then **Browse**. You should find the program icon in the folder \Program Files\Microsoft Image Composer.

Getting to Know Image Composer

Image Composer is such a powerful tool that it can be overwhelming at first. If you've only used simple graphics editors like Windows Paint, you may be disoriented by the extensive range of features. Don't fear. You can get up to speed quickly in Image Composer if you concentrate on specific tasks. In the following sections, you'll learn some basic techniques that you can accomplish in just a few minutes. With these skills under your belt, you'll be able to add the more advanced tools without much trouble.

The first step is to become familiar with the interface. Figure 9.1 shows the major elements in Image Composer.

Microsoft FrontPage 97: HTML and Beyond

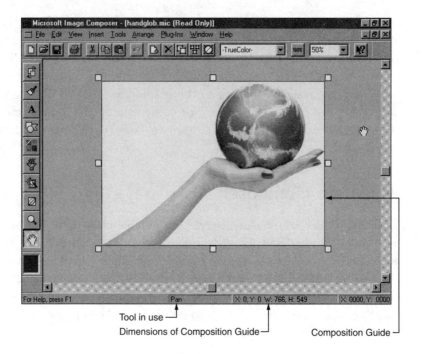

Figure 9.1a

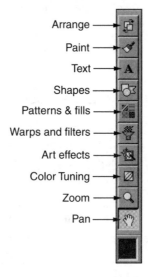

Figure 9.1b The Image Composer interface.

CHAPTER 9—Creating and Perfecting Graphics with Image Composer

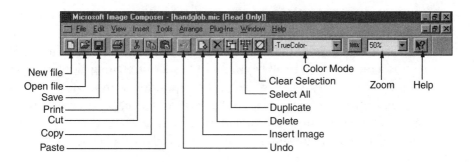

Figure 9.1c

The tools that run along the top of the display control the file and image being displayed. For example, there are cut-and-paste commands, control over color display for the entire image (color or grayscale), and control over image size (from 10% of the actual size up to 1000%).

The tools that run along the left side of the screen allow you to change the image, ranging from shapes you can add to artistic effects you can use in place of existing patterns in the image.

Right-Sizing Images before You Begin

Whenever you begin work on a new Image Composer file, it's important that you consider the place where you want to use the image. Web pages are normally composed of many different images and text elements, so you'll want to be sure you're designing an image that works well in the allotted space. While FrontPage Editor can make it fit (using the **Sizing** option in the Image Properties dialog box), if your image is squeezed into a tight space, it may look cramped and the text may be illegible.

It may take some time to get used to the concept of working with pixels. Start by thinking of the basic dimensions of a screen as 640 pixels wide and 480 pixels high. Many systems display Web pages at higher resolutions (for example, 800 pixels wide and 600 pixels high), but 640 by 480 is the lowest screen resolution in popular use. You may want to use 800 by 600 as your normal dimension, but do this only if you're confident that most of your audience runs their displays at this resolution.

Once you decide on the resolution you'll use, assume that about 10% of the display will be used for menus and borders. Now you can make a rough approximation of the sizes you'll want to use. For example, if you're creating a menu bar that will be used as a header, stretching along the top of a screen, you may want to create a composition with a width of 600 pixels and a height of only 80 or 100 pixels. For an image based on a photograph of a person from the shoulders up (a head shot) that will appear next to text, you might want a width of 120 pixels and a height of 200.

TIP Web pages that have a professional look tend to have small graphics. Not only will small graphics download faster, but they also leave more room for text and other design elements on a page.

You can set the default size for new Image Composer files with the **Tools**, **Options** command. The dialog box is shown in Figure 9.2.

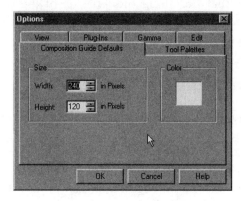

Figure 9.2 Setting the default dimensions for new images.

Image Composer shows the size of the graphic by displaying a rectangle called the *composition guide*. When you first begin to work on a new image, this rectangle is white, but its color will change if you alter the background color.

Everything inside the composition guide is included in the image; anything outside the white box is not part of the current image. As you work on graphics and rearrange things, you'll want to use the gray areas outside of the composition guide as a holding area. But be sure everything you want included on the image appears inside the composition guide.

You can change the dimensions for the current file at any time using the **File**, **Composition Properties** command.

Zooming and Panning for a Better View

To gain a better perspective on your work, you'll want to zoom in or out frequently as you work. There are several ways to change the zoom level. A drop-down menu lets you choose the size, from 10 to 1000%. Next to the drop-down menu, the **Actual Size** button will display the image at 100% with a single click. And on the toolbar at left, the **zoom** tool (a magnifying glass) will not only increase the image size by one level, but it will also pan the image so that the spot where you click is now in the center of the screen.

When working on images for Web pages, you'll often want to work with the image at 50 or 33%. This will allow you to see the entire composition guide and the objects that you're keeping off to the side.

Use the **pan** tool (the small hand) on the left toolbar when you want to move the image within the window. If you haven't heard the term before, think of film making. Cameras don't move when they film, they pan. To pan across the images on your display, select the **pan** tool, move to a spot in the display, click, and drag. The display will shift.

SPRITES: OBJECTS WITHIN IMAGES

There's one last concept to understand before you delve into the process of creating images. *Sprites* are the basic element used in Image Composer files. When you insert text, create a new shape, or insert a file, you are adding a sprite. Image Composer keeps tabs on each sprite independently so you can manipulate the various elements without affecting other parts of the image. You can have as many sprites in an image as you find necessary to achieve the proper effect. Figure 9.3 shows an Image Composer screen that is composed of ten sprites.

Figure 9.3 Images are collections of sprites.

This image is composed of two photographs that come with the FrontPage Bonus Pack CD-ROM and eight lines of text.

The Image Composer workspace is very easy to control after you begin to think of it as a collection of sprites. Just about any type of graphics special effect you want to achieve is accomplished by adding sprites or changing the properties of sprites that are already part of the image.

You can have Image Composer identify each sprite by selecting the **Select All** toolbar icon or **Edit**, **Select All** from the menus. When a sprite is selected, Image Composer displays a *bounding box*. Figure 9.4 shows the same image after the **Select All** command was used.

CHAPTER 9—Creating and Perfecting Graphics with Image Composer

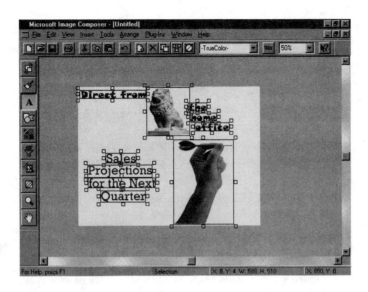

Figure 9.4 The **Select All** command displays sprites in bounding boxes.

You can also show the bounding box for an individual sprite by moving the mouse pointer near the object and clicking when you have selected any of the tools that control the properties of an image, such as the **Arrange**, **Text**, **Paint**, **Shapes**, or **Patterns** tool.

Moving and Resizing Sprites

When you select a group of sprites, you'll see a bounding box that doesn't provide editing tools since you'll need to use toolbar icons or menu commands to work with a group of sprites. But when you select an individual sprite, the bounding box will display resizing handles, indicating that you can change this sprite by dragging on the box with your mouse. Figure 9.5 shows a sprite after it was highlighted.

189

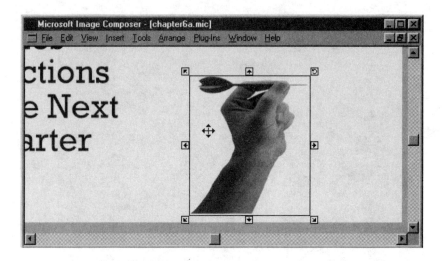

Figure 9.5 A sprite in a bounding box with resize handles.

- *Move* the sprite by holding down the left mouse button and dragging the sprite to its new location.
- *Delete* the sprite by pressing the **Delete** key. It will be permanently removed from the file (you can reverse a deletion with the **Undo** key but not if you have already performed another action).
- *Cut* the sprite and place it on the clipboard with the **Edit**, **Cut** command. Or, **Edit**, **Copy** to create a copy of the sprite on the clipboard.
- *Change the size* of the sprite by selecting one of the diagonal arrows in the corners and dragging it; the size of the box will change as you do. When you increase or decrease the size using the corner arrows, the image will retain its original proportions.
- *Stretch* the image by selecting one of the arrows on the edges on the top, bottom, or sides. When you stretch the image, the dimensions of the image will be distorted.
- *Rotate* the image by selecting the curved arrow in the upper-right corner.

When a sprite is selected, you can also use the **Color Tuning** and **Arrange** commands to change its appearance.

Selection Sets and Groups of Sprites

You'll often want to select several sprites at once so that you can change the properties of only a few sprites. For example, you might want to change the color of several words of text and leave other words unaffected. Or you may want to align text. Image Composer has two ways of working with sprites, which are shown in Table 9.1.

Table 9.1 Two Ways of Working with More Than One Sprite

Type	Status	Purpose
Selection sets	Temporary	Change properties
Groups	Permanent	Rearrange

To select more than one sprite, first select the tool you plan to use (for example, **Color Tuning** if you are going to change the colors). Then, hold down the **Shift** key and click on the sprites you want to change. A bounding box will appear on each. A group of sprites selected in this way is known as a *selection set*.

You can also use a different technique to select several sprites, which Image Composer calls a *group*. You select a group with the **Arrange** command or by selecting two sprites, right-clicking, and choosing **Group** from the menu. You cannot change the properties of sprites in a group. Instead, you use a group to simplify the alignment of groups. Normally, you would select a group and then open the Arrange toolbox to fine-tune the appearance of the sprites in the group.

A selection set is temporary. As soon as you select a different sprite, the selection set will disappear. A group is permanent. It will remain a feature of this file, even after you save it, unless you use the **Ungroup** command on the Arrange menu.

TIP Groups and selection sets work different commands, so at times you'll want to move between the two. For example, you may want to convert a group to a selection in order to change colors. After the colors are changed, you can re-store the group.

You can convert a group to a selection set with the **Explode** command. You can change a group to a single sprite with the **Flatten** command; beware that the **Flatten** command can only be reversed with the **Undo** command before you select a new tool.

CREATING NEW SPRITES

Image Composer provides a powerful range of tools for drawing and editing images. In this section, you'll learn how to begin a new image and insert a sprite using one of the tools.

Text Sprites

It may sound odd, but one of the most important uses for Image Composer is to format text. In earlier chapters, we've discussed HTML's limited options for controlling the appearance of text. As a result, GIF images that add color to words have become one of the most important tools in a Web developer's bag of tricks. Image Composer gives you the opportunity to format text to your heart's delight. Not only can you choose the exact size and font you prefer, but you can also choose colors, rotate text, and even create special effects like a drop shadow. Text can be very effective when used together with an image; for example, you can add text on top a photograph for labels or captions.

You begin the process of adding text to an Image Composer file by clicking on the **text** tool (the *A* icon). The Text dialog box opens, as shown in Figure 9.6.

Figure 9.6 The Text dialog box shows the selected style.

Click on the **Select Font** button. You can choose any font installed on your system and you can select any type size. If you want to use a point size that's not listed on the drop-down list, type the number directly into the Size box.

NOTE

Image Composer comes with a variety of fonts. They can be installed from the FrontPage setup program; if they weren't installed, you can repeat the setup routine by running the Setup program on the FrontPage Bonus Pack CD-ROM.

Once you've selected the font and size, select **OK**. You can now type in the Text dialog box. Your text will appear in the style you select. The text will appear in the currently selected color; you can change the color by double-clicking on the **Current Color Swatch** box. When the Color Picker dialog box opens, choose a new color and select **OK**. In the Text dialog box, click on **Apply** and the text will be inserted into the page in the color you selected. You can also control degree of opacity by moving the slider bar in the Text dialog box. A low setting for opacity will produce a very faint color; use an opacity of 100 for the most vibrant color possible.

TIP

You can only insert a single line of text with the **text** tool. If you want more than one line, you'll need to insert separate sprites, one by one. To align text, group the individual lines and then use the **Arrange** tool.

Fitting Text into a Space

A well-designed page is no accident. Unless you're incredibly lucky, you won't be able to simply choose a font size, type in the words, and then expect it to fit perfectly. You'll often need to try a few different type sizes to get it right. The text must fit inside the borders of the composition guide. If it doesn't fit, like the text in Figure 9.7, you have several ways of fixing it.

193

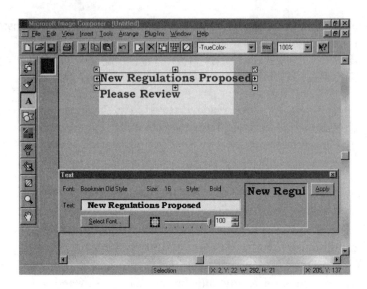

Figure 9.7 Text that doesn't fit inside the composition guide.

After the text is added to the page, you can make it fit by dragging on the bounding box handles; be sure to use the resizing tools at the corners to retain the correct proportions of the font. Use the **shrink** or **expand** tools on the top, bottom, left, or right sides only when you want to distort the text.

When you're adding several lines of text rather than resizing the text by dragging on the bounding box, a better technique is to select a different font size. Using the best font size is a better technique than resizing if you're adding multiple lines of text, since it will help to ensure a more uniform look. When you resize text by dragging on the bounding box, you won't be able to duplicate the dimensions of the font when you add new text to this graphic. If you choose a new font size, you need to delete the text sprite you used to add it; the **text** tool will not change the point size after it is added to a page.

Sometimes when you have difficulty making text fit into the composition guide, the problem isn't the type size you selected. It may be that the dimensions of your image are too small. You can resize an image by selecting the **File**, **Composition Properties** dialog box. Type in new values for the width and click on **Apply**. Image Composer will immediately resize the composition guide; if the text is still too wide, try again.

Creating a Shadow Effect with Text

To create a shadow effect (also called drop shadow), use a low setting of about **30** for Opacity and select **Apply** to add the text sprite to the page. Then, without changing any other text settings, change the opacity to **100** and select **Apply**. The two text sprites will be inserted directly on top of the other. Drag one of the sprites a short distance away. Click on a blank space in composition guide to remove the bounding boxes so that you can see the effect. Your text should be similar to the text in Figure 9.8.

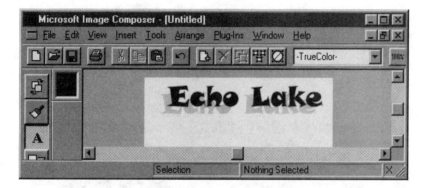

Figure 9.8 Creating a shadow effect by changing a font's opacity.

You can also create a spinning effect if you use the same technique several times but rotate the text. For example, start out with an opacity of **10** and apply the text. Then increase the opacity to **20**, apply the text but rotate it slightly. Repeat the process until you reach an opacity of **100**.

Arranging Text

Image Composer can help you create stunning effects with text but it's not a word processor and you have to put in a little extra to keep lines of text neatly aligned. Every time you add text, it becomes a standalone sprite. That can create a ragged group of lines. To properly manage text, you'll want to align the text and then group it so that it can be moved as a solid block.

Arrange the text after you've inserted each line. Then, carefully position one line of text into the correct position; normally, you'll want to do this with the top line. Then you can arrange other lines below the first line. Highlight the line that should appear directly below the top line and select the **Arrange** tool.

The Arrange dialog box is organized into several sections; you'll use the Align area. When you move your mouse pointer slowly over the Align area, a help window will open as you move the mouse pointer, indicating the type of alignment you can select. To left-align text, select the **Left Sides** area of the **Align** tool. Figure 9.10 shows the Align dialog box with the **Left Sides** area highlighted.

Figure 9.10 Lining up text.

Click and a dialog box will open, prompting you to select the sprite to be used for as the left margin. Click **OK** and then select the top line. Image Composer will immediately line up the two text sprites. Repeat the process for each line of text.

After all the text is neatly lined up, highlight each line and select **Arrange, Group** (you can also use the **Group** tool on the Arrange dialog box). Now you'll be able to move the text in a single block, without disturbing the text alignment.

Creating New Shapes

Shapes are the basic graphic elements in Image Composer. Whether you plan to use Image Composer to enhance an existing graphics file or create an original image, you'll often use the Shapes toolbox to add a new sprite. Once you've added a new shape, you can edit it or arrange it with other sprites.

Adding a Sprite with the Shape Tool

Whenever you want to add a graphic element, click on the **Shape** tool orselect **Tools**, **Shapes**. The Shape dialog box, shown in Figure 9.11, opens.

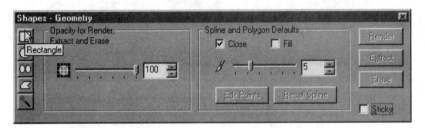

Figure 9.11 The Shapes toolbox.

To add a shape to an image, make your selections from left to right.

1. Select a shape: rectangle, oval, spline, polygon, or color lift.
2. Adjust the opacity level: **100** is a solid color; **1** is transparent.
3. Move your mouse pointer to the drawing and begin to draw the shape. If you're drawing a polygon or spline, you have more options to select in the right side of the Shapes toolbox.

The following sections describe the process for each of the shapes.

Drawing Rectangles

To draw a rectangle, after you've completed steps 1 and 2 above, click in the spot where you want the upper left corner to appear. The outlines of a box will appear. Now, drag the mouse toward the lower right corner and release the button when it is the correct shape. If it's the correct size and shape, select the **Render** button or click on another tool and the shape will be filled in. If it's not the correct shape, you can resize it.

Drawing Ovals

To draw an oval, after you've completed steps 1 and 2, you actually create a box that Image Composer will use to define the oval, as shown in Figure 9.12. Start by clicking in the upper left corner and then drag your mouse toward the lower right corner. When you release the mouse button, a box will be drawn. If this is the correct size, select another tool or click on the **Render** button and the oval will be drawn inside the box.

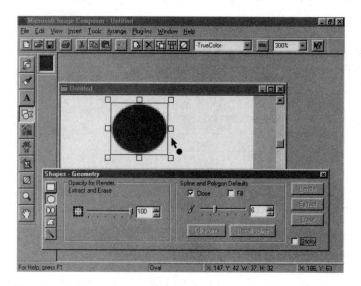

Figure 9.12 Drawing an oval.

Drawing Curvy Shapes with the Spline Tool

The **spline** tool creates complicated, curvy shapes, and it will probably require a bit of experimentation before you achieve the results you want. It's worth the trouble because, after you understand how the **spline** tool works, you can create with very little effort impressive shapes with elegant curves.

CHAPTER 9—Creating and Perfecting Graphics with Image Composer

After you select the **spline** tool and set the level of opacity, you have two more options to select.

- Click on **Close** if you want a solid object; do not select the **Close** option if you want a curvy line.
- If you select **Close**, you have the option of using **Fill**. Leave **Fill** off if you want a hollow shape; select **Fill** if you want a solid shape.

Figure 9.13 shows three sprites created with the **spline** tool. The top spline is a curvy line created with the **Close** and **Fill** options off. The middle spline is a solid shape created with the **Close** option on and the **Fill** option off. The bottom spline was created with both **Close** and **Fill** selected.

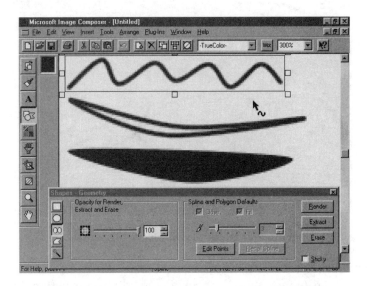

Figure 9.13 Three sprites created with the spline tool.

A spline begins as a straight line. After you've selected the tool and chosen the options, click twice to draw the first line. You then extend and enhance your line by clicking again to add new sections. For example, to create a curvy line, start by defining a short line, by clicking on two end points; a straight line will appear. Now, move your mouse to the spot where the next curve should appear and click; the original line will be extended. Continue to add line segments, and the **spline** tool will curve the line as it adds new segments. After you have a general shape, you can fine-tune the shape of the line by selecting the **Edit Points** button. Tiny squares will appear on your line at every spot where you clicked the mouse. Drag these points to a new location, and the **spline** tool will redraw only that segment of the line.

To create a solid shape, click the mouse repeatedly in the general outline of the shape you want to draw. As you draw, the spline may be monstrously inappropriate. Figure 9.14 shows the steps in drawing the five points of a star.

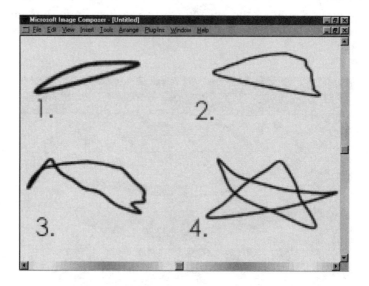

Figure 9.14 Drawing a star with the spline tool.

After you have finished adding points to the spline shape, you can refine the contours of your shape by clicking the **Edit Points** button. Each of the mouse clicks will be represented by small points on the shape. Clear near a point and drag the mouse to change the shape.

TIP

As a general rule, use very few clicks to create simple, elegant spline shapes. Click repeatedly when you want to create a complex shape with many angles.

After you finish drawing a shape, you may want to add new points so that you can introduce a curve. To add a new point, click on a section of the spline and press **I** on the keyboard.

If you want to smooth a section of the shape that is too curvy, remove some points from the line. To delete editing points on the spline, click on the point and press **D** on the keyboard.

After your spline is the correct shape, click on **Render**. The options you selected for line thickness, opacity, and fill will be added. Carefully examine your spline before your select **Render**; the spline cannot be edited after you use **Render**. You can edit the shape, however, if you use the **recall spline** tool. You can delete the old sprite and edit the duplicate.

Drawing Polygons

Polygons and splines are added and edited with the same techniques. The difference between the two is that polygons are composed of straight lines rather than curves. For example, you could build a five-point star in the same fashion as we built the star shown in Figure 9.14 using the **spline** tool. But when you use the **polygon** tool, the lines of the star will be straight, as shown in Figure 9.15.

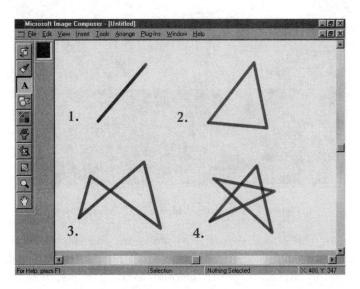

Figure 9.15 Drawing a star with the polygon tool.

To create a polygon, first select the **polygon** tool, set the options, and click in the composition guide to define the shape. After you have defined every corner, adjust the dimensions of the polygon by selecting **Edit Points**. You can add new points by selecting the new point and pressing **I** on the keyboard; you can delete points by selecting the point and pressing **D**.

Adding 3D Effects with Shapes

It's easy to add some dimension to a graphic image by duplicating an image at a different opacity. When you insert the second image with a significantly lower opacity setting and move it just slightly away from the original, it looks like a shadow. You can repeat the shadow several times to create the illusion of movement. Figure 9.16 shows a spline that was rendered first at an opacity of **25**, and again at **50**, **75**, and **100**.

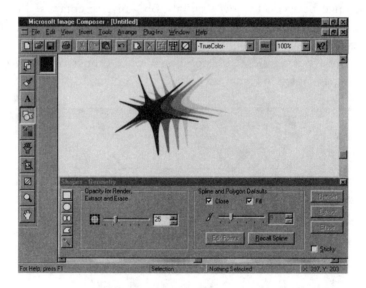

Figure 9.16 Creating shadow effects with splines.

Producing this effect is easier with polygons and splines because Image Composer provides the **recall spline** tool only for these two shapes. To produce this effect, first create the original polygon or spline. Then, select

Recall Spline. Change the opacity and select **Render**. The duplicate will appear directly on top of the original. Drag it to its new position.

You can also create a sense of distance by using **Recall Spline** and then flipping the image. For example, you could create a city scape that seems to be reflected in a pool of water. The image in Figure 9.17 was created with a single polygon.

Figure 9.17 A polygon after it was rendered at a lower opacity and flipped.

After the image was rendered with an opacity of 100, it was duplicated with the **Recall Spline** command. The opacity level was reduced to 20 and the duplicate was rendered. A mirror image was created by selecting **Arrange**, **Flip**. Once the image was flipped, it was dragged into position and resized and rotated slightly.

Special Effects with Color Lift

The **Color Lift** tool on the Shapes toolbox allows you to create 3D and mirroring special effects while changing the color of the original. See Figure 9.18.

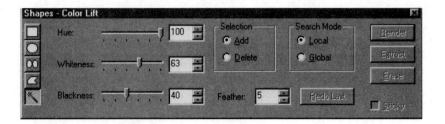

Figure 9.18 The Color Lift tool in the Shapes toolbox.

You use the **Color Lift** tool to duplicate the shapes in a sprite by selecting only one color; this makes it possible to duplicate shapes that exist within a group of sprites. The **Color Lift** tool provides settings you can use to change the color and brightness of the sprite and then duplicate it.

To use the tool, first highlight the sprite. Then select **Shapes, Color Lift**. The pointer changes to a wand; move the wand to the desired color and click. You can change settings in the box for the new color or double-click on the **Color Swatch** box to open the palette for your new color. Select **Render** after you've made your selections. The new sprite will appear directly on top of the original.

T I P

For an interesting special effect, select a value for the **Feather** option of **4** or **5**. The edges of the new sprite will be softened.

ADDING IMPACT WITH ARTISTIC EFFECTS

Once you have a variety of sprites in an Image Composer desktop, you can create the final, stunning effects with the tools that control colors and patterns.

Controlling Color Effects with Patterns

The Patterns and Fills tools allow you to change the overall appearance of a sprite by selecting a special effect that is applied evenly throughout the sprite. These are similar to the effects you might create in a paint program with tedious work. Using the tools in Patterns and Fills, it takes seconds to dramatically alter the color of a sprite.

To use any of these special effects, click on the desired Patterns and Fills tool and choose the effect from the lists. Some tools will have a choice of patterns that you select from a drop-down list. A preview of these effects appears in the dialog box. When you find a tool you want to try, select the sprite you'll want to change and select **Apply**. The new pattern will take effect immediately. If you're not pleased, use the **Undo** command to restore the original.

One of the most subtle effects you can add is a gradient ramp, which applies a gradually changing range of colors across the entire shape. You can use the entire color spectrum or choose any two colors from the available spectrum of 16 million colors, and Image Composer will apply the gradient. A more dramatic impact can be achieved with Patterns. Figure 9.19 shows two patterns: stripes and gray noise.

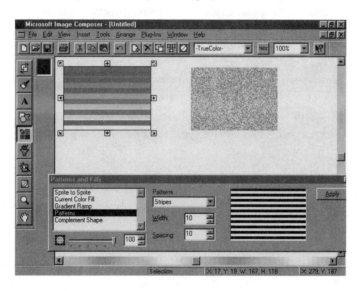

Figure 9.19 The patterns for stripes and gray noise.

Before applying the Stripes pattern you can set the width of each stripe and the distance between stripes.

TIP You can achieve unique special effects by combining two or more patterns. Try adding a stripe pattern on top of a gradient ramp. Or combine two stripe patterns, selecting a different width and spacing before you apply the second stripe pattern.

You can also control the opacity level for each pattern.

Sending Sprites behind Other Sprites

Sprites can overlap one another to create interesting graphic effects. For example, if you want a person to seem to be looking out from behind your company's logo, drag a text sprite on top of a photo. As long as the text is set to a high-level of opacity, it will seem to be sitting in front of the photo.

TIP Sprites may seem to be lost if they've been moved behind a larger sprite. Any time you seem to have lost a sprite, click on the largest object and select **Arrange, Send to Back**. Sprites that were hidden will become visible.

You can also move sprites from layer to layer using commands on the Arrange menu. First, select the sprite. Then select the appropriate **Arrange** command. Use the **Send to Back** command to move a sprite to the bottom layer. Select **Bring to Front** to move a sprite on the bottom layer to the top.

Changing a Single Color

When you want to change the color of a sprite to a solid color, with no special effects, use the **Current Color Fill** pattern. First, select the sprite you want to change. Then, select the new color by double-clicking on the **Color Swatch** box, as shown in Figure 9.20.

CHAPTER 9—Creating and Perfecting Graphics with Image Composer

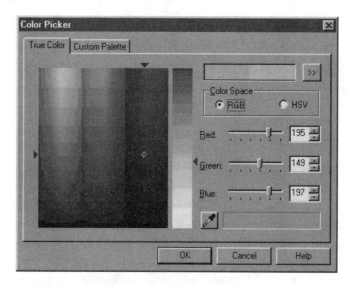

Figure 9.20 Selecting a new color.

You can choose the color by setting values for red, green, and blue, or you can point at a color on the spectrum. The small color bar in the upper right corner shows you the color selection before you opened the box, and the newly selected color. When you've settled on a new color, click on **OK**. You can now apply the **Current Color Fill** setting in the Patterns and Fills dialog box. The sprite will change to this new color.

T I P

When you copy a color that is already used in an image, you don't need to guess. The **Color Picker** option will match it perfectly. Select **Color Picker** from the Tools menu. When the Color Picker dialog box opens, select the **Eye Dropper** icon and then move it to the color you want to copy and click. This color is now selected as the current color.

Warps and Filters

Warps and filters can have a dramatic impact on an image's overall appearance. There are several broad categories available with the warp and filter tool. First, select one of these categories from the drop-down menu.

Then, you can select a specific application for that effect from the list. Many of these applications also have a series of options.

WARNING Warp and filter effects perform dramatic changes to a sprite, and you may not be pleased with the result on your first try. Play it safe and save the current file to disk before adding a warp or filter effect. You can use the **Undo** command to reverse only the last effect you tried.

A filter can be very subtle or dramatic, depending on the amount of blur you add. Blur adds a feather effect to the edges of a sharp image or sharpens the edges of a soft image. Figure 9.21 shows the effect of applying the blur filter to an ordinary rectangle. The original rectangle appears at the far left. Next is the same rectangle after a setting of 10 was applied to the horizontal plane with the vertical set to 0. To the right is the original rectangle with a setting of 0 applied on the horizontal place and the vertical set to 10. The image at the far right is the original rectangle with the both the horizontal and vertical setting of 10.

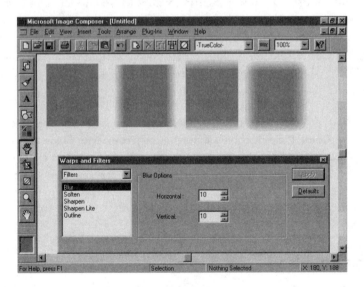

Figure 9.21 The blur effect applied to a rectangle.

Even more dramatic effects can be applied with the warp tools. A *warp tool* changes the entire shape of a sprite by applying a geometric pattern. This effect is often used to create distorted text or add a psychedelic feeling. Figure 9.22 shows eight different warp patterns applied to text. The left side of the screen shows the original text and the name of the warp; at right, the text is transformed using that warp effect.

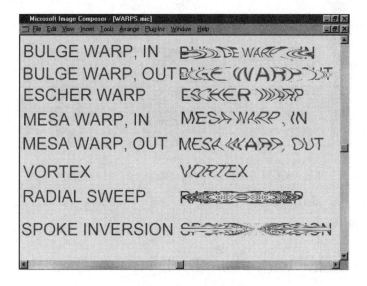

Figure 9.22 The warp effect applied to text.

Warp transforms are not quite as dramatic. The transformation takes place on a broad scale, so it can be very effective in drawing attention to a line of text. Figure 9.23 shows the different effects possible with the three major categories of warp transforms.

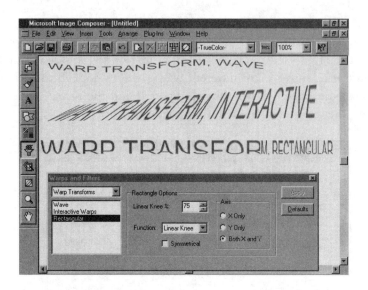

Figure 9.23 Applying a warp transform to a line of text.

Each line of text in Figure 9.23 identifies the warp transform applied to the sprite.

Adding Color with Paint Tools

If you've ever used a paint program, you needed to use paint tools to create many effects. In Image Composer, you can create many of these same effects using the tools covered in earlier sections: filters, patterns, and shapes. You'll probably find that the paint tools aren't needed very often. In general, the paint tools require some artistic skill; you need to be able to draw straight or well-proportioned curves to achieve the desired effect with paint tools. The **spline** and **polygon** tools, filled with patterns and altered with filters, can be more effective for those of us without those skills, since Image Composer can create the symmetry we'd be unable to achieve by painting.

To use the paint tools, first select a sprite. Then, open the paint toolbox, shown in Figure 9.24, by either clicking on the **paint** icon or selecting **Tools, Paint**.

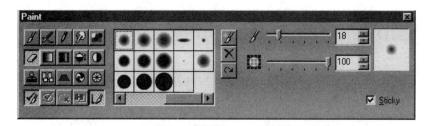

Figure 9.24 The Paint toolbox.

When you use the paint tools, you're applying color to a sprite using the currently selected color swatch and a tip that you select from the paint toolbox. Before you begin to work with paints, highlight the sprite you'll be painting and select the color by double-clicking on the color swatch box. You'll usually need to change colors before you begin to work with the paint tools.

WARNING

Be sure you've selected the right color before painting. If you don't change colors before beginning to use the paint tools, you're likely to be using the same color as you used to create the last sprite. You won't see the effect of the paint tool; it will be painting in the same color.

To begin working with paints, first select a tool such as the **paintbrush**, **airbrush**, or **pencil** by clicking on the icon. As you select a paint tool, the toolbox will show the size and style of the brush tip. After you've made your selections, move the pointer to the sprite. Once the brush is resting on the right spot, hold down the left button and drag the mouse. Figure 9.25 shows the **airbrush** tool in action.

In Figure 9.25, the **polygon** tool was used to create the sprite and the **airbrush** tool was used to add some irregular designs on top of the polygon.

You have an infinite variety of settings for the paint tools. You can select different brushes, such as a **pencil** or an **airbrush**, and then choose the diameter of the brush. You can also select any color to use for the brush.

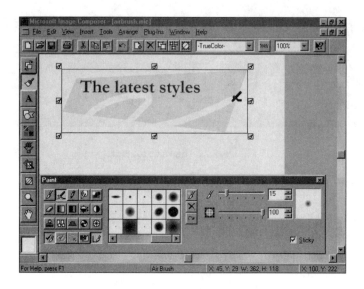

Figure 9.25 Painting with the airbrush.

Touching Up with Paint

Occasionally, an image needs just a minor adjustment. Perhaps a spot of dirt is marring a scanned image. Maybe two lines don't meet at exactly the right angle. Or perhaps the lapel pin someone's wearing in a photograph offends your boss.

You can use the paint tools to perform "fat-bit" editing, changing one pixel at a time. To do this, you need to zoom at a very extreme level until each pixel can be seen and then use the pencil with a brush size of 1. Figure 9.26 shows the process, using the hand that appeared in Figure 9.3.

1. Select the sprite that requires work.
2. Set the zoom level to **700**, **800**, or higher. Pan through the image until you find the spot.
3. Select **Tools**, **Color Picker**. Use the eye dropper to select the color you want to use to correct the problem area. If you're trying to blur over some dirt, you'll want to select a color that's next to the smudge.
4. Select the paint tools.

CHAPTER 9—Creating and Perfecting Graphics with Image Composer

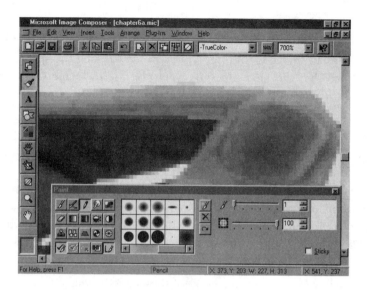

Figure 9.26 Touching up colors with the pencil.

5. Select the **pencil** and set the brush size to 1.

6. Move the **pencil** icon over the problem area and click in each pixel box, one at a time. If it's a large area, you can drag the pencil and change the color of several pixels with each pass of the mouse.

7. To determine whether you've fixed the problem, set the zoom level to **100%** and inspect it. Return to the extreme zoom level and repeat steps 5 and 6 until the problem is solved.

Making fine adjustments is precision work, so don't expect to get it right on the first try. Be sure you keep a backup copy of the file and don't overwrite the backup version until you're confident that you want to replace the original.

SAVING SPRITES, JPGS, AND GIFS

As you use all these tools, be adventurous. Some of the most interesting new images being used on the World Wide Web are being created by layering one image on top of another, and that's Image Composer's specialty.

Image Composer tracks every sprite in an image separately while you work with it. And, when you store it as an Image Composer file in the MIC format, Image Composer will continue to track the sprites independently so that the next time you open the file in Image Composer, you can continue to edit each sprite and change the way the sprites interact.

However, when you've finished creating the image you want to use in your Web pages, you'll want to save the file in either a GIF or JPG format. As explained in Chapter 3, GIF images are your best choice for images that don't require lots of colors, such as spot illustrations or text combined with shapes. JPG images are best for photographic-quality images that require many color levels. When you save an image in GIF, JPG, or any other graphic format aside from MIC, all information about the sprites will be lost. The image will be treated as a bit-mapped image as specified by the format you chose.

You'll want to keep one copy of the image in Image Composer's MIC format and another in either GIF or JPEG. When you use the **Save As** command, you'll have different options, depending on which format you select. For example, when saving an image in JPG, you can apply compression, as shown in Figure 9.27.

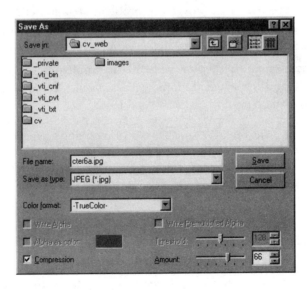

Figure 9.27 Adding compression to files in the JPG format.

To save an image in JPG format, select the drop-down arrow for the **Save As** format. When you choose **JPG**, the compression option will be enabled. You can choose the degree of compression on a scale of **1** to **100**. There is some loss to image quality when very high levels of compression are used, but if your Web site will be on the public World Wide Web, you'll want to use as much compression as is possible. You can test the images after compression by displaying them in a Web browser. To perform the test, you may want to save three different versions of the file, one compressed at about 33%, another at 50%, and another at 66% (or any other values you want to try). Be sure to give each file a unique name after you change the compression level. After you display the three images in a browser, if you find no difference in quality, keep the image stored with the highest compression (for example, 66%) and discard the others.

When saving images in GIF format, you have two different options. You can choose among a color format, a grayscale format, or a black-and-white format. Normally, you would want to select the color format; choose the grayscale or black-and-white formats only if you are specifically designing a site for a no-color application.

You can also choose to save a color in the GIF file as transparent. Checking off this option can save you the work of using the **Make Transparent** tool in FrontPage Editor. On the other hand, since you may sometimes want to use the image with the background color, you may want to leave the transparent color option unselected.

CHAPTER 10

LAYOUT MAGIC WITH TABLES

If there's one technique that separates polished, professional-looking Web sites from the many amateur pages, it's tables. Using tables, you can give your Web pages a structure that's impossible with the ordinary HTML styles. Whether you want to use the style of a newsletter, catalog, or brochure, tables are an essential ingredient.

Tables come with dozens of options in the HTML specification, but they aren't hard to master. FrontPage has a variety of dialog boxes and menu commands that can guide you through all the options. In this chapter, you'll learn how to create tables, add elements, and perfect the formats of tables. You'll learn how to integrate tables into your pages and how to take common printed designs and apply them to your Web pages, using table options.

You'll soon be able to design a Web page following the style of any printed publication.

GAINING NEW PERSPECTIVE ON TABLES

The HTML specification first approached tables the same way tables have been used for decades in printed publications: a format for presenting information in columns and rows. Whether it was financial results, comparison charts, schedules, or product specifications, the first tables on Web pages looked like tables in academic papers. They were well-organized but dull.

That's not true any more. Tables are now used at Web sites to create original designs. The Web site of *Rolling Stone* magazine uses tables in creating a splashy overview of its site. The page shown in Figure 10.1 is one big table, where each cell is occupied by a graphic image. Each of the images is clickable so that you can use this page to navigate through the

Rolling Stone magazine Web site. You might not believe that the page you see is one big table because the cell borders are turned off, but if you display the HTML source code for the page, you'll find that almost every graphic and text element is in a table cell.

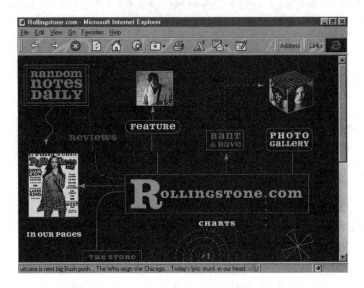

Figure 10.1 A table filled with graphics.

Tables are flexible enough to let you change the text or graphic displayed in a single table cell without changing the basic appearance of the page; if the graphic or text is a different size from the original, the cell will change its size dynamically to fit the new element. As a result, tables are often used for opening pages at Web sites where the Web designer wants to provide a clear sense of the choices available in a Web site.

NOTE

Originally, the HTML table spec required a border around each frame, making them look formal and static. But when the option to turn off borders was added, tables became a secret ingredient for designing Web pages with the polished look of a newspaper or magazine.

Many sites create opening pages using the more traditional columns that are filled with text and graphics. The iWorld site in Figure 10.2 uses tables to present a list of the pages available at the site. Some of the items are

CHAPTER 10—Layout Magic with Tables

graphics used to identify the different sections, others are short titles while still others are lengthy text descriptions of the pages. When the page is updated every day, the layout doesn't need to change; only the text or graphics inside the layout need to change. The page looks the same, even though the options available to visitors will change.

Figure 10.2 Tables can help organize the pages in a site.

But tables aren't used only to organize information. Any page that needs to have a polished appearance will benefit from the structure that a table can provide. That's because tables offer a vital design element not found elsewhere in HTML—margins. You can come close to setting the exact spot on a page where the data in a table will appear. Remember that the browser has ultimate control over how a page is displayed, so you can't be sure that everything will line up just as you plan. But a table provides far more control over a page's appearance than is possible without a table.

As a result, tables are often used by sites that want to display text in a magazine-style layout. The left and right margins can be specified precisely; knowing where text will appear makes it possible for the designer to line up different elements. For example, a graphic can appear directly below a line of text, and a background image can provide a graphic border.

At the *Rolling Stone* site, the text in the reviews section is displayed in a table. The page shown in Figure 10.3 uses a table to specify the left margin making it possible for the text in the article to line up with the text in headers and graphics (the word *reviews* is displayed as a GIF image in order to use a stylized font, instead of the browser's default font). And since the page designer knows exactly where the left margin for the text will appear, a background GIF image was designed to display the dotted vertical line, emphasizing the layout.

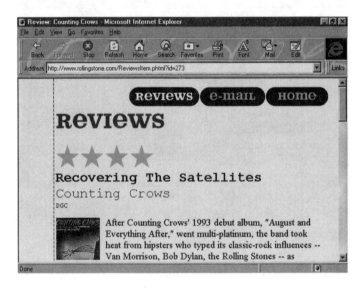

Figure 10.3 A table provides margins for lining up text and graphics.

If you examine the page carefully, you may notice that Figure 10.3 shows two tables that are unrelated. The three rounded boxes on the top line of the page are in one table; all the words and graphics that appear below are in a second table.

Once you begin to think of tables as a design tool, rather than a spreadsheet replacement, you'll find that you can create innovative, striking pages. Virtually any design used on paper can be re-created with a Web page, once you understand the powerful options available with the table settings.

CHAPTER 10—Layout Magic with Tables

CREATING A TABLE

Whether you're planning a stunning design effect or just want to display words in a column-and-row format, you begin to work with tables in the same way. You add a table to any page in FrontPage Editor by using the **Table, Insert Table** command. The dialog box shown in Figure 10.4 will appear.

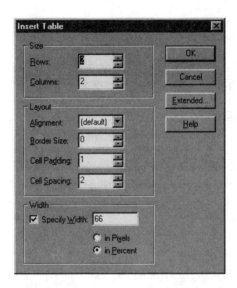

Figure 10.4 The Insert Table dialog box.

FrontPage uses the settings you entered in the Insert Table dialog box to create the initial framework of the table. When you click on **OK**, a table is added to the page using these settings. The new table's outlines are indicated with dotted lines if you set a border value of zero. These dotted lines will not appear when the page is displayed in a browser. FrontPage Editor displays these dotted lines only as an aid to your work with the table.

You can type words directly into cells, paste text, insert images or insert text stored on disk in a file. You can even insert multimedia objects like video clips into the cell of a table. Any formatting option that can be applied to text or graphics in FrontPage can be applied inside the cell. You can format cells individually, by highlighting the text in the cell or by selecting **Table, Select Table** and then setting format options. And you can format groups of cells using the **Select Row**, **Select Column**, or **Select Table** commands.

TIP

It's easier to highlight a table using the **Select Table** command. If you try to select an entire table using the mouse, you may end up selecting only data inside cells without the cell structure.

Adding Rows and Columns

The first settings you need to choose when creating a new table are the number of cells that you determine by selecting the number of rows and columns. The settings are entered in the size dialog box. This is an unfortunate label; while the number of cells is related to the overall size of your table, there are many other factors that affect size, too.

TIP

Don't spend too much time planning your layout when you create a new table. Insert the table and see if it works. You can change any of the table settings at any time as you work on the page. The final table may have very little in common with the original settings.

Rows are counted from top to bottom. You can enter any number from 1 to 100 in the Rows dialog box. Columns are counted from left to right. You can enter any number from 1 to 100 in the Columns dialog box. Figure 10.5 shows a table with three rows and two columns.

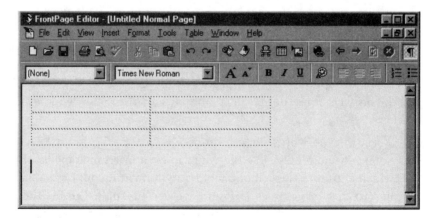

Figure 10.5 An empty table with three rows and two columns.

To add new rows or columns once a table has been inserted, you must use the **Table, Insert Row** or **Table, Insert Column** command. Before you add a new row, select a cell in the row adjacent to the spot where you want the new row or column to appear.

Deleting Rows and Columns

After you insert a table, you can't remove cells from a dialog box. To delete an entire row or column, first select a cell and then use the **Table, Select Row** or **Table, Select Column** command to highlight the entire row or column. Once you've highlighted the correct line, use the cut (**Ctrl-X**) command or the **Delete** key.

Be sure to use the **Select Row** or **Select Table** command when you want to remove the entire line. If you highlight a single cell and then use **Cut** or **Delete**, only one cell will be removed. FrontPage will remove the dotted line around part of this cell, but you may not realize that you removed only once cell because the outline of the cells that border the deleted cell will remain.

Controlling the Size of a Table

Tables are not only flexible, they're organic. They grow as you add content. The height of any cell will expand to fit all the text or graphics you insert. Figure 10.6 shows the blank table in Figure 10.5 after varying amounts of text were inserted into different cells. Every cell in the table started out the same height but grew to accommodate the text that was entered.

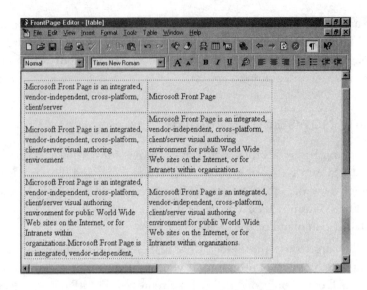

Figure 10.6 A cell's height increases to fit the contents you add.

The width of a cell is not as flexible. You can set limits on the width of a page, but if you don't, the table will expand only to the width of the widest line on the page and no wider.

You cannot directly control the width of a column. Instead, you set the width of the entire table; each cell receives an equal share of that space. If the table is 100 pixels wide and you have two columns, each column is exactly 50 pixels wide. If you add a third column, each column will now be 33 pixels.

When text is inserted into a cell, the text will be wrapped to the next line when it reaches the end of the designated width. Note in Figure 10.6 that the width of each cell remains the same; only the height is changed.

You have a choice of two methods for controlling the width of the table: pixels or percent. When you choose a width for the table in pixels, the table's width will always occupy the finite number of pixels you enter. When you enter a width using percentages, the browser will determine how wide the table should appear. For example, if you set a width of 75%, 25% of the available space along the table will be used as a buffer area.

TIP No other objects can appear next to a table, so normally you'll want to use a wide width for the table. If you want to insert an object near the table, you can insert it into a cell.

When you use percentages, the same table could appear many different ways on the same system: every time the user resizes the browser window, the table will change its dimensions. But that's normally the best technique, especially if you're using the table to hold text. The browser is able to determine the most efficient way to display text. When you specify the width in pixels, if you select a value wider than the browser window, part of the table will not be visible unless the user scrolls to the right or changes the display area.

Adjusting the Width of a Cell

While there's no setting for changing the width of an entire column, you can set the minimum width for a single cell. Using the **Cell Properties** command, shown in Figure 10.7, you can set a minimum width for a single cell.

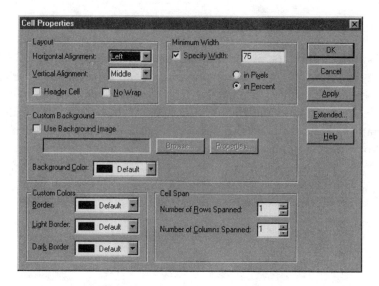

Figure 10.7 The Cell Properties dialog box.

Because most browsers will display the entire column using this minimum width for the cell, the end result is the same as if you were changing the width of the entire column.

To change the width of a cell, place your pointer inside the cell and click. Then select the **Table, Select Cell** command; the cell will be highlighted. Choose **Table, Cell Properties**. After you enter a new setting for the minimum width, click on **Apply** to see the table adjusted to reflect the new setting.

CONTROLLING THE APPEARANCE OF TABLES

Designing Web pages with tables is complicated by the fact that you can control the properties of a table overall and the properties of individual cells. You can control the way both cells and tables are aligned, the spaces that separate cells, and the colors used for backgrounds. You can also change a setting that makes all the difference between using a table for displaying columns of figures and using a table to layout a page full of a text and graphics—the border setting.

Aligning Tables on a Page

You can control the alignment of a table, affecting where it will be displayed within the page on the horizontal plane. You can set the alignment when you first insert a page, but you can also change it at any time by selecting the table and then choosing the **Table, Table Properties** command (or by right-clicking on the table and then selecting **Table Properties**).

You can choose **Left**, **Right**, and **Center** alignment. Figure 10.8 shows three different tables, aligned with each setting.

Chapter 10—Layout Magic with Tables

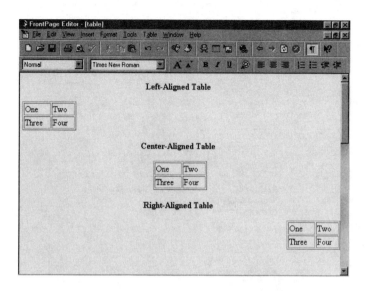

Figure 10.8 The three different alignment settings for a table.

Remember that no other object can appear next to a table on a page, so you won't use this command to arrange a table next to an object. But you might want to line up the table with text or a graphic that appears nearby.

Aligning the Contents of a Cell

You can also choose the alignment for text or graphics inside a cell. It can be a time-consuming process on a large table, since the alignment must be set individually, cell by cell. First, select the cell and then select **Table**, **Cell Properties** (refer to Figure 10.7).

You can control the horizontal alignment and vertical alignment. Figure 10.9 illustrates the different choices. The left column shows—from top to bottom, text aligned to the center, left, and right. Since the text occupies the entire cell, the vertical alignment doesn't matter.

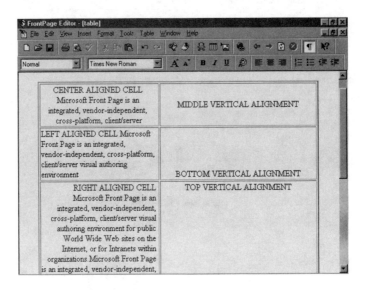

Figure 10.9 Different alignment settings for a cell.

In the column to the right, the text doesn't occupy the entire cell, so vertical alignment has an affect on the display of the text. For consistency, each of the cells are center-aligned on the horizontal plane, but the three different choices for vertical alignment are shown, from top to bottom: center, bottom, and middle.

WARNING

When adding text or other objects near a cell, be careful to insert the pointer outside the cell. The selection area for a table extends to the far left and right of a table. Move your mouse pointer above or below the table in order to select an area outside the table.

Cells That Span Other Cells

You can control the alignment of a cell in another way: you can have one cell span the height or width of several cells. This technique can be especially effective when you want to use a table to display graphics and text. In Figure 10.10 the graphic image in the top row spans three columns. The cells in the columns below are used in this table to carry labels for the image.

Figure 10.10 An example of a cell that spans three columns.

To specify a cell as spanning other cells, select **Cell Properties**. You can have a single cell span other cells or columns. The size of the cell will be increased to cover the selection you make. There's a side effect you'll have to deal with, however: other cells will push over.

When the table width is already at its maximum width, the cells at the end of the row or column will be squeezed together to make room for the expansion of this cell. When the table has room to expand, a new cell will be inserted at the end of the row or column. You can delete those cells by selecting **Table**, **Select Cell** and pressing the **Delete** key.

Adding and Removing Borders

Borders help clarify the display of material that is normally displayed in tables, like columns of numbers. But when you use tables for laying out graphics or creating newsletter-style columns of text, you'll want to see the border value to 0. You have the option of displaying a border between each frame.

Figure 10.11 shows two different settings for the border. At the top the table has a border value of 12; the same table below has a border value of 0.

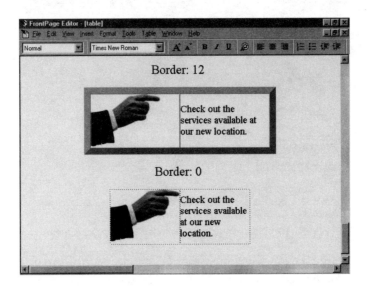

Figure 10.11 Two tables with different settings for the border value.

FrontPage will display a thin dotted line around cells when you have a border value of zero to help you keep track of your work, but when the page is displayed in a browser, no border will appear.

You can also create interesting effects with borders by changing the colors used for the shading. Browsers usually display tables that have thick borders as if they are solid objects with angled sides and light is shining from the top left corner of the screen. To achieve this effect, the top and left sides of the table are displayed with a light border, and the bottom and right sides of the table are displayed with a darker border, as though they were in shadow. By default, the table borders are displayed in shades of gray.

From the Table Properties dialog box, you can choose other colors for the thin line that runs around the edge (normally black), the light border (normally a light gray), and the darker border (normally a dark gray). You can set colors for the entire table, or you can set a different background color scheme for individual cells using the Cell Properties dialog box.

Cell border color settings were a recent addition to HTML, added by Microsoft with Internet Explorer 3.0. Netscape Navigator added support for color borders with Navigator 4.0. Earlier versions of these browsers will display the same color for the entire border using a standard shading.

Cell Padding

The appearance of text and graphics in a table can be changed dramatically using two controls that can create the effect of an object floating inside the cells of a table: cell padding and cell spacing.

You can set a buffer zone around the contents of each cell using the cell padding option in the Table Properties dialog box. When you set a value for cell padding, you're adding blank space that will surround each cell. Figure 10.12 shows the same table with two different values for cell padding.

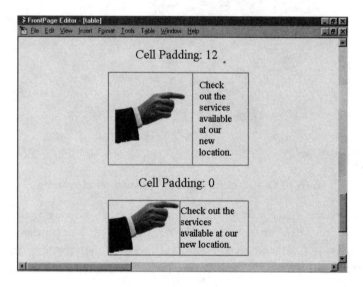

Figure 10.12 Two tables with different values for cell padding.

The table in the top of the display has a cell padding of 12. As a result, there is plenty of room between the text, graphics, and borders. The table in the bottom of the display has a cell spacing value of 0. As a result, the text and graphics are very close to the borders.

Normally, a table like this combining text and graphics would be created with no borders. Borders were displayed here for the purpose of illustrating the affect of changing the cell padding value.

Cell Spacing

Cell spacing is similar to cell padding in that it also adds a buffer zone around the contents of a cell. But when you increase the cell spacing value, the width of the border is increased, too.

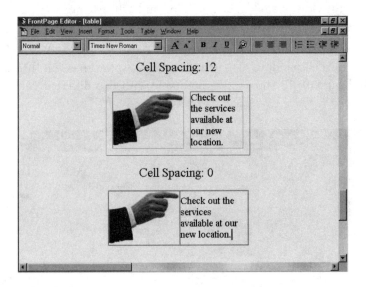

Figure 10.13 Two tables with different values for cell spacing.

In effect, the size that each cell occupies doesn't increase with cell spacing, but the distance between cells does increase. The border fills in the gap between cells so that when you increase cell spacing, the border seems bigger even when you don't change the border thickness.

Nesting Tables inside Tables

Tables can spawn new tables, and those tables can spawn new tables. And cells can spawn new cells. If you can imagine a complicated grid, you can create it in a page.

WARNING Tables nested in tables work in all versions of Netscape Navigator from 2.0 on and in Microsoft Explorer from 2.0 on. But many other browsers may be completely confused by nested tables, displaying a disjointed page full of unaligned objects instead of any columns or rows.

Inserting Tables within Tables

When you insert a table within a table, you can set all the options for the new table, independent of the settings you chose for the original table. Figure 10.14 shows a table inserted into a table.

Figure 10.14 A table inserted into a table.

To create this table, the mouse pointer was inserted into a cell in the original table (see Figure 10.13). Then, the **Table, Insert Table** command was selected. The new table is two rows and two columns.

The addition of a new table is handled no differently that the addition of new text or graphics to a cell. The table expands the height of the cell where it's inserted to accommodate the addition.

Splitting Cells within Table Cells

When you want to retain the properties of a cell but divide the cell into smaller groups, you can split a cell. Split cells rather than insert a new table when you want to keep most of the properties for the table consistent, rather than begin a new table.

When you select the **Table**, **Split Cells** command, the dialog box shown in Figure 10.15 opens.

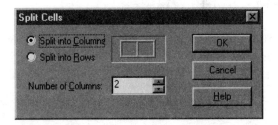

Figure 10.15 The Split Cells dialog box.

This command is similar to the effect you can achieve by spanning one cell with another cell. But it's easier to split cells than to use the span cells property since you can simply select the cell you want to change and choose the command. The dialog box doesn't obscure your view, and it shows a visual representation of the new cell. When you span cells, you have to choose settings from the large Cell Properties dialog box, which obscures the cells you're choosing.

GETTING CREATIVE WITH TABLES

When you use a table to lay out financial data or the results of clinical tests, you will want to approach tables and their options in a fairly consistent, logical manner.

CHAPTER 10—Layout Magic with Tables

When you use a table to achieve a graphic design effect or you want to add impact to page, be sure you experiment with tables. You don't need to insert a single object in each cell. Some cells can be empty, and others can include more than one graphic and text. The table in Figure 10.16 is being used to create a company newsletter; the table has a border size setting of 0, so the dotted lines that appear in FrontPage to show the outline of each cell will not appear when the page is displayed in a browser.

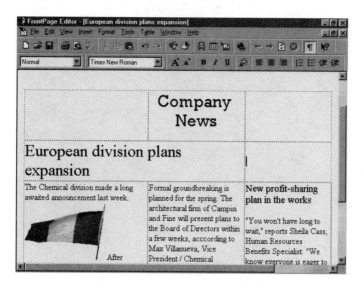

Figure 10.16 Creating a newsletter using a table.

The cell at bottom right includes text with a JPG graphic file inserted directly in the middle of a sentence. It occupies one cell. In the cell directly above, the text "European division plans expansion" is a headline. To give it extra impact, this text occupies its own cell that was adjusted to span two columns. But to the far right, one cell includes both the headline and text for a story that will be less prominent on the page. Other cells on the table are empty since the design works better if there's extra white space.

Being creative does carry a price. You need to invest more time in testing your design. FrontPage Editor does not faithfully render the design, and it may appear radically different in a browser. Be sure to preview the page in as many browsers as you need to support. If you're creating a newsletter that will be seen only by people inside your corporate network, you may be able to test it only on the browser used within your company. But if your page is on the public Internet, you'll need to test it with some of the older browsers, too.

CHAPTER 11

ORGANIZING A SITE WITH FRAMES

Most of the formatting options used on Web sites are based on models familiar to us from printed publications. Color graphics, font formats, and table layouts help to make Web sites have the same polished look as professional magazines. Frames bring the techniques of software design to a Web site, helping to bring several different concepts to the same page.

In this chapter, you'll learn how to use frames in designing a Web page. You'll learn where frames are appropriate, how to create pages with frames, and how to set the options. Perhaps most importantly, you'll learn how to edit the HTML code used to create frames. While FrontPage can help you get started with frames, you'll need to learn how to edit these codes directly in order to refine your pages.

The use of frames is a fairly advanced technique most useful as a way of organizing a large collection of pages. You won't want to start bringing frames to your Web site until you have reached the point where you feel you have so much material available, you need a way to show it all off.

UNDERSTANDING FRAME TAGS

As Web sites became stuffed to the gills with different types of material, frames were a natural evolution. Without frames, a Web page can become very long, and important information may end up buried near the bottom.

Frames do two things: they make it possible to create separate windows in a single screen, and they make it possible to have scrolling lists inside a page. Figure 11.1 shows how the TrustGroup in the United Kingdom, a group of information technology managers, uses frames to organize its Web site.

Figure 11.1 Using frames to provide an overview of a Web site.

One frame runs along the left side of the screen, serving as a table of contents for the site; this frame includes clickable graphics that will open major pages within the site. The main frame, to the right, is a fairly long text document that describes the purposes of the group. You can scroll down as you read this document, without changing the menu choices that appear in the left frame. Finally, a third frame runs along the top as a banner so that when you're scrolling down the page, you'll always see the group's logo.

This type of style is likely to become an important way to display information in years to come, but today, frames are a work in progress. The HTML specifications that define frame tags have been under review for years. The first generations of frames caused problems when displayed with some browsers, and the tags used by FrontPage may change over time.

NOTE

If the visitors to your site on a corporate network are standardized on Microsoft Internet Explorer, there's no reason to hesitate in using FrontPage's Frames wizard. But if the site is open to the public, be sure to test any pages you create with frames using Netscape Navigator.

The problem is so sticky that a frames subcommittee of the W3 HTML is working on a unified standard. Netscape and Microsoft have been at odds over the specification for frames, and the friction is expected to continue, even after the final standards are published. The frame tags in FrontPage 97 may turn out to be in full compliance with the final specification, but minor adjustments are possible. One indication of the problem is that FrontPage Editor is still not able to display pages with frames that you create using a FrontPage wizard; you need to preview pages with frames in a browser.

As a general rule, add frames to pages that you plan to keep current and don't use frames on pages that you were hoping would remain untouched.

The Structure behind Frames

Building frames is a complex task because you cannot simply divide the page. You need to establish guidelines that a browser can use to create frames depending on the size of the window available when the frame page is being displayed. You don't need to know the HTML frame tags to create frames in FrontPage, but you'll be better equipped to select the many options available with frames if you understand the way frame pages are constructed.

And while FrontPage provides a wizard that guides you through the process of creating a frame set page, revising the design is not easy with the wizard since you can't see the effect of your changes as you run the wizard. FrontPage Editor cannot display frame set pages; you need to preview them in a browser.

You may find it's easier to edit the HTML tags directly with a word processor instead of relying on the wizard for all your changes.

How Frame Tags Work

Browsers treat Web pages that display frames differently from ordinary pages. To identify the page as a frame set page, rather than a normal page displaying data without frames, the HTML code must include a different set of tags. A frame set page does not include the standard tag

```
<BODY>
```

Instead, a page with frames uses the tag

```
<FRAMESET>
```

The frame set page can be used as an opening page for your Web site (if it's named correctly as `index.htm`), or it can be opened by links from other pages at your site. But a frame set page does not need to contain any text or graphics. Instead, the frame set page consists of links to source files.

TIP A page with frames can be the opening page for your Web site. Normally, you'd rename the existing `index.htm` and give your frame set page the name `index.htm`. You'll probably want to use your original opening page as one of the more prominent frames.

The `<frameset>` tags specify the rows and columns in the page using a style that's similar to tables. Both columns and rows are defined. You can use either pixels or percentages to define the size of the columns and rows. For example, the following tag defines a page with three rows of equal height, extending across the length of the screen; each frame will be 33% of the width.

```
<FRAMESET ROWS="33%, 33%, 33%">
```

Columns are inserted using a similar style. The following tag would create two columns, one is 25% of the width, the other is 75%.

```
<FRAMESET COLS="25%,75%">
```

The similarities between frames and tables ends there. The frame set tag divides up the entire page, not just a small area. But the frames are not created at once. The order in which column-and-row frame tags are inserted in a page plays a major role in determining how the page will appear.

The first frame tag to appear in the HTML file divides up the entire page into either rows or columns. These frames are then divided up by the tags that follow. For example, a row tag establishes a grid for the page that consists of three rows. Then, a column tag may break up the first row into two columns, the second row into three columns, and the third row into two columns. Virtually any combination is possible.

Once you understand the nested structure of a frame set instruction, it's not too hard to follow the style. The following code displays the frames that appear in Figure 11.2.

Figure 11.2 A page with three rows; the center row has two columns.

If you're following along, note that the first frame set tag defines the three rows. Then, an image is inserted in the top row; the next row is divided into two columns, and the bottom row displays a graphic

```
<frameset rows="15%,40%,45%">
<frame src="cvlogo.gif" name="logo">
<frameset cols="25%,75%">
<frame src="services.html" name="CV Services">
<frame src="index.html" name="Index page">
<frame src="sports_bar.gif" name="graphics">
</frameset>
```

This excerpt shows only barebones frames, without any of the many options available for displaying frames, such as turning off the scroll bars, setting margins, or changing the border appearance.

The Importance of Good Sources

Each frame that is created must specify a source file. If no source URL is supplied or the file can't be found, the page won't display at all in most browsers.

The file that defines the frame does not normally include text. Instead, you set a "source file" for each frame, choosing graphics and text files that will be displayed in the frame.

This design makes frames the perfect tool for opening pages or other pages that feature changing content. You can update the text or graphics in the source files without changing the frame page. For example, a site that features news can replace the featured stories simply by copying a new version of the file to the Web site. You don't need to be concerned with the length or format of the text files; the browser will adjust the text to fit inside the designated frame.

CREATING PAGES WITH FRAMES

The wide range of options involved in building frames is too complex for ordinary menu commands. You won't find a frames tool anywhere on the FrontPage menus.

That doesn't mean you need to write your own HTML code. FrontPage will generate frame set pages using a wizard. Once you've created a new page, you can revise it. You may find that it's easier to make changes by editing the HTML with a word processor like Windows Notepad (you can't use FrontPage Editor's **View HTML** command with frame set pages). But you'll certainly find that running a wizard is preferable to writing the code from scratch.

Starting the Frames Wizard

You begin the process of creating a frame set page with the FrontPage Editor's **File**, **New** command. The dialog box shown in Figure 11.3 opens.

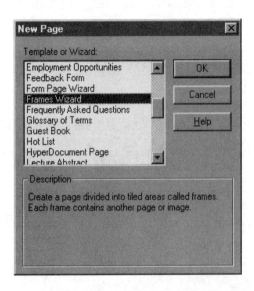

Figure 11.3 Selecting the Forms wizard in FrontPage Editor.

Select the **Frames Wizard** and click on **OK**. The Frames wizard runs as a series of dialog boxes. Each one poses a question. Be sure to complete all the entries in every box; leaving even one option blank may result in a frame that doesn't work. Before you finish, you can review each of the steps and change your answers at any time by selecting the **Back** button.

TIP

It's a good idea to specify an alternate page to display in case the browser loading your frames page doesn't support frames. The Frames wizard can specify the page, but only if it's already part of the current Web. You may need to import the alternate page into your Web before you use the Frames wizard.

The first selection you must make when running the Frames wizard is to choose between picking a template and doing it yourself by defining a custom grid. The templates are a good way to get your feet wet in designing frame set pages. After you've used the wizard with a template to save your first frame set page, you'll be able to customize it further.

Choosing among the Frame Templates

The selection of frame templates covers the most common types of applications for frames. You can choose among several types of contents pages (some with a banner for a corporate log, some without). Figure 11.4 shows the list of choices.

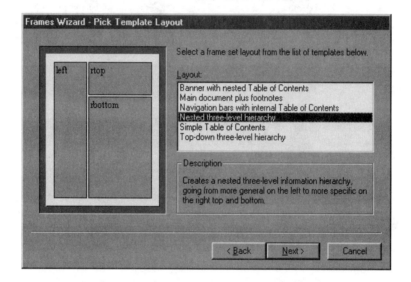

Figure 11.4 The choice of templates available for frames.

With the Forms wizard open and the dialog box shown in Figure 11.4, follow these steps to help you make the correct choices.

1. Click on the name for each layout and an outline of the page frames is displayed in the dialog box. Once you select a layout, click on **Next**.

2. Since many browsers are not able to display frames, it's a good idea to enter a page that will load if the browser is not able to display frames. Click on the **Browse** button, and the wizard will display a list of the HTML pages that are part of the current FrontPage web. It's okay to display a page that will also be used in a frame. If you want to link to a page that's not in the Web, select **Cancel** and stop the wizard. Switch to FrontPage Explorer and import the page into the Web; then continue with the Frames wizard.

3. Enter a title that describes the purpose of the page (it will be used in the title bar when the browser displays the page) and the file name to be used, with an HTM extension.

4. Click on the **Finish** button, and the wizard will add the frame set pages to the current Web.

The frame pages are not yet complete. The next step is to open the file from FrontPage Editor. Instead of displaying the page, however, FrontPage will launch the Frames wizard again. This time, it will open with values for the page you just created rather than a blank page.

Adding New Columns and Rows

Whether you create a custom grid or choose from a template, the Frames wizard will walk you through the same steps in choosing among frame options. The only difference is that when you use the Frames wizard and choose a template, you go in a circle. You seem to finish the Frames template, but then you end up back at the beginning of the loop.

The dialog box shown in Figure 11.5 appears immediately after you select the option to build a custom grid or after you open a file you saved using the template option.

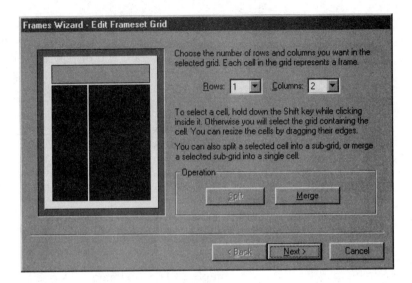

Figure 11.5 Editing the grid for a frame set page.

You can completely change the appearance of the frames on this page, but you don't have total control over the grid. Keep in mind the way frames are drawn. First the page is defined as a series of columns or rows; then other columns and rows are inserted inside. To insert new columns or rows, hold down the **Shift** key and click on the frame you want to change. Then, select the number of columns or rows from the drop-down list.

The box also provides a shortcut. The **Split** button will insert a grid with two rows and two columns into the currently selected frame. You can undo this new grid by selecting the **Merge** button.

To return to editing the entire page, click in every box until all are selected. It's easy to add frames, but it's not always possible to remove all the frames you've created. If you find the page has more frames than you wanted, press **Cancel** and start over.

After you have chosen the correct number of columns and rows, you can adjust the height and width of each frame by dragging the frame borders. This is not a crucial step since frame borders are often resizable after the page is completed.

Adding Source Files

Once you've completed the grid, you need to assign source files to each frame. This is an essential step; the page will not display at all in many browsers if valid source files are not entered for each frame. Consider this the moment of truth if you're just experimenting with frames. If you aren't sure which files will be displayed, you might as well stop now and do some planning. You cannot specify a "file to be named later." You must have a file already stored on disk; however, it doesn't need to be finished. You can edit the source files repeatedly, but each source must display a valid URL. To enter the source file or URL for each frame, click on the frame. The frame is highlighted, as shown in Figure 11.6.

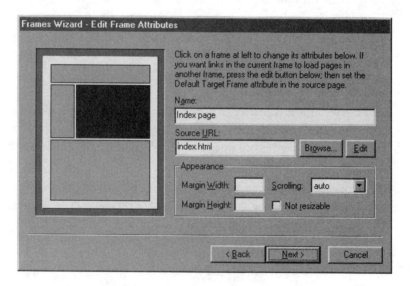

Figure 11.6 Adding a source file to a frame.

Type in the URL or select a file in your Web site by clicking on the **Browse** button. Only the files in your current Web will be displayed. (Another reminder: If you haven't imported the files you want to use into the current Web, cancel the wizard and move the files before you go any further.) The dialog box organizes the selections into HTML, images, and "any type" but only files in the current Web are available.

You can enter files at other locations as long as you enter the complete URLs. If you enter the URL for another Web site, be sure to include the full address, including "http://" and the name of the server.

NOTE

When a browser displays a frame, all links in that frame will work. If you display a remote Web site in a frame, visitors to your site may end up surfing the Web as they click from one site to another, inside the frame.

While you've selected the current grid, you can set options about how the frame will be displayed. You can enter a margin that will be used as a buffer zone around the file. You can choose to make the frame not resizable. With this option left blank, visitors to your site will be able to drag the borders for the frame to increase or decrease their view of the frame. You'll want to consider the purpose of the frame in setting this option. If you consider the information in this frame essential, you'll want to choose **Not resizable**. For example, a frame devoted to an advertisement would not be allowed to be resized.

The last option is a choice of whether scroll bars will appear on the frame. The **auto** option is best if you're not sure. Frames will have a scroll bar only if the source text or image cannot fit within the size allotted.

Finally, be sure you've entered a source file or URL for each grid. Before you leave this dialog box, click on each frame and review your choices. Your selections will have a big impact on the success of the page's design, and most problems can be fixed here.

Displaying an Alternate Page

The next dialog box allows you to specify a page that will run if the browser doesn't understand the frame set tags. If your Web site will run only on a private intranet and you're confident all visitors will have a recent browsers, you can leave this setting blank. Everyone else will want to enter a page in the current Web. You may want to choose one of the pages used as a source file for a frame or another file.

Wrapping Up and Revising

The last step in creating the frame set page is to name the page. You need to enter a title that will be used to identify the Web page in a browser as well as the file name. After you've entered your names and selected **Finish**, the wizard will generate the file, add it to the Web, and update links between this page and other files in the Web so that the Explorer view is accurate.

Unfortunately, you won't be able to view your page in FrontPage. You need to open it with a browser. Be sure to test the page thoroughly. Unless you're extremely good *and* lucky, the page will probably require some adjustments. Be sure to test all links and attempt to display all the source files.

Text and graphics displayed in frames may not be completely visible. One way to fix the problem is to change the option **Not resizable**, and another option is to change the grid size.

To fix all these problems, you can either run the Frames wizard again or edit the HTML source code directly. Since you can't display the frame set page in FrontPage Editor, you'll need to open the HTML page in a word processor.

Fixing HTML Frame Tags

You can fix most frame problems by editing the HTML source code. Just be sure that you don't add any stray characters or delete essential parts of the tag. Every comma and quotation mark matters in an HTML source file. Use the following definitions to help you understand the function of each tag. In the next section, "Editing and Refreshing Pages," you'll learn how to use this information to edit the source code for frame set pages.

The following tags will appear within these bookends. Remember that all HTML tags must begin with an opening angle bracket (<) and conclude with a closing angle bracket (>). The frameset tag indicates the beginning of HTML code for displaying a frame; the first tag can be either a row or column setting.

WARNING Be sure to keep a backup copy of the original HTML file before you edit it. And be sure that you save it in a text format using the same file name and without any word processing format options. Windows Notepad is a good choice since it is not capable of adding nontext formatting.

Frameset rows defines the number of rows and the height of each row. The rows can be defined using pixels or percentages. An asterisk (*) indicates that the last row receives the remainder of the page. A sample of a valid statement follows:

```
<frameset rows="15%,40%,45%">
```

Frameset cols defines the height of each column in the page. The rows can be defined using pixels or percentages. An asterisk (*) indicates that the last row receives the remainder of the page.

```
<frameset cols="25%,75%">
```

Frame src defines the file or URL that will be displayed inside the frame. It can be a file within the Web or a complete Internet address. Several optional settings may be added to this frame. *Name* is a title for this frame that must appear within quotation marks. *Marginwidth* and *marginheight* are relatively small numbers (2 or 3), which define space between the source file and the frame borders; they must appear within quotation marks. *Scrolling* defines whether scroll bars will appear for this frame; valid settings are **yes**, **no**, and **auto**; they must appear within quotation marks. *Noresize* determines whether the frame can be resized in a browser; there is no optional setting for noresize.

The following is a sample tag for frame source with all options.

```
<frame src="Logo.gif" name="logo" marginwidth="2" margin-
height="2" scrolling="yes" noresize>
```

Noframes displays the text and graphics that will appear as an alternate, when the browser is not capable of displaying frames. FrontPage inserts a WebBot for the noframes display. Edit this section of the frame set page only if you understand the various HTML tags.

Each frame set tag must be concluded with the tag

`</frameset>`

A typical frame set page will have two concluding frame set tags; one concludes the rows, and the other concludes the columns.

Editing and Refreshing Pages

Since you are not able to display frame set pages in FrontPage Editor, you may want to edit the page using Microsoft Internet Explorer and the Windows Notepad.

First, display the frame set page in Internet Explorer. You'll need to use Internet Explorer's **File**, **Open** command. Then select browse and navigate to the Front Page Web folder where you stored the frame set page. Select it, and Internet Explorer will display the page.

When the page is open, select **View**, **Source**. Internet Explorer will launch Notepad (unless you changed the default word processor, in which case a different editor will load).

Remember that FrontPage Explorer keeps index files that record the location of each file in the Web. Don't rename the file with Notepad unless you plan to export the HTML page to a different Web site.

WARNING

You can change the values directly in the Notepad window, as shown in Figure 11.7.

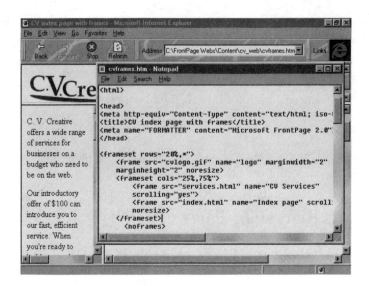

Figure 11.7 Editing the frame set HTML tags using Notepad.

When you're satisfied with your changes, select **File**, **Save**, and Notepad will replace the file. Minimize Notepad and click on the **Refresh** button in Internet Explorer. The changes you made will be reflected in the new version of this page. Repeat the process of editing, saving, and refreshing the page until you're happy with the results.

CHAPTER 12

CREATING FORMS TO GATHER INFORMATION

Until this point, we've seen how to use FrontPage to publish and share information. But a Web site can also gather information. The easiest way to interact with visitors to your site is to create a form. While forms are commonly used to invite visitors to request information or provide feedback about the site, you can also gather any type of information you want. On a public site, you might want to conduct surveys. Or, on a private network, you can use forms for all types of internal correspondence, ranging from requesting vacation to submitting reports.

In this chapter, you'll learn how to create forms and tailor them to your needs. You'll learn the process of adding form fields to pages, setting up form properties, validating data entries, and formatting the data you'll record.

FORMS PROCESSING BASICS

Forms have become popular on the Web thanks to the simple ability of Web browsers to generate a variety of input fields with brief HTML instructions. But displaying those fields is the easy part. Taking the information entered at a Web page and processing it requires some type of scripting.

FrontPage makes the entire process very easy. First, you create *form fields* by selecting from a variety of common input styles (text boxes, drop-down lists, and check boxes) and giving a label to each. For example, you would select a text box and assign it the label "first name." Or you would ask people at your Web site to identify their department by listing all the divisions with an organization. Rather than risk the possibility that they'll type it incorrectly, you can have them choose from a list.

Once a user enters the information in a browser window, the data need to be returned to you. A Web server needs a *forms handler* to process the data, assigning the information that users type to the correct field and then storing the data in a file.

WARNING

Pages you create with forms will run only on Web servers with Microsoft FrontPage Server extensions installed. While the HTML tags that FrontPage uses for displaying form fields will display in all browsers, the forms will not be processed correctly unless the server extensions are running.

Most Web sites process forms using a CGI (or the common gateway interface) form handler, written specifically to handle each form. FrontPage, however, doesn't require you to write a script in order to create a form. When you insert and edit form fields to a page, FrontPage adds the HTML code that makes it work. Some of the code is standard HTML tags that generate input fields and labels. But rather than use CGI forms handling and scripts, FrontPage will insert a WebBot to process and save the data in a file at your Web site. At your convenience, you can use FrontPage Explorer to export the file from the server and open it with a Web browser, word processor, spreadsheet, or database program, depending on the options you choose. Or you can display it at the site with a Web browser.

TIP

If you're using a form simply to collect interesting information that you want to share, you can invite visitors to review the data you've collected. Store the results to an HTML file and add a link to the file from one of your current Web pages.

CREATING A FORM

The process of creating a form begins by adding form fields to an open page. First, create the page where you want the form to be displayed in FrontPage Editor. Then, select **Insert**, **Form Field** from the main menu. The menu in Figure 12.1 will open.

Figure 12.1 The menu list of form field choices.

This menu clearly describes the form fields available and so working with this menu is a good way to become familiar with the options as you create forms. But it's cumbersome to use since you need to pull down the menus and select from a list for each field.

An easier method is to use the Forms toolbar shown in Figure 12.2. You can display this toolbar by selecting **View**, **Forms Toolbar**.

Figure 12.2 The Forms toolbar.

The Forms toolbar provides the same six form fields available on the drop-down menu. FrontPage will display the name for each of the form field icons if you move your mouse near the icon and hold it for a few seconds.

TIP

The Forms toolbar appears below the other toolbars at the top of the FrontPage window when you first select it, but you can "tear it off" and move it anywhere in the display. To select it, point near an edge of the toolbar until the entire toolbar is highlighted and then drag it.

Inserting Form Fields

The first step in building a form is to select the spot in your page where you want the form to appear and then choose a form field using either the drop-down menus or the Forms toolbar.

255

As soon as you select a form field, FrontPage will insert the form field—text box, drop-down menu, scrolling text box, radio button, or check box—into the page. Whenever your mouse cursor passes over the form field area, it changes from a pointer to a robot-like character. Whenever you see this robot pointer, your mouse is passing over an area controlled by a WebBot.

FrontPage Editor will also indicate that this area of the page is a form by displaying dotted lines above and below the fields you've inserted. These lines will not appear when the page is displayed in a browser. Figure 12.3 shows a display after a scrolling text box was inserted.

Figure 12.3 Inserting a form field.

After the field is inserted, you need to add the label that will appear with the field. When the field is inserted, your cursor is to the left of the field. If you want the label to appear in the standard position left of the field, move it before you enter the text.

Editing the Fields

Once fields have been added to the page, you can edit them like other objects. You can drag and drop fields to rearrange your form, or you can cut and paste them. To remove a field, select it and cut, or simply backspace over it.

Most forms on the Internet are boring, but yours don't have to be. You can format the labels using colors and font styles. Figure 12.4 shows a form using each of the six form fields.

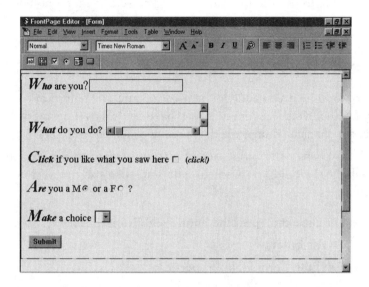

Figure 12.4 You can format the labels for each field.

Don't insert graphics into the form area unless you're planning to assign a form field function (such as "submit") to the graphic. Everything in the form is treated as a database field, and the forms handler will attempt to assign a value to each form; a graphic inserted into the form will be identified as a field. You can display graphics on the same page as the form; just keep them outside of the dotted lines that indicate the beginning and end of the form.

CONTROLLING THE DATA YOU COLLECT

After form fields are added to a page, you need to choose properties. Some of the properties will affect the display of the field, and others will affect how the input is processed.

When setting properties, keep in mind that a form is actually a way of inputting records into a database. The properties for each field are needed in order to store the data in a form that a database can handle. Whether you open the information in a database, spreadsheet, or word processor is your choice. But the properties you select will have an impact on how you're able to use the information. As you select the properties, consider how you plan to use the file this form will generate.

Form Field Properties

Every form field you add will be used to store one record in one database field. When you set properties, you have control over a variety of settings that are characteristic of the data usually collected from such a device.

You change the properties of a form field from a dialog box. First, highlight the field you want to edit, and then use one of four different techniques:

- Right-click and select the **Form Field Properties** menu.
- Press **Alt-Enter**.
- Select **Edit**, **Form Field Properties**.
- Double-click on the field.

The dialog box that opens is unique for each type of field. The one setting common to all fields is the name of the field. FrontPage will assign a name by default, such as T1 for the first text field, T2 for the second text field, and D1 for the first drop-down list. You'll want to change the name to help you identify the field results, and you may want to use the abbreviated version of the label as the name. But try to keep it short. This name will be used as the header for the field, so don't use a name that's longer than the expected results. For example, it's okay to change a text box name from T1 to "name," but if you're using a check box, the field results will be only one character long so you probably don't want to create an excessively long header for this narrow column.

WARNING Don't use characters outside of the alphabet or numeric fields for the name of a field (for example, don't use @, #, or a blank space). FrontPage is not be able to perform validation on fields with nonstandard names.

Let's look at the other choices available for each form field.

Text Box Properties

Text boxes are often used for collecting names or other short bits of text. The Text Box Properties dialog box, shown in Figure 12.5, is mainly used to control the length of the field, but you can also use it to validate the data entered.

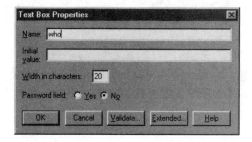

Figure 12.5 The Text Box Properties dialog box.

Any text you enter in the Initial Value field will appear in the browser display. This is usually left empty; otherwise, a user will assume it's already completed. You can set the length of the field; the default of **20** is commonly used for names. The width of the text box is determined by the width you enter here, so if you're looking for a short answer, enter a low number.

If you are using passwords to protect access to a type of data, select **Yes** in the password field. You don't establish password protection simply by clicking on this option; you need to validate the entries in addition to checking here. Selecting **Yes** will result in the browser showing asterisk (*) in place of text for entries in the field.

You can perform an extensive amount of validation to the entries in the text box field in order to restrict entries to specific values. Since you could set up a code system that would be required for users to enter, you may use password protection in conjunction with a validation to perform a rudimentary type of security. See the section on validation later in the chapter.

Scrolling Text Box Properties

A scrolling text box gives users a chance to write long comments. The Scrolling Text Box Properties dialog box, shown in Figure 12.6, is similar to the text box in that you want to set a limit on the amount of data that can be entered.

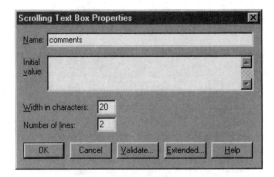

Figure 12.6 Scrolling text box properties.

Since a scrolling text box is designed to collect a lot of text, you can control the width and the number of lines it will occupy. You can also control the size without opening the dialog box; just resize the borders from the Editor display.

T I P

A form can be used on an intranet Web site to collect reports from members of a team. Use multiple scrolling text boxes to encourage people to organize their reports into sections. For example, in creating a meeting report, create fields for "purpose of meeting," "topics discussed," and "follow-up items."

Changing the values for width and number of lines does not restrict the amount of text that a user will be able to enter. To restrict the length of the message, click on **Validate**, select the text data type, and enter the number of characters under Max Length.

Check Box Properties

Check boxes collect answers to a simple question, and so the check box field is normally used to assign a logical "true/false" validation. As a result, the Check Box Properties dialog box, shown in Figure 12.7, provides very few options.

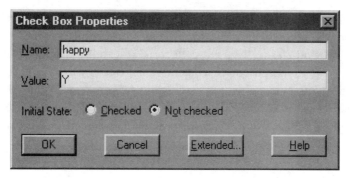

Figure 12.7 Check Box Properties dialog box.

You can name the field, select the value that will be stored in the results file, and select whether a check appears in the box when the form is displayed. You may want to change the default setting for value from "on" to something that fits in with your database, such as Y for *yes*.

Radio Button Properties

Radio buttons are a way to allow users to select only one item from a list. When FrontPage inserts new radio buttons into a form, it gives every radio button in the group (defined as the buttons on the same line) the same name (R1) by default, as shown in the Radio Button Properties dialog box.

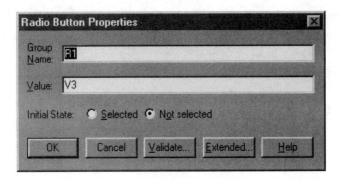

Figure 12.8 Radio Button Properties dialog box.

But it provides the default value in a sequence in order to differentiate the choices. The first button in the line will return the value of V1, the second V2, and so on. If you're collecting an extensive amount of data, you may want to assign codes to each value, but if you're collecting a form you'll review personally, you may want to assign a value that identifies the selection. For example, V1 could be "male" and V2 could be "female." By default, the first radio button on the line is selected, but you can choose to have any of the buttons be the default.

Drop-Down Menu Properties

Drop-down menus are used whenever someone can choose from a long list. A popular use is to allow people to select their state name from a drop-down list.

WARNING

It's essential that you edit the properties for a drop-down menu. No values will appear in the list until you add them in this dialog box.

You add each item to the drop-down list in the Drop Down Menu Properties dialog box. It's a good idea to enter a full description of the information as the choice so that users won't guess and then enter an abbreviated version of the choice as the value. As shown in Figure 12.9, you could use the full name of a state as the choice and the two-letter abbreviation as the value.

CHAPTER 12—Creating Forms to Gather Information

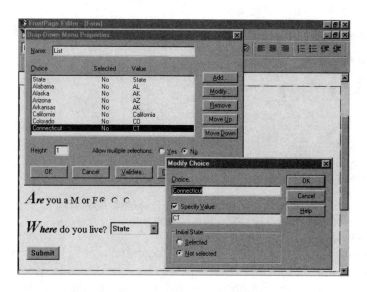

Figure 12.9 Adding an item to a drop-down menu.

When you add or modify choices, a second dialog box opens, allowing you to enter the choice and value. If you click on **Selected** for this choice, it will be included in your default list; the Main Properties dialog box allows you to restrict users to only one selection or multiple selections from the list. You can change the height of this box, but you cannot edit the width. FrontPage will display the box as wide as the longest entry on your list.

Push Button Properties

The final field in your form is also the most important. The push button is the field that triggers the processing of the data you're collecting. No data are collected with the push button field. But you use the Push Button Properties dialog box, shown in Figure 12.10, to specify what the server will do with the data you've collected from the other fields.

263

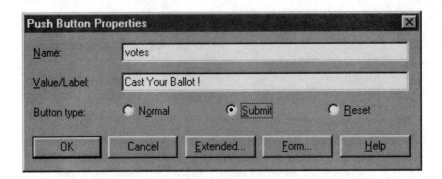

Figure 12.10 The Push Button Properties dialog box.

By default, FrontPage names the buttons, B1, B2, and so on, depending on how many you insert. If you're creating a simple form to collect information, you need only one button, and it must be designated as the **Submit** button. The **Reset** button is optional; it allows a user to correct mistakes easily by refreshing the page with a blank version of the form. If you are writing a script that will create a special processing routine for form, select the option **Normal** and then use the **Form** button to assign the script to this button.

WARNING

If you fail to include a push button and assign it to a forms handler, your form will seem to work on a Web page but it won't capture the data. You must name a file so that the server knows where to store the data you're collecting.

In the interest of creating a more enticing form, you'll want to change the button name from the rather doctrinaire "submit" to something more appealing, like "Cast Your Ballot!" or "Thanks for your input."

The **Form** button allows you to configure the form handler that will be used to get the data from your visitor's browser to you.

CONFIGURING THE FORMS HANDLER

Browsers do much of the work when you create a form. The form field buttons, boxes, and menus are created with standard HTML tags. But the browser merely collects the data and gets it ready to send out. A forms handler must be able to process the data after a user types it in.

The default handler that FrontPage provides for gathering data in ordinary forms is the WebBot Save Results Component. The processing is done on the Web server running code that is part of the FrontPage Server Extensions, but you need to select options that the WebBot will use.

Selecting a Forms Handler

You begin the process of configuring the WebBot Save Results Component with the Forms Properties dialog box, shown in Figure 12.11.

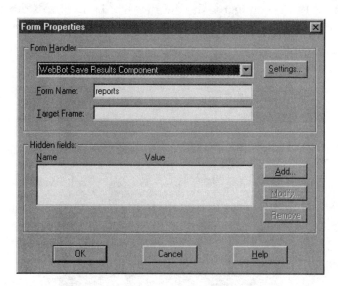

Figure 12.11 Configuring the forms handler in the Forms Properties dialog box.

You select this dialog box by selecting Forms from the Push Button Properties dialog box, or by right-clicking anywhere in the form and selecting it from a menu. You have the option of several forms handlers. For ordinary forms where you're collecting data that will be stored in a text or HTML file on your server, select **WebBot Save Results Component**. Two other WebBots are provided for using a form in special circumstances (registering visitors to a site with a password and using forms to create discussion groups); both are covered in Chapter 14. Select

Custom CGI if you want to send the form to a CGI script on the server for processing. Select **Internet Database Connector** if your server has OBDC or other database drivers installed.

When you select the **WebBot Save Results Component** you need to select settings for where the form data will be stored, the format it will be stored in, and what happens after the form is completed.

Sending the Results to a File

When you select the **Settings** option for **WebBot Save Results Component**, a dialog box opens for all the settings. The first table, shown in Figure 12.12, configures the file that will be used to store the results and controls how the data will be formatted.

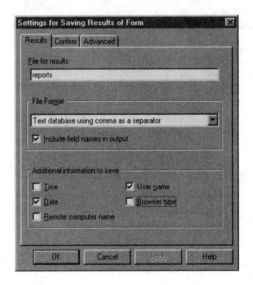

Figure 12.12 Configuring the file where form results are stored.

The most important entry is the name for the file; you need to type it in (you can't pick it from a list). Then, select the format. You have a choice of many common text formats used for collecting data including comma-delimited, tab-delimited, and space-delimited text. Or you can choose from several ways of HTML formatting including bulleted lists and definition lists.

You have the option of recording the field names in the output and recording the name of the time and date when the form was filed.

If you're on a closed network, you may want to record the user name, too. Even though this option is available on an Internet network, it rarely provides the full user name; instead, you will probably receive the user's domain name and an alias assigned by the user's Internet service provider. Select the option to record the browser used by the person completing the form if you're interested in gathering information about your users' software. Some browsers use code names, and many will also supply the operating system being used (for example, Netscape Navigator 3.0 running on Windows 95 will be identified as "Mozilla 3.0").

To retrieve this file, use FrontPage Explorer to open your Web on the server. Highlight the file and select **File**, **Export**. You will be able to save a copy of the file locally.

Splitting the Results

You can also create a secondary results file in a different format. You may want to use this option to generate an HTML file that can be displayed at the Web site, while recording results in a text file that will be used with a database. You configure this second file from the **Advanced** tab of the dialog box, shown in Figure 12.13.

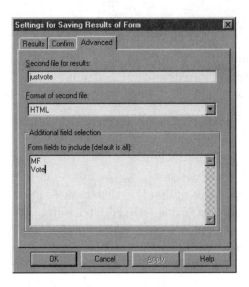

Figure 12.13 Configuring a second results file.

Thanking Clients and Explaining Failures

After a user has completed the form, you need to specify the next page they'll see. The server will display a default page that reports the form was successfully transferred, but why not take advantage of this opportunity to send a message of your own. You can thank them for their input, suggest a new link for them to visit, or include a link back to your home page. You may even want to display the results report if you saved it in HTML format.

You specify the page that will display from the **Results** tab of the Setting for Saving Results of Form dialog box, as shown in Figure 12.14.

Enter the URL or name of the file that will load. If it's in your Web site, you can select it with the **Browse** option. You may also want to enter a different file if the form fails. Normally, the server displays a message based on the problem. Since you aren't likely to know why there's a problem, you won't be able to provide as much help in solving the problem as the server can; however, you will want to use this file if you're using validation for any of your pages.

CHAPTER 12—Creating Forms to Gather Information

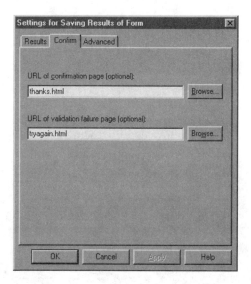

Figure 12.14 Choosing files displayed after form is submitted.

Validating Data before You Collect It

Several of the form fields allow you to validate data, helping to limit access without installing an enterprise server with advanced security. For example, on a corporate Web site, you may want to require that only users who know the correct codes can complete a form. Or you avoid errors in forms by restricting some fields to only valid ranges.

TIP

If you set up a validation field, be sure to create a Web page that will explain the possible reasons why the form would not be processed. Then, list the page on the **Confirm** tab of the Settings for Saving Results of Form dialog box.

To control validation properties, you first insert the field into a form. Then, you select the form and right-click. If the field has validation settings, you'll see an option for **Form Field Validation**. You can set validation properties for each field except check boxes and submit buttons.

Each of the Text Box Validation dialog boxes allows you to specify a display name. The server will use this field in identifying when a validation error occurs. When you don't enter a name, the server will use the form field name.

Validating Text Entries

The options for setting text validation are the same for both the single-line text box and the scrolling text box, which are shown in Figure 12.15.

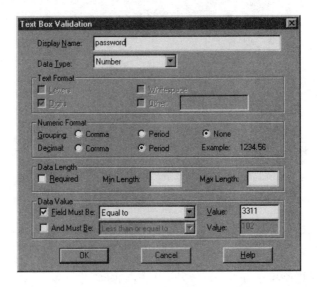

Figure 12.15 Validating a text box.

Validation can be used for a variety of purposes. You may want to require that a user enter a code or a value within a specific range. (If you want to use password protection to limit access to certain pages at a Web site, see Chapter 14 for a full discussion of the WebBot Registration Component.)

When setting up validation options, first choose the data type from a choice of text, integer, or number. The range of options available will change based on this first choice. To limit the length of comments that a user can enter, enter a value under data length. To restrict access based on codes, enter a range under Data Value. You can require that users enter an exact value or set a range (greater than, less than). If the values entered don't match the constraints, the form will not be processed, and the browser will display the message specified by the forms handler.

Validating Radio Buttons

The only constraint you can place on a radio button is that one of the buttons must be selected. If a user tries to submit a form without selecting one of these options, the form won't be processed. If you use this type of validation, be sure that you create a page that explains how the problem can be fixed. See the section entitled "Thanking Clients and Explaining Failures" earlier in this chapter to learn how to specify the file that displays when validation fails.

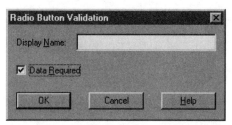

Figure 12.16

Validating Drop-Down Menus

You have the same option for validating a drop-down menu: you can require that users make a selection. But you have one more option in this dialog box, which is shown in Figure 12.17.

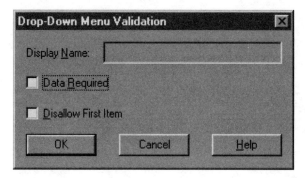

Figure 12.17 Setting validation requirements for drop-down menus.

You can require that users do not select the first item on the list. This option is useful if you use the first listing to identify the choices. It's become common for Web sites to display an instruction instead of a choice in the first item. For example, the first item in the list might read "Select one." Use this validation option to be sure that they actually do.

PART III
ENHANCING YOUR SITE

CHAPTER 13

ORGANIZING A SITE WITH TIME-SAVING WEBBOTS

In Parts I and II, we explored FrontPage techniques for creating a robust Web site that you can use to publish information and to gather data from visitors at the site. In Part III, we'll look at techniques you can use to enhance the site with multimedia and to connect it to other types of documents like databases and spreadsheets. We'll also look at tools you can use to improve management of the site, ranging from maintaining the basic site to automating the replacement of documents with new material.

This chapter examines FrontPage's unique WebBot technology and shows you how you can use these components to accomplish more with less work. This chapter will explain how you can insert WebBots into a page to

- Include the contents of one page in another page.
- Schedule the display of material for specific times.
- Display a time stamp.
- Generate a table of contents automatically.
- Provide a "search the site" feature.

WEBBOT COMPONENTS

WebBots are dynamic objects that you can insert in your pages. The purpose of a WebBot is to eliminate the need for scripting to accomplish routine chores. They work only when FrontPage extensions is running on the server or when you're using the FrontPage Personal Web Server on your system.

The forms you create in FrontPage (covered in Chapter 12) require WebBots for processing data input. Other WebBots are inserted in an HTML page using FrontPage's **Insert**, **WebBot Components** command; Figure 13.1 shows the list of WebBot components that opens when you select this command.

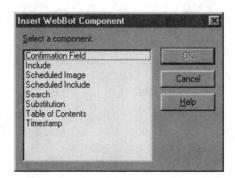

Figure 13.1 The Insert, WebBot Components command.

A few of these WebBots are included in the FrontPage wizards and templates. In Chapter 5, we saw how the Project Web wizard and Guest Book templates use WebBots. FrontPage includes WebBots in the wizards and templates partly as a way of showing off the potential for these time-savers. Let's see what each can do.

Editing WebBot Component Properties

Since WebBots are objects, you can move them and edit them using the same techniques that apply to other objects on a page, like graphics. You can cut them from one spot and paste them somewhere else. Or you can remove them entirely by selecting the WebBot and pressing the **Delete** key.

After a WebBot has been added to a page, you can edit the properties from a dialog box or by directly editing the HTML code. To review the dialog box with the WebBot properties, first select the spot on the page where the object was inserted. You can display the properties dialog box by pressing **Alt-Enter**, right-clicking, or making selections from the Edit menu.

Chapter 13—Organizing a Site with Time-Saving WebBots

However, while you are able to view the HTML tags that a WebBot component adds to a page, FrontPage will not allow you to edit them. You can use the **View, HTML** command to reveal the WebBot tags, as shown in Figure 13.2, and you can make changes to the text display in the window. But FrontPage will not record the changes you type; it will display an error message when you close the window.

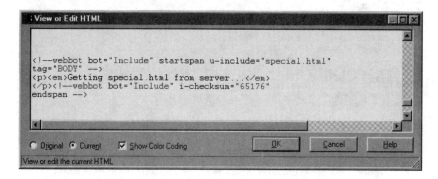

Figure 13.2 Viewing the HTML tags in a WebBot.

And don't try to out-fox FrontPage by editing the code in a text editor. You'll be able to save your changes, but the WebBot Component may not work properly.

Reusing Pages and Graphics

The Include WebBot has enormous potential for simplifying the management of a complex Web site. This simple object will display the contents of a page or graphic in another page.

One Navigational Toolbar for Every Page

One very productive application for the Include WebBot is to display the same navigational toolbar in every page at your site. You create the graphic image for the toolbar just once, including options for visiting the most important topics at your site, and create a clickable image map with links to the opening pages. Figure 13.3 shows a sample navigational toolbar.

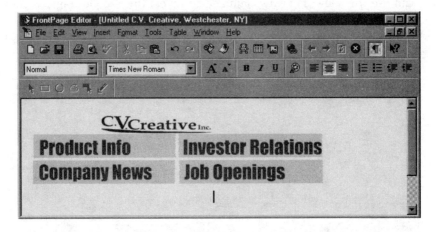

Figure 13.3 Navigational toolbars work well with the Include WebBot.

But rather than display the navigational toolbar with ordinary image source HTML tags (using the **Insert**, **Image** command), you save the page as a single Web page and give it a name that will remind you or its function (for example, `menu.htm`). Then, insert the toolbar in any page using the Include WebBot Component.

Keeping Information Current

The Include WebBot can also help you keep information accurate across you entire Web site while you maintain only one file. For example, if prices on your products change frequently and you need to mention the prices on several different pages, you could make your life much easier if you changed the price in just one file. If you display product-price information using the Include WebBot, you can store the information in one Web page display. When a change needs to be made, just update the one file. Every page in your Web will display the most current version of the file.

Inserting the Include WebBot

The Include WebBot is added to a page with a single dialog box. The key to using it properly is to be prepared. Before you are ready to insert the command, be sure that you have created the source file and saved it.

WARNING

Only files that are stored in the same Web can be selected with the Include WebBot. If you want to use a page that is not in the Web, import it to the current Web using FrontPage Explorer's **Import** command.

When you're ready, open the page that will display the source file in FrontPage Editor. Move your cursor to the spot on the page where the source file should appear and select **Insert**, **WebBot Components**. Select **Include**, and the dialog box shown in Figure 13.4 will open.

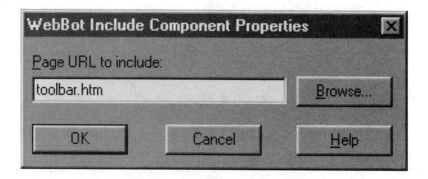

Figure 13.4 Inserting the Include WebBot.

Click on the **Browse** button to display the files in the current Web. You can select files stored in folders, but you cannot select files that are outside of the current Web.

PUTTING YOUR SITE ON A SCHEDULE

You may occasionally take a day off, but your Web site never will. Unless the network your Web server uses to connect with the world goes down, it will be open for business 24 hours a day, 7 days a week.

Occasionally, you'll need to make temporary changes. Perhaps some of the pages at your site may not be available for a few days while a server is being replaced. Or maybe you just want people to know that you're on vacation and may not be able to answer e-mail.

FrontPage provides two WebBots that can establish a schedule for the display of pages or graphics.

Inserting the Include WebBots

The Scheduled Include and Scheduled Include Image WebBots are very similar: they are added in the same way and provide the same options. The only difference is that Scheduled Include allows you to display the contents of a complete Web page in another page. And the Scheduled Image WebBot allows you to insert a single graphic in a page. Figure 13.5 shows the Scheduled Include WebBot dialog box. The Scheduled Include Image dialog box is virtually identical.

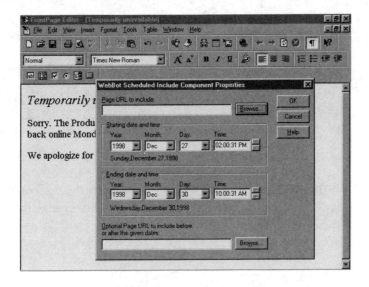

Figure 13.5 The Scheduled Include dialog box.

Like the Include WebBot, you must create the source material and store it in the current Web before you select either one of the scheduling WebBots. From the dialog box, you can specify the exact time (down to the second) when the file will be displayed as part of this page, and when it will no longer be displayed. After you insert the WebBot, FrontPage Editor will observe the schedule for displaying inserted files as you work on the page.

NOTE: The Scheduled Include commands use the system clock of the server in determining when to display or stop the display of a file. So if find there's a problem with the timing of scheduled includes, the server's clock may be wrong.

The beginning and end times are determined by the server when the page is loaded. The display will not change after a page is loaded into memory. If you display a file in FrontPage Editor or browser a few minutes before a scheduled interval, you may need to wait until the time passes on the system clock and then refresh the page. The current time is displayed by Windows 95 and NT on the system menu.

Keeping Visitors Informed about Updates

We're all swamped with more information than we need and don't want to waste time reading information that's outdated. So as a courtesy to people who visit a site, many Web managers like to let users know when the pages were last updated. Visitors can then decide whether they want to spend time at the site looking for information. If your site becomes an important source of information, people will start to pay close attention to any changes you make. Adding a Time Stamp WebBot can encourage loyalty: visitors will be grateful that you're honest. And they won't bother asking if you've got news about something that happened yesterday if your time stamp reveals that the pages were last updated a week ago.

You add a time stamp by selecting **Insert**, **WebBot Components**, **Time Stamp**. The dialog box in Figure 13.6 opens.

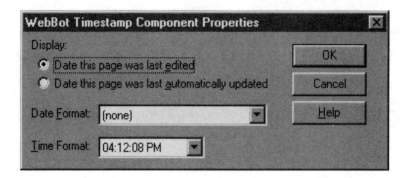

Figure 13.6 Adding a Time Stamp WebBot.

You have two choices of when FrontPage will generate the time stamp: you can display the date when the page was last edited or the date when an automatic update occurred (for example, if an Include WebBot is used on the page, the update may be later than the date the page was edited).

You can select from nine different formats for the date display (for example, 7/4/97 or July 4, 1997). And you can choose from eight different formats for the time including a choice of whether the time zone (TZ) is included.

WARNING

ou can use the time stamp to help you keep track of updates without revealing the date. Select **None** for the date, and insert the WebBot at the very bottom of the page without a label.

Be sure to add text before the time stamp appears in the page. The WebBot inserts only the date or time. You need to insert a label so that visitors know the purpose of the date or time.

Providing a Search-the-Site Button

As your site grows larger, visitors may have a hard time finding information. Although you can help make information easy to find by organizing the site well, the Search WebBot will add a brief form to your pages that can find text in any page within your site, as shown in Figure 13.7.

CHAPTER 13—Organizing a Site with Time-Saving WebBots

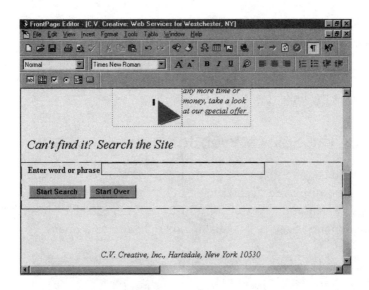

Figure 13.7 A Search WebBot added to a page.

Before you add the Search WebBot, be sure your site is presentable. The Search WebBot looks for text in every page. Normally, visitors to your site will be able to see only the main or `index.htm` page and pages that are called with a link. But the Search WebBot will open any page, including a file you haven't linked to others because it's not finished. The only files excluded from the search are those stored in folders that begin with an underscore character. Many of folders that begin with an underscore are maintained by FrontPage for maintenance, but the folder

`_private`

is created in order to allow you to store files that you want to exclude from a search.

WARNING

Don't add the Search WebBot to your site unless you are confident visitors should be able to look through all the pages. The Search WebBot can display pages you did not intend to make public.

That doesn't mean that you must keep all pages in the `_private` folder until they're completed. When you publish your site, just be sure you do not move pages from your system to the public server unless you're ready to make them public. If you have finished pages that you want to keep private, move them to the _private folder using FrontPage Explorer; FrontPage will adjust the links to show the new location. Don't move files using a different file management utility since FrontPage will not be able to adjust the links.

Inserting the Search WebBot

Once you're sure you want to add a Search WebBot, open the page where it will be displayed. Typically, searches are placed on an opening page, but you can add a search option to any page. Select **Insert**, **WebBot Components**, **Search**. The dialog box in Figure 13.8 opens.

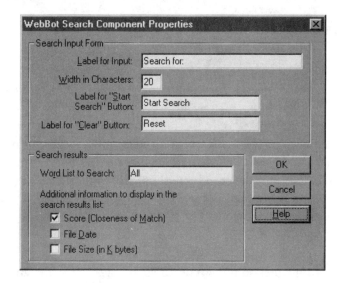

Figure 13.8 Adding a Search WebBot.

The WebBot Search Component Properties dialog box gives you control over the appearance of the form. You can choose the text that will be displayed next to the text-entry dialog box, specify the width of the dialog box and enter the text that will appear on the buttons that begin the search and that allow users to reset the search term.

NOTE You may want to add text to your page advising users how to enter a search term. The Search WebBot can accept search terms with the Boolean operators AND, NOT, and OR. Users can also restrict the search to a phrase by using parentheses.

When the Search WebBot is run by a browser, it will display a list of all the pages at your site that produced a match. From the dialog box, you can control how the results of the search will be displayed. You can display a score indicating the relative quality of the match, the size of the file, and the date when the file was created. Unless you're willing to have visitors dissect the pages in your site, you probably don't want to display the size of pages and the dates when files were created.

Displaying an Overview of Your Site

If you've done a good job of organizing pages in your site, you may want to show visitors the structure. The Table of Contents WebBot will automatically generate a list of the pages in your site, showing the titles of the pages and providing links. The WebBot will also update the table of contents as you add new pages, change titles, or change the URL.

You would normally add a table of contents to the home page or to the opening page of a large section. Before you add a table of contents, you'll want to have most of the pages already started. They don't need to be finished, since you can continue to edit the pages after the table of contents has been generated.

Inserting the Table of Contents WebBot

Open the page where you want the table of contents to appear and select **Insert**, **Web Components**, **Table of Contents**. The Table of Contents WebBot dialog box appears in Figure 13.9.

Microsoft FrontPage 97: HTML and Beyond

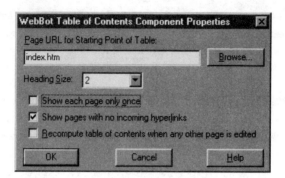

Figure 13.9 Inserting the Table of Contents WebBot.

The first option you select is the starting page. The Table of Contents WebBot will analyze the page you select as the starting point and display the title for each page that links to the starting page. Normally, you'll want to select as your starting page your home page (the one named index.htm, index.html, or welcome.html, depending on your server). But if you want to display only a subset of your entire site, you can choose a page that is the opening page for a specific category. For example, you may want to provide a table of contents to only the pages that display information about products. Choose the opening page for this section.

Since the Table of Contents WebBot is generated by analyzing the links, your options are based on how the WebBot uses the links it finds. When you select the **Show each page only once** option, you will prevent redundant listings from appearing if a page is linked more than once. The **Show pages with no incoming hyperlinks** option will result in a table of contents listing for a page that you may have intended to be hidden.

For a normal table of contents, the only option you'll want selected is **Recompute table of contents when any other page is edited**. This option will keep your contents up to date by tracking changes made to all the pages in your Web site.

CHAPTER 14

RUNNING A DISCUSSION GROUP

Whether you aspire to being the next Jay Leno, running your own talk show, or you just want to give your customers and fellow staff members a chance to talk about issues, a discussion Web is a chance to turn a Web site completely interactive.

With a discussion Web, visitors to the site can post messages for everyone to see and read comments posted by others. Message boards are famous for provoking lively exchanges that spread information rapidly. But they're also notorious for bringing out the worst in people, leading to uncivilized conduct, bruised egos, and even flame wars.

Setting up a discussion Web is fairly easy using a FrontPage wizard. But it's important to choose carefully among the many options. A discussion Web can eat up a lot of space at the server and use a lot of time, both from the Web site administrator and from the workday of every person who visits, if it's not carefully managed.

This chapter will describe the steps you can follow to set up a discussion group and to keep the level of activity within reasonable limits.

TALK SHOW BASICS

Discussion forums were once the province of bulletin board systems and online services like CompuServe and America Online. And many corporations have also added internal discussion forums with Lotus Notes, Collabra, and Microsoft NetMeetings. They're popular because they allow a wide number of people to discuss a subject. One person makes a statement or asks a question in the form of a text message. Everyone who displays the message can respond either directly to the person who wrote using e-mail or by posting another public message. As new messages are posted, the series of messages is called a *thread*, like the threads of a verbal conversation. Other threads can take place at the same time. Normally, the message is given the title of a broad topic (for example, investing in stocks). The threads follow specific topics (for example, news about the stock of a single company).

Where Newsgroups Fit In

Discussion groups came late to the Web. The initial design for the Web and HTML was to publish information without providing a vehicle for readers to talk back.

Group discussions on the Internet were supposed to take place on *Usenet*, the first network of message boards, which grew wildly as thousands of people discovered the potential for public discussions. New topics were added outside of the original confines of Usenet into the broader area that's now known simply as newsgroups.

Newsgroups exist outside of the World Wide Web but newsgroup servers are publicly available over the same TCP/IP as HTTP servers, you can create a link to a newsgroup from a Web page. In FrontPage use the **Insert**, **Hyperlink** command and select the **World Wide Web** tab of the dialog box. Then, add a link with a URL that begins with "news:" and includes the name of the newsgroup. For example, inserting this URL in a link

```
news:microsoft.public.frontpage.client
```

will display the list of messages in a newsgroup focused on discussions about using FrontPage. Figure 14.1 shows Microsoft's Internet News, a newsreader program, displaying a list of messages in this newsgroup. Microsoft has set up over a dozen newsgroups for discussions about its products, and many other corporations have done the same for their own products.

Chapter 14—Running a Discussion Group

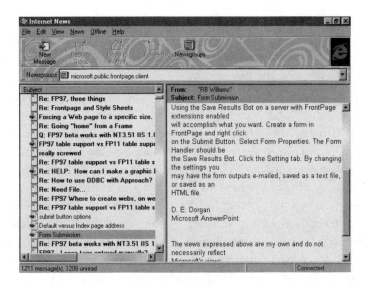

Figure 14.1 A newsgroup where FrontPage is discussed.

Although it's possible to create a new newsgroups just to discuss topics related to your site, you can't be sure the line to the newsgroup will work for all visitors to your site.

A newsgroup link works only if the client system has a newsreader installed and access to a news server. News servers (also called NNTP servers) maintain copies of the messages posted on the more than 20,000 newsgroups that currently exist.

NOTE

A newsgroup can be set up on a private server, limited only to people who know the address and have a password. All that's needed is a server running NNTP or news server software. Discussion will be limited to people who know the news server's URL, have a password, and are running newsreader software.

Internet access does not always include access to such a server. Most Internet service providers maintain their own news servers only for their own customers and restrict access to customers who log in with a password. But many corporations provide Internet access to their employees without maintaining a newsgroup server or contracting with an Internet service provider for access privileges.

289

And even if the visitor to your Web site does have privileges to access a newsgroup server, a Web designer can't be sure the links to a newsgroup will work. The client system needs to have properly configured the software for accessing the newsgroup.

Even if all the right conditions are in place—a newsgroup on the right topic is active, and you're confident your visitors can reach it—a newsgroup still has one big disadvantage. It's remote from your site. The process of linking to the site will introduce a delay for visitors. And, after the newsreader software is loaded and connection with the news server is established, a list of distractions appears. Every other news group listed on the menu is now competing for the user's attention. It's like you're running two different stores and sending people around the corner when they want a certain type of merchandise. As a Web administrator, you'll get a better level of participation if they can contribute to a discussion when they're at your site and paying attention to your topics. A discussion Web gives your Web site synergy: people respond to the material at the site, before they're distracted.

The Drawbacks of a Discussion Web

Discussion Webs are great for developing a dialog with the people who visit a site, but they carry a high price. If the discussion group becomes popular, you'll be devoting considerable server resources to it. Every time a visitor posts a message, the server needs to process an incoming form and store it on the server. Every message also requires disk space on the server. And when visitors read through the previous comments and lists of comments, they're generating hits on the server.

Before you plan a discussion Web, make sure that your server isn't already overtaxed. Be sure that you have enough disk space available to store the messages you'll generate; fortunately, you won't need much space. Since a discussion group consists entirely of text files, most messages will be short, requiring only 1 or 2 kilobytes of space. More importantly, check to make sure that your server's level of processing is not close to saturation before you add a new burden.

In the past, discussion Webs were also rare because they required fairly involved programs written in a combination of CGI and *Perl*

(Practical Extraction and Report Language). But FrontPage includes several bots you can use to spare you from writing the programs required to set up and maintain a discussion group.

CREATING A NEW DISCUSSION WEB

It's possible to add a discussion Web to a Web page by building a form, as shown in Chapter 12, and then using a the discussion Web form handler rather than the standard Save Results WebBot. But the process is much easier if you start the Web by running the Discussion Web wizard.

The first step is to decide whether you want the discussion Web pages to be stored within your current Web or generated as a new Web. The advantage of inserting it into an existing Web is that you'll be able to get it running with fewer steps, but in the long run, you'll probably find it's more work to maintain.

If you want to keep conversations restricted to only visitors who are willing to register their name and a password, you don't have a choice. The discussion Web must be created in the Root Web. If you use the Discussion Web wizard on a Web that is not identified in FrontPage Explorer as the Root Web, you will not be able to add password protection to the site.

Selecting the Discussion Web Wizard

Once you've decided where the Web will reside, you're ready to begin the Discussion Web wizard.

1. From FrontPage Explorer, select **New**, **FrontPage Web**. A list of templates and wizards opens.
2. Select **Discussion Web Wizard** and click on **OK**.
3. The dialog box shown in Figure 14.2 opens. Select the location. If you're developing it on your system, leave it at the default location of **localhost**. If you're connected to the server, use the drop-down list to select the server. If you're creating a protected Web, select the Root Web on the server.

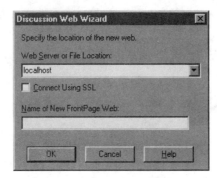

Figure 14.2 Naming the Discussion Web wizard.

4. Enter a name for this Web and click on **OK**.

5. FrontPage will set up the folder structure, generate new index files, and load the wizard software into memory. In a few seconds, the Discussion Web Wizard dialog box will appear. Each dialog box will give you the option of moving forward by clicking on **Next**, moving backward by clicking on **Back** (if there is a previous question) so that you can change your answers, or **Cancel**.

6. The first dialog box explains the purpose of the wizard. Click on **Next** to display the screen in Figure 14.3.

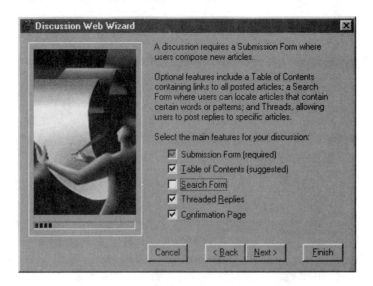

Figure 14.3 Setting the scope of your discussion Web.

7. The dialog box that opens gives you several options. Select **Table of Contents** if you expect to have a long series of messages, since it will display the title of each message. Select **Search Form** if you want to give visitors the ability to search for a specific word in the messages that have been posted (don't select this option if you're trying to conserve resources on the server). Select **Threaded Replies** if you expect to have many different topics of discussion and want to keep the messages on each topic displayed together (don't select this option if you want to keep the discussion limited to a single topic). Select **Confirmation Page** to display a message confirming when new articles are received; this can prevent people who think their message did not go through from submitting their comment twice. Select **Next** after making a choice for each option.

8. The next dialog box gives you the option of selecting the descriptive text that will appear at the top of the discussion pages at the Web and of selecting the name to be used for the folder. Your choice of descriptive text will affect what people say; be as specific as possible, as shown in Figure 14.4. If you want them to talk about your products, include the product name. The name for the folder must begin with an underscore; you'll be better able to manage your Web if you change the default to a name that means something to you. Click on **Next** after you've entered the text for both.

Figure 14.4 Entering the title for each discussion page.

9. The next dialog box gives you some control over the number of fields that will be added. Choose the layout that includes just a subject and comments format to conserve resources. If you want to encourage discussions on a variety of topics, choose the layout that includes either a category or products. Don't spend too much time with this option; you'll be able to add or change the fields after the Web is created. After you've made your choice, click on **Next**.

NOTE A discussion Web on an intranet will be restricted to only browsers who can connect to the Web site. But even in such a protected atmosphere you may want to create the Web as a protected discussion group because messages will appear with the author's name.

10. The next dialog box, shown in Figure 14.5, allows you to choose between a public discussion group that will be open to anyone who can display the opening page and a protected discussion group that will be restricted to people who have a password. One advantage of selecting the protected discussion group is that messages will be displayed with the registered name of the person who wrote the message. If you choose the option to make the discussion protected, you'll need to change the text of the opening page and permissions settings when you finish creating the discussion Web.

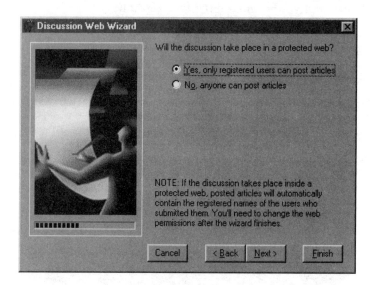

Figure 14.5 Choosing between a public and private discussion.

Chapter 14—Running a Discussion Group

11. The next dialog box lets you choose the order that messages will be sorted between newer messages first or older messages first.

WARNING

If you select the option in step 12 to make the table of contents the home page for the Web and you've already created a home page, the FrontPage Discussion Web wizard will destroy the original file.

12. The next option allows you to configure the Web's table of contents page as the home page for the Web. That will give you the ability to advertise your domain and folder as a place to go for the discussion Web. You won't want to select this option if you're adding the discussion Web to an existing Web since the original home page will be overwritten.

13. The next screen allows you to choose the information that will be displayed if you've opted to provide a search feature. You can choose to display just the subject or include the date, size, and relevancy score for this match.

14. The next dialog box allows you to control the appearance of the discussion Web pages. You can select the background color for the pages and the colors used for links. You can edit the colors after the Web is created by selecting the page properties for the title page; be sure to read the section entitled "Fine-Tuning Pages in a Discussion Web" later in this chapter.

15. The next dialog box allows you to set up the frames that can be used, as shown in Figure 14.6. The default option (**dual interface**) will provide a choice of displays so that browsers that do not support frames will be able to view the pages. However, this will create a fair amount of overhead for the server, so it's an expensive option in terms of server resources. If you're creating a discussion for an organization where you're confident every browser can display frames, you can select one of the two options that always displays frames. For a public Web site, the **No frames** option is probably best. Selecting any of the versions with frames will also add more work to the setup process. As discussed in Chapter 11, FrontPage Editor cannot display pages with frames, so any changes you make to these pages need to be performed using the Frames wizard. You need to preview pages with frames in a browser to confirm that the display options are correct.

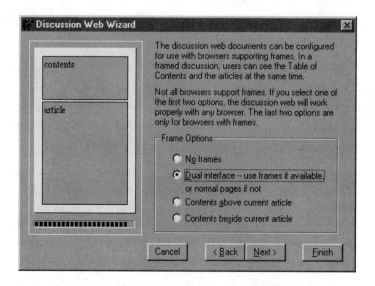

Figure 14.6 Selecting the frames used to display messages.

16. The next dialog box is the last. You will be prompted to review your answers, using the **Back** button. Or you can click on **Finish** to instruct FrontPage to generate all the files needed to run the Web.

If you selected the option to create a protected Web, the registration page will open in FrontPage Editor so that you can customize the page and complete the process of setting up permissions for the Web. If you selected an open discussion Web, you can publish the pages immediately or customize the appearance of the pages.

Controlling Access to Protected Discussions

When the Discussion Web wizard displays the opening page for a protected Web, it will provide instructions in the text of the page on how you can control access to the Web. This opening page, shown in Figure 14.7, will not match the appearance of the other pages in your Web, so you may want to set the background image and color using the page properties setting.

CHAPTER 14—Running a Discussion Group

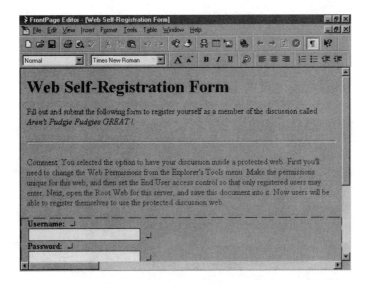

Figure 14.7 The default opening page for a protected Web.

You will want to change the text to display your own titles on the page and directions. As you edit the form in FrontPage Editor, note that when you move your mouse the mouse pointer changes to the **robot** icon, indicating that you're working within an area controlled by FrontPage WebBot. This area is a form that uses the WebBot Registration Component as a forms handler.

The registration process will add anyone who completes the registration form to the list of users who can have access to the Web. The text in the area near the top of this page explains the procedures you need to perform in order to activate registration.

Following is a detailed explanation of these steps.

1. With this Web page still open in FrontPage Editor, switch to FrontPage Explorer.
2. Select **Tools**, **Permissions** and select the **Use unique permissions for this web** option, as shown in Figure 14.8.

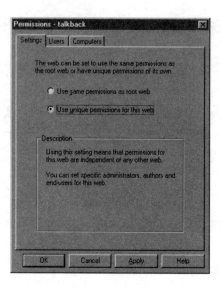

Figure 14.8 Changing permissions for a protected Web.

3. From this same dialog box, select the **Users** tab. At the bottom of the **Users** tab, click on the **Only registered users have browse access** radio button.

4. The next step is to save the self-registration form into the Root Web. If you're creating pages on a local system, you'll need to connect to the network first. Then, from FrontPage Explorer, select **File**, **Publish**. The Open FrontPage Web dialog box opens.

5. Select the server where the Web will be stored and <Root Web> from the list of webs. Click on **OK**, and FrontPage Explorer will move the files and folders from your system to the server.

Fine-Tuning the Pages in a Discussion Web

You can't customize the appearance of your discussion Web pages by opening the pages that are displayed by the browser. FrontPage structures a discussion Web with very few pages in the main folder while generating the contents of each page with an Include WebBot. In order to change the appearance of the page, including adding a logo or graphics to the headers or editing the text that displays, you'll need to open these pages with Editor.

NOTE

FrontPage stores the source pages for the discussion Web in a folder named _private because the Search function always ignores this folder.

First, you've got to find them: FrontPage stores them in a _private folder in the Web. FrontPage uses a name that begins with the folder name you selected and concludes with a description (each page has an HTM suffix). Figure 14.9 shows the list of files that appears when you select the _private folder. In this sample, the name of the Web folder is italk.

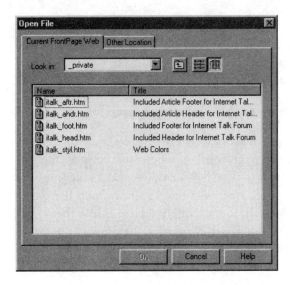

Figure 14.9 FrontPage stores discussion Web pages in the _private folder.

Fortunately, the titles aren't too difficult to decipher. The page entitled Web Colors stores a style sheet for the background and link colors. And four files control the top and bottom of each page. There are headers and footers for the HTML page displayed with each message and headers and footers that appear inside the form as part of the message.

If you don't change the default pages and your discussion Web is a failure, you may want to go in and customize the pages. Figure 14.10

shows how the main or table of contents page appears after a message has been posted using the default settings.

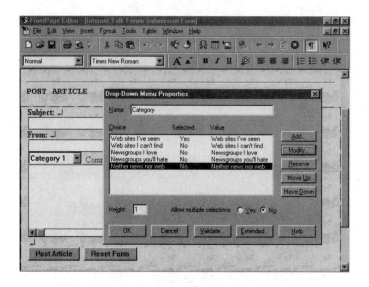

Figure 14.10 The default opening page for a discussion Web.

If you choose the option to organize topics by category, you'll need to customize the page entitled Submission Form in the main folder (not the _private folder). The default values that FrontPage adds to this page are "Category 1," "Category 2," and so on. Open the page in the FrontPage Editor, select the categories field, and edit the form field properties. When the Form Field Properties dialog box opens, select each of the default entries and click on **Modify**. Figure 14.11 shows the process.

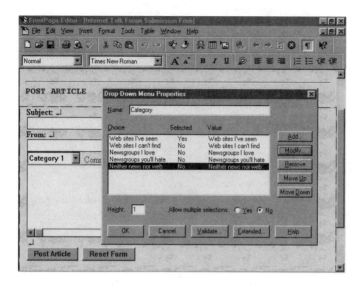

Figure 14.11 Changing categories created by the Discussion Web wizard.

CHAPTER 15

ADDING SOUND, VIDEO, AND ANIMATION

Multimedia is slowly but surely becoming a common element at most Web sites. If it can be stored in digital format, you can distribute it from a Web site with a link. There are ways to move all forms of sound files, film clips, and animated graphics over the TCP/IP pipeline that connects a Web site with browsers.

Although large multimedia files are not practical on public Web sites where many users connect with modems, some multimedia techniques don't require large files. Animations and background can be added with files that are smaller than many background images.

In this chapter you'll learn the many different options available to make a Web site more lively. You'll learn about the choices you need to make in choosing among different forms of multimedia files including plug-ins and ActiveX controls. You'll learn how to add Java applets to a site. And you'll learn how to create GIF animations and marquees that add sizzle to a site without eating up precious resources.

DEFINING MULTIMEDIA

Multimedia is a catch phrase for a number of exciting technologies. When you're in the business of marketing computers, multimedia is a great selling point, but when you're business is managing a Web site, multimedia refers to files that display moving images or play audio clips.

Planning Multimedia Applications

Before you spend too much time preparing your multimedia files, you'll need to take into account the realities of distributing multimedia files. The first step is to consider whether anyone will be able to display the files you provide. And that means you need to evaluate whether the MIME type you plan to use can be processed by browsers that display your Web pages.

Planning Multimedia: Client Issues

Before spending much effort in creating multimedia-equipped pages, you need to consider two requirements for multimedia on the system being run by your visitors: hardware and software.

Client Hardware

Silent animations can run on any system that's capable of displaying other graphics. But a sound card and a speaker or headphones must be in working condition (meaning that the sound drivers must be properly installed) to play multimedia files with music, recorded speech, or sound effects. As a Web master, you can't do anything about the available hardware—and you don't want to get involved in straightening out sound card configuration problems. Debugging problems between a sound card and the operating system can take the better part of a day (or weekend).

The hardware may also present a drawback if you want to distribute full-motion video clips. The browser PC should be equipped with a Pentium chip (rather than a 386 or 486) in order to run full-motion videos; Macs should be running a PowerPC rather than a 680x0. And full-motion video clips are practical only if the browser is connected to the network at a speed of at least ISDN levels of 128 Kbps. It's foolish to distribute full-motion video if many of the visitors to your site are connecting to the network with only a 28.8 or 14.4 Kbps modem.

Client Software

The software installed on the client's system can also be a limiting factor. Most multimedia can be displayed by a browser only when a player is installed. Players are available as either Netscape plug-ins or ActiveX controls. Browsers now come with a fair number of players installed, but older browsers may not have the player software. Netscape Navigator 3.0, for example, comes with LiveMedia players for audio in the MIDI, WAV, AU, and RealAudio formats and video in the AVI format. Earlier versions of Netscape Navigator are equipped with a player for only the AU format.

Planning Multimedia: Download Issues

Multimedia is often ignored by Web administrators because there's an assumption that places enormous demands on the server. That's true if you present a 30-second full-motion video clip that's almost a megabyte in size. But there are several techniques for providing multimedia that are very compact. Animated GIF files, for example, can be only slightly larger than ordinary GIF images. And MIDI music files can play for long periods but are even smaller than the average GIF file. In the long run, Java applets are expected to be one of the most effective techniques for displaying multimedia because they have the potential for providing extended animations with background sound with lower download requirements.

Planning Multimedia: Server Issues

Adding multimedia to a Web site is much easier if you have access to the server configuration. Every file displayed at a Web site must be recognized by the server as a MIME type. If you try to add a new Shockwave presentation to a Web site that doesn't recognize the DCR format of the file, all users will see is an error message when they attempt to play the file. Configuring MIME types must be done at the server using the setup software.

It should be obvious, but it can't be stressed enough. Multimedia files can place a heavy burden on a server. But for the types of multimedia you would normally add to a FrontPage site—WAV audio, Java applets, and AVI movies—the effect on the server is no different than if you were including a graphic file of the same size.

Web servers can also be used for a different type of multimedia application that is worth considering. Streaming video and streaming audio software can be run on the same hardware used for your HTTP server. A streaming server will allow your site to display video and audio clips in real-time. Rather than wait for a long file to download, the browser is able to begin displaying the first scenes in a movie or playing the first seconds of sound almost instantly. Figure 15.1 shows the player for RealAudio, a streaming audio product.

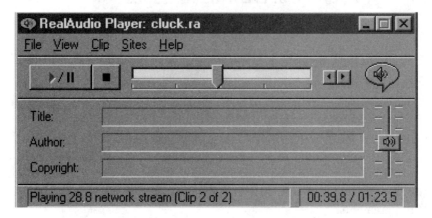

Figure 15.1 RealAudio streams audio almost instantly.

In order to provide streaming audio, you'll need either to install the server software on your own hardware or to use an Internet service provider that provides access to a server. Table 15.1 shows some of the more popular streaming servers for multimedia.

Table 15.1 Streaming Servers for Multimedia

RealAudio	Plays audio clips	www.realaudio.com
Xing StreamWorks	Plays audio or full-motion video	www.xingtech.com
VDOlive Server	Plays audio clips	www.vdo.net
Vosaic Server	Plays full-motion video	www.vosaic.com

Sending streaming audio or video is not practical when visitors to your site are connecting with modems. Even an audio stream is subject to disruption. But if you're running your site on a network where most users connect using a LAN, both audio and video servers can work quite well.

All the streaming server applications require that the browsers displaying the video or audio stream have a plug-in or player installed.

Distributing Multimedia at a Web Site

There are many specific types of formats for displaying multimedia, but thanks to the MIME spec, it all works. That doesn't mean it's simple. Fortunately, as long as you're confident your audience can use the multimedia you're generating, you don't have to choose between a plug-in or a player. You just need to make sure it's available to browsers that are equipped.

Playing with MIME

Multimedia files are digital copies of sound, animated graphics, or full-motion video. Like any other data format, they come to life only when they're processed by software. As explained in Chapter 3, Web browsers were designed to display files in HTML text, GIF graphics, and JPG graphics. But a browser can allow another software program to take over and process the multimedia files.

To help programs throughout the Internet understand the format of a data file, the MIME specification is used (see the section in Chapter 1 entitled "MIME: The Secret Behind the Magic"). As long as a multimedia file is recognized by the browser and server as a properly configured MIME type, the file can play. Figure 15.2 shows Internet Explorer's MIME type listing for sound files in the WAV format.

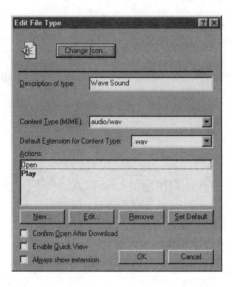

Figure 15.2 A MIME type configured in Internet Explorer.

Helper applications were the first technique used to play multimedia files. A helper application (or helper app) is any software on a system that will run when the browser encounters an unknown file type. For example, on Windows systems, the Windows Sound Recorder can be configured as a helper app so that it automatically loads whenever a WAV file is encountered during a browsing session. The helper app system is awkward since the player program is not under the control of the browser; after the helper app finishes playing the file, the browser won't retake control of the system until the user clicks on a browser control.

Plug-In Player Overview

Netscape created the concept of plug-ins to overcome the limits of a helper. *Plug-ins* are designed to work within the confines of the browser and return control of the system to the browser after playing a multimedia file. A plug-in is created solely for playing a particular file type from within Web browsers. A few plug-ins are available for static files. For example, Adobe Acrobat displays documents in the Acrobat format (based on PostScript), and Microsoft offers plug-ins for displaying Microsoft

Chapter 15—Adding Sound, Video, and Animation

Office applications including PowerPoint and Microsoft Excel. Most plug-ins, however, are created for playing multimedia files.

The first plug-ins were introduced with Navigator 2.0. Netscape also published a software API (applications program interface) so that programmers could write their own plug-ins. A small army of developers have created plug-ins and offered them for free in the hopes of popularizing the form of multimedia they work with. The plug-ins that have become popular are covered in this chapter, but dozens of other plug-ins are available at Web sites (Netscape publishes a list at www.netscape.com). Microsoft Internet Explorer began to support plug-ins in version 3.0.

To install a plug-in for a browser, you need to obtain the software, normally by visiting a Web site and downloading a file that's between about 500 kilobytes and 2 megabytes. Once the file is on the browser's system, it needs to be installed. As part of the installation, a plug-in will update the browser's configuration of MIME types. If you're not sure whether a browser can display a particular file, you can check its configuration. Figure 15.3 shows the list of MIME types in Netscape Navigator.

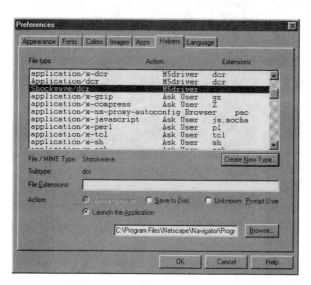

Figure 15.3 Netscape Navigator's list of helper apps.

The list of all installed MIME types (native browser MIME types, helpers, and plug-ins) can be displayed in Navigator 2.0 and higher by selecting

Options, General Preferences. A list of just the plug-ins installed in Navigator 3.0 and higher can be displayed by selecting **Help, About Plug-Ins**.

The situation is a little more complicated in Microsoft's browser because it allows you to play multimedia files using Netscape-style plug-ins and using a technology Microsoft invented called *ActiveX*. Some multimedia software developers offer players both plug-ins and ActiveX controls, and Microsoft Internet Explorer allows you to use either one. In Microsoft Internet Explorer, you can display the list of all available MIME types by selecting **View, Options** and then selecting the **Programs** tab. On the **Programs** tab, select **File Types**. The dialog box in Figure 15.4 will open.

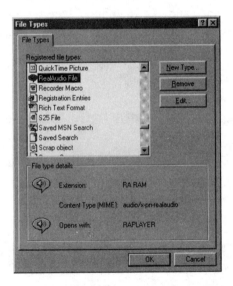

Figure 15.4 Viewing MIME types in Microsoft Internet Explorer.

CHAPTER 15—Adding Sound, Video, and Animation

Adding Files That Require a Plug-In

To add multimedia files in a format that requires a plug-in player, first, move the file into your Web using FrontPage Explorer's **Import** command. Then use FrontPage Editor's **Insert**, **Other Components**, **Plug-In** command. The Plug-In Properties dialog box shown in Figure 15. 5 opens.

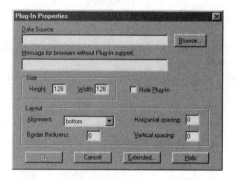

Figure 15.5 Adding a plug-in to a page in FrontPage Editor.

In this dialog box add the file name for the multimedia data on the line Data Source (you can locate it using the **Browse** button). On the following line you can enter the message that will appear in browsers that do not have plug-in support. You can also set options controlling the size of the graphic that will appear.

WARNING

When you use the **Insert Plug-In** command, FrontPage inserts an `<embed>` tag into the HTML code of your document, identifying the multimedia data file as the source file. At some time in the future, the `<object>` tag is expected to replace `<embed>` for adding data types to HTML pages.

The page will be updated to include a large **Plug** icon, shown in Figure 15.6. You'll need to preview the page in a browser in order to confirm that the correct plug-in file was identified.

311

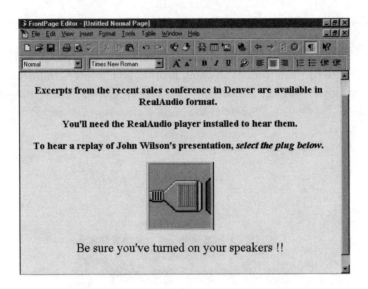

Figure 15.6 A page after plug-in properties were added.

Since the plug-in icon is a generic graphic that doesn't say anything about the type of multimedia you're playing, you will need to add text or graphics to help users identify the purpose of the multimedia data you've added.

ActiveX Control Overview

ActiveX was originally developed by Microsoft as a way to allow applications to control other applications' data files on the Windows platform. That was before the Internet became such a driving force and when the technology was still within the framework of OLE and Microsoft's Visual BASIC for Applications (VBA). Microsoft expanded the technology to give Web browsers the capability of displaying all types of data. Internet Explorer 3.0 is the first browser to support ActiveX controls and Netscape Navigator added support with version 4.0 (also called Netscape Communicator).

Most multimedia formats can be played using either an ActiveX control or a Netscape-style plug-in. Developers need to write the ActiveX

CHAPTER 15—Adding Sound, Video, and Animation

control for displaying their multimedia files, but most have. Developers were quick to write ActiveX controls for playing their files because ActiveX carries a significant advantage over plug-ins. An ActiveX control can be downloaded and installed automatically. When an ActiveX software file is added to an application, the source of the ActiveX player is identified; as a result, an ActiveX compatible browser will download the software without needing to ask the user for assistance.

TIP When developing Web pages for a network where everyone is standardized on Internet Explorer and Windows applications, you can display data files for all those applications from Internet Explorer. For example, the Web site can contain links to Office applications like PowerPoint and Excel.

When a user encounters a new data file at a Web site and is working in Netscape's plug-in environment, the setup process is tedious. Once you understand that you need a plug-in, you must navigate to the Web site where the plug-in is offered, find the right Web page to begin the file download, choose a system folder to store the download, wait until it finishes downloading, and then run a setup routine (if you remember where you stored it). Then, you must return to the page where the data file is offered. After it's over, your system includes the original downloaded file, which you're not sure whether you can delete.

ActiveX controls can install themselves because every ActiveX control carries a unique identification number: the Class ID. Every Windows 95 and NT system release 4.0 and higher maintains a table with the Class ID for every ActiveX control installed on the system. When a user clicks on a data type that's new to the browser, no work is required: the software is downloaded immediately, and the file plays when the process is complete, as long as the <object> tag at the Web site correctly identifies the source for the ActiveX control.

If you want to add a data type supported by ActiveX at your Web site, you can direct users to a URL where the file can be found. Figure 15.7 shows the message that appears when a Web administrator uses this option.

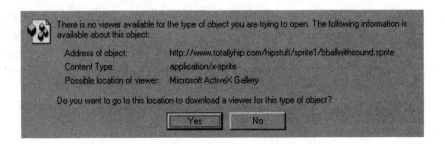

Figure 15.7 ActiveX controls are easier to track down than plug-ins.

When this option is configured properly, clicking **Yes** on this box will begin the process of downloading and installing the ActiveX control. FrontPage Editor gives you the option of specifying the URL for the code source of an ActiveX control, so your Web pages can also direct users to the Web site where the ActiveX player software will be downloaded.

NOTE If some of your visitors are on a network and can't download ActiveX controls and plug-ins from the public Internet, you may want to offer copies on your server. Most plug-ins are offered by their developers for free distribution, although you should check the copyright notice before posting them at your site.

This feature is available because ActiveX is based on a distributed model and provides a setting for the *code base*, a URL where the source can be found. The code base is normally set as an option for the `<object>` HTML tag used to insert ActiveX data in a page.

Adding Files That Require an ActiveX Control

You're probably not shocked to learn that Microsoft FrontPage offers a bit more help in configuring an ActiveX control than it offers for configuring a Netscape-style plug-in. Putting aside the competitive reasons, this is actually a result of the more extensive options that ActiveX provides for matching software objects that is allowed under the ActiveX specification.

You add a multimedia file to a page, using the ActiveX control properties by selecting **Insert**, **Other Components**, **ActiveX Control**. The dialog box in Figure 15.8 opens.

CHAPTER 15—Adding Sound, Video, and Animation

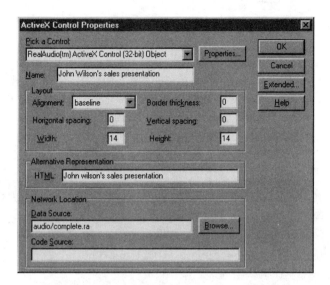

Figure 15.8 Setting the properties of an ActiveX control to play a multimedia file.

You start the process by choosing from a list of controls; any ActiveX controls installed on your system will appear here. FrontPage identifies the controls by the Class ID's recorded in your system registry. Since Microsoft Internet Explorer installs several popular multimedia formats (including RealAudio and Shockwave), you should be able to easily install controls for these data types. Adding an ActiveX control to a Web page is very easy if you have the ActiveX software installed on your system; if it's not installed, you need to obtain the Class ID number to insert the correct tags in your page.

TIP If you believe some of your site's visitors will have only a plug-in and others will have only ActiveX controls, you'll need to insert a tag for both players. Both links will refer to the same source data file, so it won't add a burden to your site maintenance after the separate tags are added.

And while FrontPage doesn't give you much control over the icon that appears when you've inserted an `<embed>` tag to refer to a Netscape-style plug-in, it gives you a lot of control over the appearance of the Active X link. You display an icon that's suggests the purpose of the player. For example, the icon used to represent a RealAudio file is an audio player that includes the RealAudio logo and slider bars to control the audio playback.

You can adjust the appearance of the **ActiveX** icon by selecting the **Properties** button from the ActiveX Control Properties dialog box. A control pad with the icon opens. To resize using the mouse, drag the control's borders. You can also resize the icon by entering pixel values. Click on the **Properties** button and another dialog box opens, as shown in Figure 15.9.

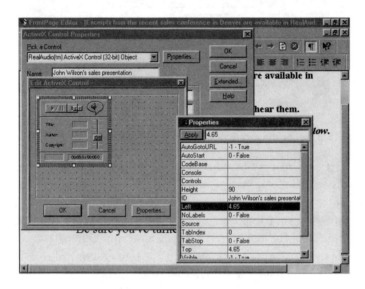

Figure 15.9 Adjusting the properties of an ActiveX control.

To change the height, select the row labeled **Height**. Enter a new value in the text box at the top of the screen and click the **Apply** button.

Java Applets for Multimedia

Java is the first programming language developed with the Web as its first priority. As a result, applets are being developed in Java to play multimedia applications without the need for players or plug-ins. A Java script can be stored at a Web site and played by any browser that includes a Java interpreter. Every version of Netscape Navigator version 2.0 and on, as

CHAPTER 15—Adding Sound, Video, and Animation

well as every version of Microsoft Internet Explorer version 3.0 and on, includes a Java interpreter.

Java scripts don't completely remove the need for plug-ins or viewers. Typically, a multimedia Java applet that combines animated graphics with sound will require a sound player, but it will generate all the graphics. But all PCs with a Web browser are capable of playing sound files are in WAV and AU formats, and all Macs are capable of playing sound files in AU format without a plug-in. With the proper programming skill, Java applets can achieve visual effects comparable to presentations created in an environment like Shockwave, which requires a player installed in the browser.

The growth in Java applets is expected to be exponential, partly as a result of development tools like Microsoft Visual J++, Symantec's Visual Caf, and others that are specifically tailored to building interactive multimedia presentations. In Liquid Motion Pro from Dimension X, for example, all the scripting tools normally found in multimedia development environments can be applied to a Java applet. Figure 15.10 shows Liquid Motion Pro with a presentation in development.

Figure 15.10 Developing multimedia with Java.

Developing a presentation using Java tools like Liquid Motion Pro is a fairly complex task but it can be accomplished by nonprogrammers.

Normally, you would use this type of tool to string together a series of graphic files and sound files. You could create the illusion of animation by using the menu commands to control the playback sequence, timing, and special effects like scene fades. (To learn more about Liquid Motion Pro, visit their Web site at www.dimensionx.com.)

Before you can add a Java applet to your Web site, you'll need to import the Java source code, class libraries, and graphics files to your Web. Once the applet is a part of your Web, you add it to a Web page using FrontPage's **Insert**, **Java Applet** command. Figure 15.11 shows the dialog box for an applet with the settings needed to include the Java applet generated by Liquid Motion Pro in Figure 15.10.

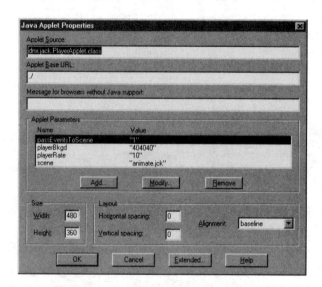

Figure 15.11 Adding a Java multimedia applet.

The Java Applet Properties dialog box requires very specific information about the source file. You must enter the class libraries included under Applet Source. If the applet was imported, you won't need to enter a URL (enter the URL when you're running a Java applet stored at another site). You'll also need to enter the names of parameters within the applet and values for each one. If you use a Java authoring tool like Liquid Motion Pro, all these values will be properly presented in an HTML generated as part of the staging process for the applet.

You can control the appearance of the Java applet in your page using settings that are similar to the way you control the display of a video image. You can align the applet and the size of the window that browsers will use to display the applet. FrontPage can not play the Java applet directly. Instead of the images within the applet, you'll see only a large J icon; Figure 15.12 shows a Web page with a Java applet in place.

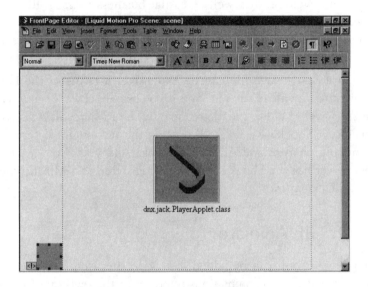

Figure 15.12 A Java applet displayed in FrontPage Editor.

You'll need to preview the page in a browser in order to test the display of the applet. You can edit the properties in FrontPage Editor by selecting the section highlighted with a J icon and selecting **Edit**, **Java Applet Properties**.

SHORT AND SILENT ANIMATIONS

Animation is something we all know too well; animations are like Saturday morning cartoons. A series of graphic images are displayed one after another. Sound may be added, but some animations are silent. The most popular technologies for animation today are Shockwave, Java scripts, and GIF animation.

Adding Shockwave Presentations

Shockwave was invented by Macromedia, a software company that develops PC and Mac software for creating all types of animated presentations. Many popular CD-ROM titles were developed with the company's software products, which is available in several levels to satisfy professional software developers, as well as casual business users. Authorware and Director can be used to develop advanced presentations combining live video, animated images, and sound. Action can be used to create a simpler animated presentation that mixes sound and graphics.

But a Shockwave file can be expensive in terms of the bandwidth required to download the file. And if you use Shockwave, your users must have a player in either the Netscape plug-in or Microsoft ActiveX format. You install Shockwave DCR files using the techniques described earlier for adding plug-ins and ActiveX controls. And you also need to be sure your server has the Shockwave format registered as a MIME type for the DCR file extension.

Microsoft GIF Animator

Simple animation can be added to a Web site using animated GIF files (often called GIF 89a animations referring to the revision of the GIF format that spells out the use of animations). A small animated graphic can be less than 20 kilobytes, rather than the 200 kilobytes or more that a Shockwave animation will require.

An animated GIF file includes multiple frames of the same image. When a browser plays the file, the illusion of motion is created if subtle changes occur from one file to the next. In essence, the different GIF files are combined to form one large GIF file with formatting information that controls the time between the display of each file.

WARNING

GIF animations will be small files only if you use relatively small files to build the animation. Every time you add a GIF file to an animation, it increases the size of the final animation file.

CHAPTER 15—Adding Sound, Video, and Animation

Microsoft GIF Animator is a free utility you can use to create these files; it's included on the CD-ROM with this book and is offered by Microsoft at its Web site (www.microsoft.com). A number of other GIF animation programs are available around the Web, but when GIF animator is installed, it has the advantage of being displayed as an option on the FrontPage's Tools menu. The interface also shares some general design guidelines with Image Composer, such as the tool for grouping objects.

WARNING

You can run Microsoft GIF Animator without running FrontPage but you'll need to import the files into your FrontPage webs in order to have the files stored in the Web indexes that FrontPage maintains for each site.

When you run Microsoft GIF Animator, the program will occupy only about half the screen, as shown in Figure 15.13. To become familiar with the software, you can open some of the animated GIFs that the program installs during setup. You may need to dig through a series of folders to find the images.

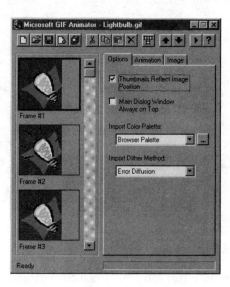

Figure 15.13 Microsoft GIF Animator displaying a series of images.

To load the files, click on the **Open Folder** icon and select the multimedia folders in your system's root directory. Select the folder **Graphics**, the folder **Web**, the folder **Animations**, and finally the folder **Microsoft GIF Animations**. Figure 15.13 displays the **Lightbulb.gif** file.

When an animated GIF file is displayed, GIF Animator displays each frame in the frame from top to bottom on the left side of the screen. You use the three tabs at the right to control the animation.

Creating a GIF Animation

In order to create a GIF animation, you need to have several GIF images. You can create the original files in Microsoft Image Composer or any other graphics program that can store files in GIF format. You'll need to create images that are slightly different from one frame to the next in order to create the illusion that movement is occurring. Figure 15.14 shows a text image being edited in Image Composer.

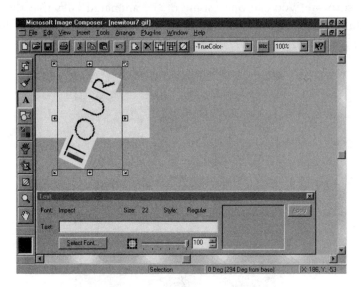

Figure 15.14 Creating the GIF files to be used in an animation.

If you want text to move, you will need to start with one image and save it. Then, make a slight change. For example, rotate it, as shown in Figure 15.14. Save this change to a file with a different name (for example, **logo2.gif**). Repeat the process, making sure that each change moves the

Chapter 15—Adding Sound, Video, and Animation

file in the desired direction. Save each change with a different file name (for example, **logo3.gif**, **logo4.gif**, and so on).

After you have a series of images, open GIF Animator and click on the **new file** button. Then, open a file, choosing the GIF file that should appear last. GIF Animator inserts each file in front of the last file, so you need to work backward. After you have inserted each file in the sequence, you will need to set the time that each appears. Select the **Image** tab and click on the first frame. Set the duration of the frame in one-thousandth of a second increments. You'll need to experiment to get the values correct, but a setting of **5** to **10** is a good start. Also set the **Undraw** method. In order to create a sense of motion, you will want to select **Restore Background** for most frames so that the next frame appears in its entirety. If you select **Leave Background**, the current frame will remain on screen and obscure parts of the next frame drawn.

After you have set values for each frame, click on the **right arrow** button at the top of the screen. A preview window will open, as shown in Figure 15.15.

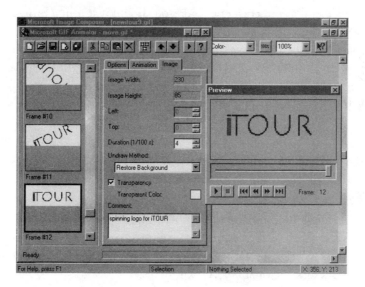

Figure 15.15 Previewing an animated GIF.

When the preview window is open, select the **right arrow** button, and the animation will play. If it's perfect on the first try, go buy a lottery ticket

323

because the stars are aligned in your favor. Otherwise, start experimenting with options to create an acceptable animation. Select the transparent background option if the objects have a solid background color that you want to fade into the page.

Try changing the duration of frames—each frame doesn't have to have the same duration. And you may want to leave the background remaining in some of the frames to create the appearance that your moving image is leaving trails in its wake.

TIP

A moving object will seem to gather speed if you set the duration of early frames high (about 10 one-thousands of a second) and set the duration of frames that follow to lower values (about 6 one-thousands of a second and 3 one-thousands of a second, progressively).

To keep the animation running constantly, select the **Animation** tab and turn looping on. You can choose the number of loops or set looping to forever. The animation will repeat as long as the file is displayed.

Although Microsoft GIF Animator will display the file in the correct sequence and at the correct speed, you should test it in a browser to make sure that the colors and backgrounds are correct. FrontPage Editor will display only the first image in the file; it cannot show animation.

ADDING SOUND TO A PAGE

Sound is normally inserted into a page using a file in the WAV (Windows audio) or AU (Mac audio) formats. Almost all browsers can play AU files. Versions of Netscape prior to Navigator 3.0 did not have support for WAV files.

But downloading sound files can take a lot of network bandwidth. WAV and AU files are digital recordings and use up disk space even to play back silent intervals in music. A WAV file with 1 minute of sound requires a disk file of about 100 kilobytes.

When your source files are in a particular format, you don't have much choice, but if you want to add sound to a Web site in order to make it more appealing, try to use MIDI sound files. They're much shorter than WAV or AU files because they're in a digital format created to convey musical information. They are often a fraction of the size of a WAV or AU file and will play longer. The disadvantage of using MIDI is that some systems don't have MIDI support. Microsoft Explorer 3.0 and Netscape Navigator version 3.0 come with support for MIDI playback.

Playing Sound in the Background

The HTML tag `<bgsound>` makes it possible for a browser to play a sound file automatically when a page is displayed. The user doesn't need to select a link or even click on a **start** button. The sound seems to begin almost by its own volition. Clearly, this isn't something you want to do at a site that displays corporate reports (unless you work for a music publisher), but it creates a pleasant effect at a casual Web page.

Select the option **Insert**, **Background Sound**, and FrontPage will let you choose from the files in a supported sound format. The dialog boxes will not display files that aren't in a supported sound format. You can search through all of the folders on your system.

Once you select a valid sound file, FrontPage will close the file and add it to the page's HTML code. The only way you'll know it's there is to preview the page in the browser in order to hear the sound file play or select **View**, **HTML** to review the `<bgsound>` tag.

Basic Text Animation with Marquees

Microsoft added a kind of limited animation with the marquee HTML tag that appeared in Explorer 2.0. It's not widely supported (Netscape Navigator 3.0 doesn't display it). But it's popular in areas of the Web where Explorer is preferred and can be very useful in intranets where everyone runs Explorer.

The marquee is easy to add to a site. It displays a line of text that moves across the screen. You insert the text using **Insert**, **Marquee**, as shown in Figure 15.16.

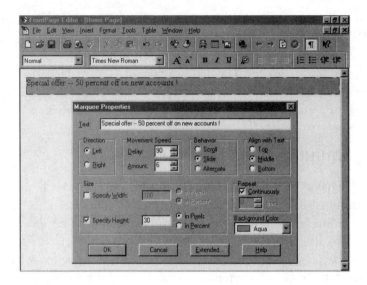

Figure 15.16 Inserting a marquee.

You can choose the direction the text will move (from left to right or from right to left). You can also set the alignment of the text within the marquee window and control the background color. You cannot choose the font for the marquee although you can select the height and width of the marquee window and change the speed at which the text moves.

INSERTING VIDEO FILES

As discussed earlier, video files are very large and can require a long wait as they download. Streaming video servers are on the market to help reduce the problem.

If you still want to publish video files from your Web site, select **Insert**, **Video**. A dialog box will open to allow you to insert any AVI video files on your system, as show in Figure 15.17.

CHAPTER 15—Adding Sound, Video, and Animation

Figure 15.17 Setting the properties for an AVI movie clip.

FrontPage displays the first image in the clip. After you insert the video clip, you can edit the properties by highlighting the image and selecting **Edit, Image Properties**. You can choose to have the video file play as soon as it is completely downloaded to a browser or have it begin to play whenever a mouse passes over the clip in a browser. You can also choose to have it play in a continuous loop. To change the size of the video window, select the **Appearances** tab.

FrontPage does not support the other popular movie formats on the Web—QuickTime MOV and MPEG files. To add these types of files, you'll need to insert the files for a plug-in, as described earlier in this chapter in the section entitled "Adding Files That Require a Plug-In."

CHAPTER 16

DEVELOPING WITH JAVASCRIPT AND VBSCRIPT

As Web sites become more interactive, HTML tags aren't enough to handle the entire load. The HTML specification was designed to display objects on a page and provide links to other pages. CGI scripting became popular as a way to provide simple interaction, but it doesn't process information on the client's computer. As a result, it places too much of the burden on the server. When a server is required to do too much processing, the performance of every Web page hosted by the server will suffer.

FrontPage offers two tools for building scripts to your site that avoid this problem: script wizards for both JavaScript and VBScript.

In this chapter, you'll learn the purpose of each language and where they fit into the larger picture of Web site development. Since the scripting languages are essentially competitors, you'll receive some guidance in choosing the environment that will work best for you. You'll learn the basic elements of each language, and you'll receive step-by-step instructions in creating two scripts you can add to your Web pages—one will display an alert message box you can use to grab the attention of visitors to your page in ways that aren't possible with HTML. The other will automatically display a different URL in the browser of anyone who displays a page; this technique is often used to manage the process of relocating a Web site. You'll have your choice of scripting languages; the two scripts are demonstrated in both VBScript and JavaScript.

THE POLITICS OF SCRIPTING LANGUAGES

Scripting languages are not neutral territory in the war over Internet standards. In fact, they're very hotly contested prizes. The tools chosen by developers to create exciting Web sites will have a profound impact on the future of Internet standards, and the leading software publishers are competing fiercely for developer loyalty.

There are two major positions. Netscape is allied with Sun in promoting Java as the leading tool for developing interactive Web applications. Java is similar to the C++ language in that just about any computing application can be written in the language: Java spreadsheets, database applications, games, and charting tools are being developed. But Java was written with the Internet in mind; it is designed to place the processing burden on the client's computer, keeping the server free to do what it does best (serve up data). In Chapter 15, the section on Java applets explained how you can insert Java programs into your Web pages.

Microsoft is the chief competitor to the Java environment. At its heart, Java is a problem for Microsoft because the language runs on all operating systems, lessening the appeal of Microsoft's Windows environment. But Java is also a threat to Microsoft's efforts to set standards for the future of computing. (The world of computing lives by the gold rule: "he who makes the rules, gets the gold.") While Microsoft does support Java with products like Visual J++ and countless opportunities, Microsoft believes it offers something better.

Table 16.1 Comparing the Development Choices for the Web

Java	A programming language similar to C++; applets are compiled and run in a browser on the client's computer. Available for all major computing operating systems, including Windows, Macs, and UNIX.
JavaScript	Scripting language based on Java; creates scripts that are interpreted by a browser as they run. Available for all major computing operating systems, including Windows, Macs, and UNIX.
ActiveX	Broad framework for developing applications that interact, based on Microsoft's Component Object Model, and the OLE specification. Works best in Microsoft Windows environment; support for other environments is in development.
VBScript	Scripting language based on Visual BASIC; creates ActiveX controls that are interpreted by the browser as they run. Available mainly for Windows; Netscape plans support in the future.

The ActiveX Environment

ActiveX is Microsoft's technology for tying together software. It is based on an object model: programs and documents have properties that can be affected by other objects. ActiveX has its roots in Microsoft's OLE (Object Linking and Embedding) specification, which was originally created to make documents interoperable between applications. The first uses were within Windows: an Excel spreadsheet could be displayed in a Word document or a PowerPoint presentation. OLE Remote Automation added object registration and class IDs so objects could reveal their properties to other objects, making it possible to do more than just link documents. Objects can be created solely to process other objects without referring to the container applications (like Excel).

Microsoft gradually expanded the OLE concept, creating the Component Object Model and OCX specification along the way. All these pieces were combined to form the ActiveX environment, which defines how objects should be created and managed within the Windows framework. Active documents are objects that can be manipulated by ActiveX controls were introduced.

Microsoft Internet Explorer 3.0 is considered a showcase for the ActiveX technology. Internet Explorer contains an ActiveX control known as WebBrowser whose main function is to support HTML. But Internet Explorer also can be treated as an object by other ActiveX controls. Microsoft Office 97 applications are capable of accessing Internet Explorer's controls. For example, the Office 97 Binder, shown in Figure 16.1, is a container that can adjust to the different properties of various ActiveX controls.

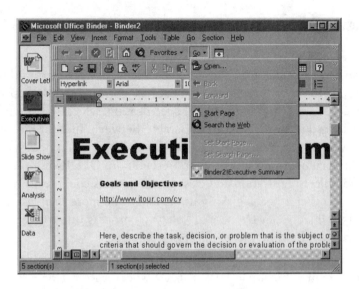

Figure 16.1 The Microsoft Office 97 Binder understands ActiveX controls.

Embracing Java within ActiveX

ActiveX coexists just fine with Java. In Microsoft's view, Java is a pleasant little environment for creating and manipulating objects. It doesn't interfere with ActiveX, so Microsoft has made sure that Internet Explorer browser can interpret Java applets without causing compatibility problems. It also gives FrontPage Editor the ability to include both Java applets and JavaScript code in FrontPage Webs.

TIP

If your Web site exists mainly on an Intranet and everyone who connects to the site runs Microsoft Windows applications, your choice is simple. ActiveX and VBScript will be the better choice.

Microsoft's strategy is to embrace and extend. It will continue to embrace current technologies like Java in the hope that it can entice developers with broader strategies like ActiveX, which will keep them firmly within Microsoft's world. Microsoft's long-term strategy is to first establish ActiveX as the essential environment for managing objects across the Web and then to establish a server model that will incorporate the older

HTTP specification with the ActiveX object model. ActiveServer is Microsoft's technical specification for this server.

Where JavaScript and VBScript Fit In

JavaScript was originally developed by Netscape as a language that could fill in some of the gaps in Web page development. Originally called LiveScript, Netscape changed the name as it allied itself with Sun to promote Java as a long-term development strategy for the Internet.

JavaScript is complementary to Java. The two share much of the same syntax, but there are key differences. Java is object-oriented in that it allows programmers to create object classes and object libraries and then to manipulate the object's properties. JavaScript cannot create objects. It lets you control only the objects within the browser's environment. JavaScript code is inserted into an HTML code and is interpreted by the browser as the page is displayed. Thus it does not require any server intervention but does require a browser that contains a JavaScript interpreter. One of JavaScript's great advantages over Java to Web administrators is that JavaScript is limited in scope. One of the weaknesses of Java is that because Java allows programmers to have access to system files, a Java program could contain a virus. JavaScript, on the other hand, cannot directly affect the system's hardware. It cannot delete files or perform any of the other tasks typically associated with viruses. As a result, a Web administrator can add JavaScript to Web pages without fearing a virus.

Netscape added a JavaScript interpreter to Navigator with release 2.0; Microsoft added a JavaScript interpreter to Internet Explorer with release 3.0.

VBScript has much in common with JavaScript. It was created solely for the purpose of manipulating data in browser pages, but its origins are in Visual BASIC. It is actually a subset of Visual BASIC for Applications (VBA), the macro language used by Microsoft Office applications like Microsoft Excel. VBScript uses the same syntax as VBA, but it can affect only objects within the Web browser. As a result, VBScript is just as safe as JavaScript; it can't contain a virus or delete data on the client's system.

VBScript must run in an ActiveX container application; because it controls only Web browser objects, it requires an ActiveX-compatible browser. Microsoft added ActiveX controls to Internet Explorer in release 3.0; Netscape plans to introduce ActiveX support in release 4.0.

Adding Scripts to Your Web Pages

Because the two scripting languages are so tightly linked to data displayed on a Web page, both are perfectly suited to the types of applications normally associated with forms. You can't generate input objects with either program, but you can process information generated with HTML form tags. That makes both environments ideally suited to creating form validation scripts.

The advantage of using JavaScript or VBScript for form processing is that you can perform the processing right in the client's browser. The calculations are handled more quickly since data doesn't move across the network. As a result, server resources are spared.

Advanced script applications require some programming experience, but FrontPage Editor includes Script Wizard, a menu-based tool for adding JavaScript and VBScript to Web pages.

Choosing between JavaScript and VBScript

The rest of this chapter will guide you through the process of adding scripts to your page. First, we'll look, step by step, at the process of adding different JavaScript routines to a page, and then we'll do the same for VBScript. If you are hoping that reading through these techniques will help you choose between the two, you'll be disappointed. The process of running FrontPage's Script wizard for JavaScript and VBScript is very similar. You will need to make your choice between the two languages on broader issues. You'll need to look at the types of applications you believe visitors to your Web site will be running. If your site is on the public Internet, you will have no way of interacting with those applications, and JavaScript is the better choice since it has no link to a computing platform. But if your Web site is on an intranet and the Web site will be used mainly by systems that are running other Microsoft Windows applications, VBScript will be the better choice in the long run. Chapter 17 will explore the possibilities of accessing other types of data when you're working in the Microsoft Office 97 environment.

CHAPTER 16—Developing with JavaScript and VBScript

Adding JavaScript to Web Pages

Because older browsers cannot understand JavaScript, the actual script is inserted into Web pages using HTML tags that essentially hide the page from the browser. Browsers ignore HTML tags they don't understand, and so several techniques are used for inserting JavaScript code. FrontPage will begin a JavaScript program with these tags. The first tag informs a JavaScript-compatible browser to pay attention to the following lines.

```
<script language="JavaScript"
<!–
```

The second line indicates the beginning of the JavaScript; browsers that don't understand JavaScript will ignore the tags. The JavaScript program will end with the following two lines.

```
//–>
</script>
```

The FrontPage JavaScript wizard will insert these tags automatically when it generates code. You can edit the JavaScript directly using the **View**, **HTML** command or using a word processor.

You can also insert JavaScript programs directly into your pages using a word processor.

Overview of JavaScript

A complete discussion of JavaScript is beyond the scope of this book. If you plan to make extensive use of JavaScript, you'll want to spend some time learning the complete syntax. A good resource is *Practical JavaScript Programming* by Reaz Hoque.

But it is possible to take advantage of JavaScript for simple scripting without learning the entire language. The most important concept to understand is the object model. JavaScript comes with built-in objects. Each represents a major element in the Web browsing environment. Table 16.2 shows the objects in JavaScript.

Table 16.2 JavaScript Objects

Navigator	The Web browser displaying the current page.
Window	The current browser window (each framed window has its own window object).
Location	The current URL information (includes protocol, domain name, path, and port).
History	The recent URLs displayed by the navigator.
Document	The current page.
Form	A form on the current page.

Every object has a predefined list of properties and methods. *Properties* are settings of the object you can change; *methods* are actions you can set into motion. There are few built-in types of event: a form and the opening of page in a browser window are the most important events, although you can add new events. A JavaScript program is essentially a series of changes to the properties or methods of JavaScript objects that are triggered by an event.

For example, the window object has a method known as alert messages. When you define this method in a JavaScript statement, the current window will display an alert box, as shown in Figure 16.2.

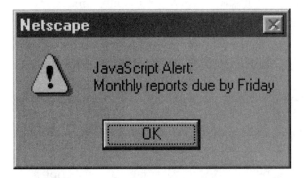

Figure 16.2 An alert message generated by JavaScript.

You don't need to describe the alert box or tell JavaScript to include the **OK** button. It is created by JavaScript as a result of executing the alert message box method with the window object.

CHAPTER 16—Developing with JavaScript and VBScript

You can assemble a JavaScript program by using the JavaScript wizard. The basic technique is to select objects and then set the properties and methods. You can create some simple programs without much programming. For sophisticated routines, like developing a calculator customized to a specific application, you'll need to apply programming techniques.

The next two sections will show you how to use JavaScript for adding two helpful routines to your pages: displaying an alert message and sending browsers to a different URL. No programming skills are required; although if you are a programmer, you should have little trouble adding these routines to other scripts.

Displaying an Alert Message with JavaScript

An alert message box can be a useful technique for grabbing the attention of visitors to your page. For example, if this same page is displayed by users on a regular basis, you can display an alert message to direct their attention to a new feature.

An alert message box can be very useful on a corporate intranet when you want to use your Web site to spread new information. For example, the alert message box may inform employees of a change in the company's schedule.

You can begin the process of inserting the JavaScript alert message box by opening the page where you want the box to appear. The following steps will create a script that opens the alert box as soon as the page is displayed, using the JavaScript event onLoad.

1. Display the page where you want the message box to appear in FrontPage Editor.
2. Select **Insert**, **Script** from the main menu. The dialog box in Figure 16.3 opens.

337

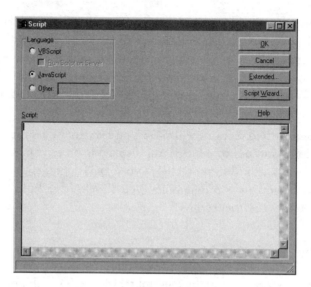

Figure 16.3 Choosing between JavaScript and VBScript.

3. Select the option **JavaScript** and click on the **Script Wizard** button. The dialog box in Figure 16.4 opens. This window is divided into three panes. The top left pane allows you to select an event. The top right pane allows you to insert actions (that is, select objects or variables and define the properties and methods). The bottom window displays each event and the action as you define them. To use the Script wizard, you begin by selecting an event in the top left pane and creating an action in the top right pane that occurs when the event is triggered.

4. Begin the scripting of the alert message box by double-clicking on the Window event. The **window** icon expands to display the choices **onLoad** and **onUnload**.

5. Double-click on the choice **onLoad**. The bottom pane displays your choice. Click on the code view. The dialog box changes to show the actual JavaScript instruction you're building.

6. In the Action window, double-click on the **window** icon to display a list of methods and properties for the window object. Select the first method, **alert**.

CHAPTER 16—Developing with JavaScript and VBScript

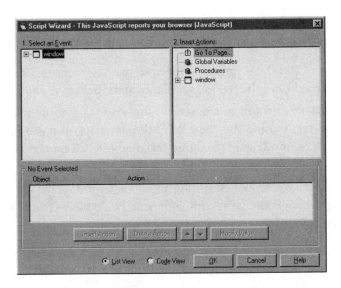

Figure 16.4 The opening display for the JavaScript wizard.

7. The bottom pane displays the JavaScript code using the word *msg* for the text that will appear in the button. Change the text to the message you want to display, as shown in Figure 16.5.

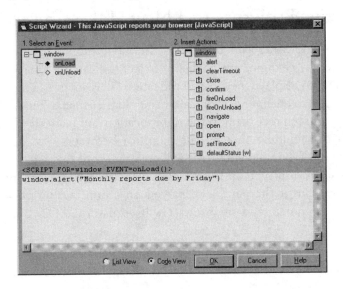

Figure 16.5 Inserting text for the message box.

339

8. Select **OK**, and the dialog box closes. FrontPage inserts the code into your page and displays a small J icon to represent the script.

In order to test the script, you'll need to preview the page in a browser. Be sure that you save the file in FrontPage Editor before you preview it.

To make changes to the script, you may want to edit the JavaScript source directly using the **View**, **HTML** command. You can make changes using the Script Wizard if you prefer; double-click on the J icon, and the Script wizard will open.

If you have problems getting the code to run, compare it to the following, which is the JavaScript code you would have created by following the preceding steps.

```
<script language="JavaScript" for="window" event="onLoad()">
<!--
window.alert("Monthly reports due by Friday")
//-->
</script>
```

Redirecting Browsers to a New URL with JavaScript

One of the JavaScript options is the navigational component of the browser. By changing the navigator object, we can use a simple JavaScript program to display a new page or location. This script can be useful if you ever need to change your domain name. Rather than ask users to click on a link, you redirect them to the right location automatically. You may also want to include a link on the page for browsers that don't support JavaScript. The following steps will create a script that will run as soon as the page is displayed on JavaScript-compatible browsers, so the link won't be seen. But if the page is displayed on a non-JavaScript browser, the script is ignored, and the browser will display the HTML tags with the link.

The JavaScript program that accomplishes this is a single statement. You can create the script in the JavaScript wizard by following these steps.

Chapter 16—Developing with JavaScript and VBScript

1. Open a new page in FrontPage Editor. If you're replacing an existing URL, you may want to rename the original page using FrontPage Explorer.
2. Select **Insert**, **Script**.
3. Select **JavaScript**.
4. Select **Script Wizard**. The Script Wizard dialog box opens.
5. In the Event window, double-click on **Window**.
6. Select **onLoad**. In the bottom pane, the wizard will begin to generate the line of script. The dialog box changes to show the actual line of script.
7. In the Insert Actions window, double-click on **Go To Page**. The Go To Page dialog box opens.
8. Enter the new URL. If it's a page in the same folder at your Web site, type the file name including the HTM extension. If it's at a different Web site, include the complete URL with protocol.
9. Click on **OK** to close the Go To Page dialog box. The line of code appears in the bottom pane. If you need to correct the URL, select **Modify**. The dialog box shown in Figure 16.6 will open.

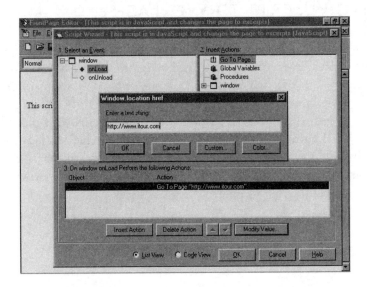

Figure 16.6 Modifying the URL for the navigator location.

10. Click on **OK** to close the Script Wizard dialog box. FrontPage will insert the script in your Web page. A small **J** icon will represent the script.

To test the script, you'll need to save the file in FrontPage Editor and then preview the page in a browser that supports JavaScript. You can edit the page using the **View, HTML** command to display the script or by double-clicking on the script to open the wizard.

If you need to debug the script, compare it to the following code, which accomplishes the URL redirection.

```
<script language="JavaScript">
<!–
{
Window.location.href = "newpage.htm"
}
// –></script>
```

ADDING VBSCRIPT TO WEB PAGES

Like JavaScript, VBScript is not understood by older browsers (remember that it's not even understood by Navigator 3.0 or Microsoft Internet Explorer 2.0; the first browser to come with a VBScript interpreter is Microsoft Internet Explorer 3.0). To allow VBScript to be inserted into Web pages without causing compatibility problems with older browser, the actual script is inserted into Web pages using HTML tags that essentially hide the page from the browser. FrontPage will begin a VBScript program with tags that informs a VBScript-compatible browser to pay attention to the following lines.

```
<script language="VBScript"
<!–
```

CHAPTER 16—Developing with JavaScript and VBScript

The second line indicates the beginning of the VBScript; browsers that don't understand VBScript will ignore the tags. The VBScript program will end with the following two lines.

//-->
</script>

The FrontPage VBScript wizard will insert these tags automatically when it generates code. You can edit the script directly using the **View**, **HTML** command or using a word processor.

You can also insert VBScript programs directly into your pages using a word processor.

TIP

Microsoft publishes a gallery of VBScript programs you can examine at http://www.Microsoft.com/vbscript. Some are freely distributed so that you can insert them into your own Web pages.

Overview of VBScript

Anyone who's written programs with Visual BASIC or who's written advanced macros in Microsoft Office will readily understand VBScript. Because it is a subset of Visual BASIC and Visual BASIC for Applications, it follows the same rules. A complete discussion of VBScript concepts is beyond the scope of this book. If you plan to make extensive use of VBScript, you'll want to spend some time learning the complete syntax. A good resource is *teach yourself ... Visual Basic* by John Socha.

You don't have to master the language to use VBScript in simple techniques for enhancing your Web pages. The most important concept to understand is the object model. VBScript comes with built-in objects. Each represents a major element in the Web browsing environment. Table 16.3 shows the objects in VBScript.

343

Table 16.3 VBScript Objects

Object	Description
Navigator	The Web browser displaying the current page.
Window	The current browser window (each framed window has its own window object).
Location	The current URL information (includes protocol, domain name, path, and port).
History	The recent URLs displayed by the navigator.
Document	The current page.
Form	A form on the current page.
Links	Hyperlinks in the current page.
Anchors	Internal links within the current page.
Frame	A frame within the current page.
Scripts	Other VBScript code in the current page.

Every object has a predefined list of properties and methods. Properties are settings of the object you can change; methods are actions you can set into motion. There are few built-in types of event: a form and the opening of page in a browser window are the most important events, although you can add new events. A VBScript program is essentially a series of changes to the properties or methods of VBScript objects that are triggered by an event.

For example, the window object has a method known as alert messages. When you define this method in a JavaScript statement, the current window will display an alert box, as shown in Figure 16.7. If you're comparing VBScript to JavaScript, you'll notice one advantage of using VBScript for generating an alert message.

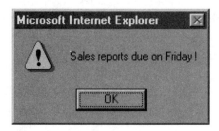

Figure 16.7 An alert message generated by VBScript.

Chapter 16—Developing with JavaScript and VBScript

The VBScript message is cleaner: it doesn't add the text "JavaScript alert." Only your message is displayed.

In every other way, developing a short script that displays an alert box is identical in VBScript and JavaScript. You don't need to describe the alert box or tell VBScript to include the **OK** button. VBScript has a different syntax. VBScript is procedure-oriented and rather than simply declare the object, as JavaScript does, VBScript creates a procedure and calls it.

You can assemble a VBScript program using the script wizard. The basic technique is to select objects and then set the properties and methods. You can create some simple programs without learning much about the language.

The next two sections will show you how to use VBScript for adding two helpful routines to your pages: displaying an alert message and sending browsers to a different URL. No programming skills are required; although if you are a programmer, you should have little trouble adding these routines to other scripts.

Displaying an Alert Message with VBScript

An alert message box can be a useful technique for grabbing the attention of visitors to your page. For example, if this same page is displayed by users on a regular basis, you can display an alert message to direct their attention to a new feature.

Begin the process of creating a VBScript alert message box by opening FrontPage with the HTML page where you want the box to appear. The following steps will create a script that opens the alert box as soon as the page is displayed.

1. Display the page where you want the message box to appear in FrontPage Editor.
2. Select **Insert**, **Script** from the main menu. The dialog box in Figure 16.3 opens.
3. Select the option **VBScript** and click on the **Script Wizard** button. The dialog box in Figure 16.8 opens. This window is divided into three panes. The top left pane allows you to select an event. The top right pane allows you to insert actions (that is, select objects or vari-

ables and define the properties and methods). The bottom window displays each event and the action as you define them. To use the Script wizard, you begin by selecting an event in the top left pane and creating an action in the top right pane that occurs when the event is triggered.

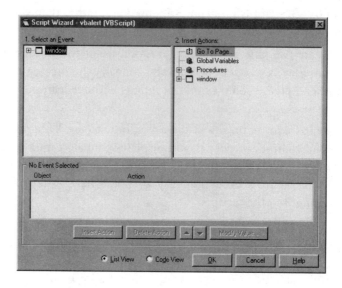

Figure 16.8 The opening display for the VBScript wizard.

4. Begin the scripting of the alert message box by double-clicking on the Window event. The **window** icon expands to display the choices **onLoad** and **onUnload**.

5. Double-click on the choice **onLoad**. The bottom pane displays your choice. Click on the code view. The dialog box changes to show the actual VBScript instruction you're building.

6. In the Action window, double-click on the **window** icon to display a list of methods and properties for the window object. Select the first method, **alert**.

7. The bottom pane displays the VBScript code using the word *msg* for the text that will appear in the button. Change the text to the message you want to display. Figure 16.9 shows a script being developed with the message "Sales reports due on Friday!"

CHAPTER 16—Developing with JavaScript and VBScript

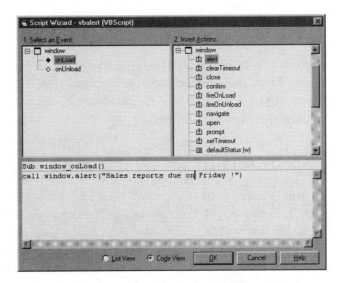

Figure 16.9 Inserting text in a VBScript message box.

8. Select **OK**, and the dialog box closes. FrontPage inserts the code into your page and displays a small icon to represent the script.

In order to test the script, you'll need to preview the page in a VBScript-compatible browser. Be sure that you save the file in FrontPage Editor before you load it in the browser.

You can edit the script source code directly using the **View**, **HTML** command in FrontPage Editor or you can make changes using the Script wizard if you prefer; double-click on the **VBScript** icon, and the Script wizard will open.

If you have problems getting the code to run, compare it to the following, which is the VBScript code you would have created by following the preceding steps.

```
<script language="VBScript">
<!–
Sub window_onLoad()
call window.alert("Sales reports due on Friday !")
end sub
```

```
-->
</script>
```

If you compare the technique for building this script in JavaScript and VBScript, you'll find that the methods are identical with the Script wizard. However, if you compare the code generated by the two, you'll see that the programs are clearly different.

Redirecting Browsers to a New URL with VBScript

Like JavaScript, VBScript lets you control the navigational component of the browser. By defining and then calling a new procedure for the navigator object, we can use VBScript to send visitors to our page to a new location, without asking them to click on a link. This script can be useful if you ever need to change your domain name. Rather than ask users to click on a link, you redirect them to the right location automatically. You may also want to include a link on the page for browsers that don't support VBScript. The following steps will create a script that will run as soon as the page is displayed on VBScript-compatible browsers, so the link won't be seen. But if the page is displayed on a non-VBScript browser, the script is ignored, and the browser will display the HTML tags with the link.

You can create the script in the VBScript wizard by following these steps.

1. Open a new page in FrontPage Editor. If you're replacing an existing URL, you may want to rename the original page using FrontPage Explorer.
2. Select **Insert**, **Script**.
3. Select **VBScript**.
4. Select **Script Wizard**. The Script Wizard dialog box opens.
5. In the Event window, double-click on **Window**.
6. Select **onLoad**. In the bottom pane, the wizard will begin to generate the line of script. The dialog box changes to show the actual line of script.
7. In the Insert Actions window, double-click on **Go To Page**. The Go To Page dialog box opens.

CHAPTER 16—Developing with JavaScript and VBScript

8. Enter the new URL. If it's a page in the same folder at your Web site, type the file name including the HTM extension. If it's at a different Web site, include the complete URL with protocol.

9. Click on **OK** to close the Go To Page dialog box. The line of code appears in the bottom pane. If you need to correct the URL, select **Modify**. The dialog box shown in Figure 16.10 will open.

10. Click on **OK** to close the Script Wizard dialog box. FrontPage will insert the script in your Web page. A small icon will represent the script.

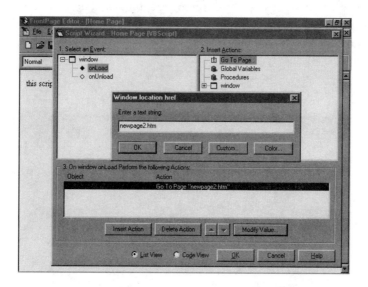

Figure 16.10 Loading a new URL with VBScript.

To test the script, you'll need to save the file in FrontPage Editor and then preview the page in a browser that supports VBScript. You can edit the page using the **View**, **HTML** command to display the script or by double-clicking on the script to open the wizard.

If you need to debug the script, compare it to the following code, which accomplishes the URL redirection.

```
<script language="VBScript">
<!–
Sub window_onLoad()
Window.location.href = "newpage2.htm"
end sub
–>
</script>
```

If you're comparing VBScript and JavaScript, notice that the same task is accomplished with slightly different techniques. The JavaScript program is a single line, while VBScript declares a procedure, calls it, and needs to identify the end of the procedure.

CHAPTER 17

CONNECTING WITH OFFICE 97 AND REMOTE DATABASES

The ability to work with data in many different forms is one of a Web site's most important functions. You can't possibly create HTML pages with all the information your site is capable of publishing. Whether you want to publish information about your company's product lines at a public Web site or share corporate spreadsheets on an intranet, setting up links to other sources of data can not only save you work, but it can also help you tap into the best resources available for achieving your Web site's goals.

In this chapter, you'll learn about some of the many techniques available for connecting to other data sources in FrontPage. Since FrontPage was created by the same Microsoft division that created Microsoft Office 97, there are some synergies between these two products. Learning about them may help you decide whether you can benefit from moving to the full Office 97 environment. If not, this chapter will show you how to use a variety of other connectivity techniques for working with other applications.

We'll be using some specific applications and file type as examples, but the possibilities are endless. Almost any type of data can be funneled into your Web site. This chapter will help you understand the basic techniques needed for realizing all these possibilities.

RECEIVING FILES FROM CO-WORKERS

As a Web administrator, you may often be able to benefit from having your co-workers send you files using their own applications. You can be spared from typing text into your pages that already exists in files they have on their hard disks. And since typing is probably not your best skill, you'll be more likely to have accurate information if you receive the originals.

Since HTML is a text format at heart, the basic requirement for receiving raw data is that it is in a text file; every word processor has an option to save the file as text. While you can import any text file directly into your FrontPage Web pages, using Editor's **Insert**, **File** command, you may find that it's often possible to obtain files in HTML. Recent version of the leading word processors and spreadsheets, including Lotus Smart Suite and Corel Suite with WordPerfect, now offer the ability to save most data files in HTML format. When you receive files in these formats, rather than in the native application formats, not only will you be able to open the files right away without going through a painful conversion process, but many of the formatting selections made by users will be retained. The saved HTML files are usually formatted with very simple choices: plain text for most parts of the document with either headers or large font sizes where a document used special fonts. In Microsoft Word, files that contain tables will be correctly converted to HTML format from the original Word DOC format, too.

Microsoft Office 97 offers an additional feature: wizards that allow some customization of how the files are formatted in HTML.

Receiving Files from Office 97

All the major applications in Office 97—Word, Excel, Access, and PowerPoint—can export data files in HTML. Section headings and the use of italics in Word documents will be preserved. Spreadsheets created in Excel will be exported to tables. And database tables created in Access will be exported to tables. You can begin this process of group collaboration by letting you co-workers know that if they are submitting material to be published at the Web site, they should save the file in HTML format.

Office 97 provides two techniques for saving files in HTML. The simplest method is to use the **Save As HTML** command. This method will be best if you want to select the final format options for the page so that they fit in well with other pages on your Web.

The other technique is available for Excel and Access. These two programs generate data that can be handled in so many different way on a Web site that Microsoft has created HTML conversion wizards. By running these wizards instead of the **Save As HTML** file choice, users are guided through the process of formatting the HTML document, offering a chance to select from different choices.

WARNING

The ability to save files in HTML and to run the HTML Export wizard is available only if these features were selected during Office 97 setup. If they're not available, the setup program will need to be run in order to install the necessary components. You'll need to select the **Custom** setup option since the **Typical** setup does not install the wizards.

Saving Excel Spreadsheets with the Internet Wizard

In Office 97, Excel provides an additional **File, Save As** command; rather than select **HTML** from a list of file types, Excel provides the Internet Assistant wizard. When you select **File, Save As HTML**, this wizard runs asking a series of questions about how the file should be formatted before it is saved to HTML. See Figure 17.1.

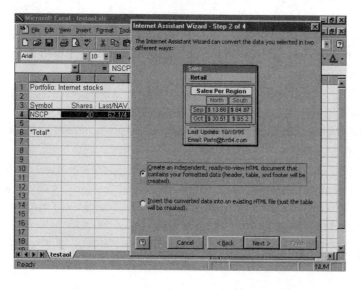

Figure 17.1 Excel's Internet Assistant wizard.

The first screen in the wizard asks you to choose the range of data. The wizard will begin with the currently selected data, but you can edit the range of data that will be exported and add new ranges. The wizard will allow you to specify several different ranges to export.

The next screen asks you to choose between saving the file as a self-contained HTML page, which will have its own headers; adding the selected ranges to an existing screen. In either case, the next screen gives you the chance to select the options needed in either case. If you're saving the page to a self-contained file, you can enter the text to be used as the header, insert some horizontal lines to improve the page's appearance, and insert a link to your e-mail address if you wish.

If you're saving the page to an existing file, the wizard will prompt you for the file where the range should be inserted; however, you'll need to do a little work, too. You need to insert the following HTML comment tag in the desired HTML file before the wizard can complete its work.

```
<!-##Table##->
```

You'll find that it's easier if you edit the HTML files to include this string before you run the Excel wizard.

When you've finished selecting options about how the page will be saved, Excel will give you the option of saving it within a FrontPage Web. This option can save time and disk space; you won't need to import the file, it will already be within the correct FrontPage folder as part of the Web.

The file that Excel's Internet Assistant wizard creates is filled with HTML comment tags, so when you open the file in FrontPage, you may think there's something wrong. Figure 17.2 shows a page generated by the wizard.

The wizard inserts a series of comment tags which FrontPage displays as **exclamation point** icons. These tags will not be displayed when the page is opened with a browser, but they do occupy a fair amount of space within FrontPage. Don't remove the tags if you plan to keep the file updated using the Excel Internet Assistant wizard again, since the wizard will use the tags to isolate the range that needs to be updated.

Chapter 17—Connecting with Office 97 and Remote Databases

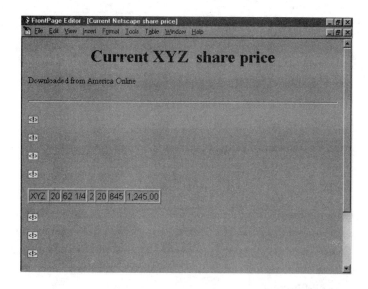

Figure 17.2 An Excel table exported to FrontPage by Excel's Internet Assistant wizard.

You can remove all the markup tags if you will not update this file again. Before you begin removing tags, you'll want to see what they do. To reveal the code inside each of these comment tags, highlight the icon, right-click, and select the menu choice **HTML Markup Properties**. Figure 17.3 shows one of the tags as displayed by this command.

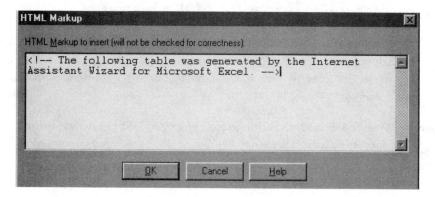

Figure 17.3 HTML comments inserted by Excel's Internet Assistant wizard.

Whether you keep the markup tags or delete them, you can edit all other properties in the page or insert new elements.

Connecting Web Sites to Databases

As a site grows, it's appetite for new data is voracious. The more successful your site becomes, the more you'll want to publish. The trail for new sources of information will usually lead to a database.

WARNING

FrontPage uses WebBot software to generate data queries so you'll be able to interact with remote databases using the IDC wizard only if your sited is hosted by a server with FrontPage extensions already installed.

The design and maintenance of database queries is a major branch of computer science, and entire careers are devoted to mastering it. Many large Web sites employ teams of programmers to maintain the links between the HTML front end of the site, and the vast database stores on remote computers.

Using FrontPage, you have a few tools that can help you tap into databases without spending that much effort. As you might expect, FrontPage can work very well with the Access database manager in Microsoft Office 97. The rest of this chapter will show you some of the techniques available for connecting to Access and other databases.

Microsoft's IDC Format for SQL Queries

FrontPage can reduce some of the work in linking Web pages to databases by helping to construct SQL (Structure Query Language) files for accessing databases directly. You add database queries to your pages in a two-step process.

WARNING

FrontPage Editor simplifies the process of creating links to database, but you need to construct valid SQL queries. The wizard will not walk you through the process of constructing the correct syntax of the query.

The basic technique is to give users the opportunity to query a database by constructing the query in a form that you add to a Web page. But rather than send the form to an HTML file as shown in the discussion of forms for gathering data in Chapter 12, you would send the form to an the IDC (Internet Database Connector) file that contains the query. The IDC format is supported by Microsoft's Internet Information Server as a way to send extract information in SQL from databases that have ODBC drivers. The IDC file contains information to help the server establish contact with the source data file, and it contains the actual query statements. Since the original database may have password protection, the IDC file can carry login information.

The results of queries will be displayed in an HTML format known as HTX. Pages in the HTX format are templates that contain HTML formats for displaying the results of database queries. You can edit the appearance of an HTX page using the FrontPage Editor's **Edit**, **Database** commands.

Unfortunately, the process of connecting a Web site to a database is awkward and time-consuming, using FrontPage's tools. If you plan to provide many database links to your Web sites, you may want to consider other products that make the process easier. Borland's IntraBuilder and Macromedia's Backstage Enterprise Studio are two of the many products on the market that can manage database connections with much less work than FrontPage requires. Before you make the decision, read over the process and ask yourself if you really want to be doing this every time you need to edit the queries displayed at your Web site.

The following sections describe the individual steps.

Creating IDC Files with the Database Connector Wizard

You begin the process of creating IDC files by selecting **File**, **New** in FrontPage Editor. From the list of templates and wizards, select the **Database Connection Wizard**. The first screen, shown in Figure 17.4, allows you to specify the source file for the data and any login information that may be needed to open the file.

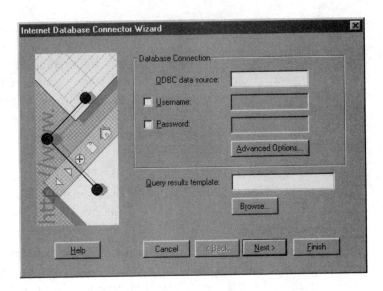

Figure 17.4 The Database Connector wizard.

If you plan to move the database up to your Web site, you may want to import it before running the wizard. You'll be saved from the need to enter the entire path for the file. You can also name the query results page on this dialog box. You enter the first part of the name; FrontPage will give the page an HTX extension.

The next dialog box allows you to construct the query. You add the statement by selecting the **Insert Parameter** button. The dialog box shown in Figure 17.5 opens.

Enter the entire statement in this text box. The FrontPage wizard will encapsulate the statement using the $ character after you close the dialog box by clicking on **OK**. If you compose more than one SQL statement, the dialog box gives you the option of selecting whether the new statement is executed before or after the statement already entered.

After you've entered the entire query, click on **Next** to open the next wizard dialog box, shown in Figure 17.6. Here you can choose default values for any of the parameters. When your SQL query is run as part of a form that specifies the IDC file as the form handler, the default parameters are combined with the parameters passed. But if the SQL query runs from a link directly from an IDC file, only the default parameters are used.

CHAPTER 17—Connecting with Office 97 and Remote Databases

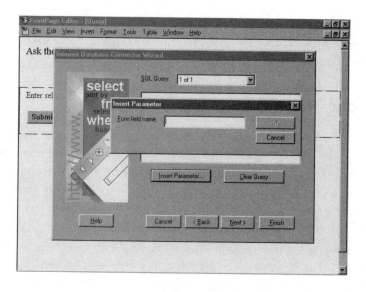

Figure 17.5 Adding the SQL statement.

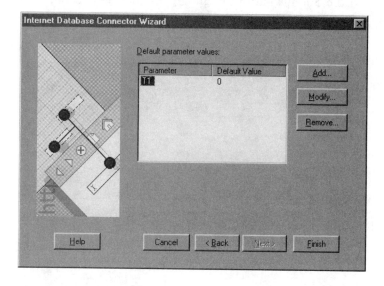

Figure 17.6 Setting default values for the query parameters.

The wizard will create an IDC file in your current Web; you'll be prompted for a folder you can use to help keep the query scripts separated from other files.

Activating Your IDC Query

Once the IDC file is created, you need to specify it either by directing a link to the file or by using the more common practice of creating a form. If the IDC file is run from a link, the browser will have no input into the search. When you construct a form, the browser can enter parameters for searching, making it possible for you to create a form that lets visitors find database entries that match their own criteria.

You create the form using **Insert, Form Field**. Be careful to design the form so that it will create a valid query that will be sent to the server when a push button is selected. Chapter 12 provided extensive detail on form creation. After you've created a form, you need to assign a form handler to the **Submit** button. Highlight the button and select **Edit, Form Field Properties**. The Push Button Properties dialog box opens, as shown in Figure 17.7.

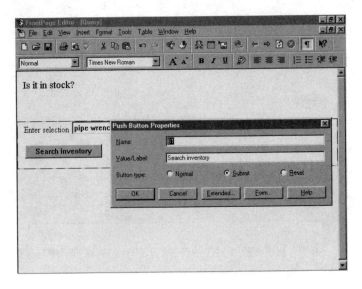

Figure 17.7 Editing the properties of the Submit button.

Be sure you're entering the values for a button chosen as **Submit** or **Normal** (not **Reset**) and then click on the **Form** button. This menu allows you to select the form handler that will be used by the server for processing the data submitted by the browser. FrontPage uses its WebBot software for handling forms, so you'll be able to use only the forms on a server where the FrontPage Server Extensions are installed.

Select the option **Internet Database Connector** and click on the **Settings** button. A dialog box opens, as shown in Figure 17.8, where you can specify the IDC file you just created with the Internet Database Connector wizard. You can search for the file name using the **Browse** button.

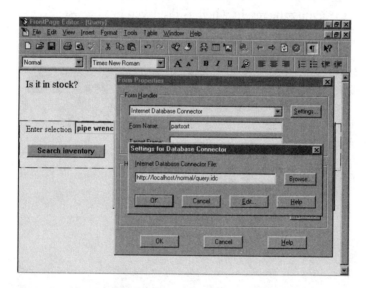

Figure 17.8 Configuring the IDC file to process a form.

To test the form, save it and then preview it in a browser.

Customizing Your HTX Database Results

When the query results are returned form the server, the IDC file will display them in an HTX database results page. FrontPage can begin the process of creating this page using a template. Select **File**, **New** from the FrontPage Editor menu and choose **Database Results** from the list. A page opens, as shown in Figure 17.9. It includes some text, explaining the purpose of the page.

You will not be walked through the creation of this page. You need to use the **Database** commands on the Edit menu to insert field codes so that the query results will display on the page. You may also want to add explanatory text or graphics to help browsers understand the results being displayed.

You control the display of results using commands on the **Edit**, **Database** menu. The first two commands allow you to display the names for fields. Choose the **Database Column Value** if you want to specify the name based on the original database fields; choose the **IDC Parameter Value** to enter names based on the IDC parameter selection. Be sure to add headings or labels to identify the results when it's displayed in a browser.

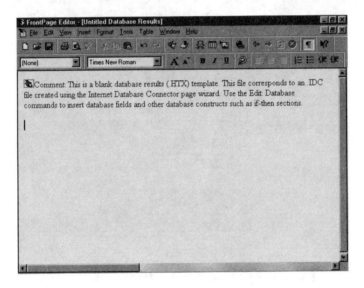

Figure 17.9 The HTX page generated by the Database Results template.

You can also create conditional statements for controlling the display of results using the **If-Then Conditional Section** command, as shown in Figure 17.10.

Chapter 17—Connecting with Office 97 and Remote Databases

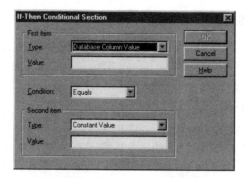

Figure 17.10 Controlling HTX display with conditional values.

Publishing Pages Data Directly from Microsoft Access

The Internet Database Connector is useful when the databases are in publicly available SQL formats and are outside of your direct control. When you or your colleagues are using Microsoft Office 97 with Access, you can tailor tables without using ODBC (Open Database Connect) connectivity and SQL programming. Instead, you can use Access to generate the HTML files you'll want to display. The files will display more quickly, and there will be less overhead on the server since you'll be displaying HTML data stored at your Web site. And you won't need to have the server process a WebBot forms handler and wait for the database to return results. The downside is that the HTML pages available at your site will be frozen in time—the Web site will display old data if the source data file was updated after the page was exported to HTML.

Microsoft Access can also generate HTX and IDC files using its own wizard technology. Co-workers can generate the files directly and send them to you. You could then create the forms in HTML pages and specify the correct IDC file as a form handler in order to add database queries to pages.

Saving Access Tables to HTML Files

Microsoft Access provides both types of Web support from the **Save to HTML** command on its File menu. The command turns on the Microsoft Access Web Publishing wizard, allowing users to select any table, query, form, or report to be saved in HTML format.

The wizard will save the data in an HTML page that can be very simple or be inserted into an existing template. Figure 17.11 shows a database table exported to an HTML file without any formatting.

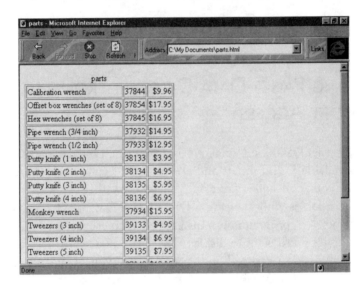

Figure 17.11 An Access table exported to HTML.

The Access table was converted directly to an HTML table without any special use of fonts. The wizard does provide some control; you can have the data added to an existing HTML page or select from a template.

The Access Web Publishing wizard can also be used to generate an entire Web site, complete with an index page. It lets users include many different parts of a single database; every individual report, form, table, and query may be added or left out. If you're using a large database file with many individual parts, a fairly complex Web site can result from including all of the pieces.

The wizard provides three choices for the format of the page output, as shown in Figure 17.12.

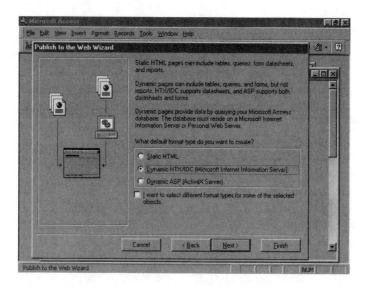

Figure 17.12 Access can generate ordinary HTML or IDC/HTX queries.

The simplest option is to generate a static, HTML page that will be stored on disk in individual files (Figure 17.11 is an example of such a page without a template). Dynamic pages are stored as a combination of IDC query/HTX results pages or as an ActiveX object, which can be processed by an ActiveX server.

Do not attempt to use the Access Web Publishing wizard to move files to a FrontPage Web site. The wizard uses the Internet FTP for moving files but FrontPage does not support this protocol. Files placed in a FrontPage Web folder with FTP may cause damage to the file or links in your existing Web site. You should move files to a FrontPage Web only through the FrontPage Explorer's **Publish** or **Import** tools. If you're working with a colleague, have the files sent to you by e-mail or through a disk copy, rather than FTP transfer.

WARNING

Attempting to add files to a FrontPage using the Access Web Publishing wizard over an FTP connection can wreak havoc on the Web's structure. Any pages added to a FrontPage Web using external file transfer won't be included in the FrontPage index files.

CHAPTER 18

PERFECTING YOUR WEB SITE

By now, you should be well on your way to building an elaborate site. Each of the previous chapters focused on a specific concept that's part of the Web building process or a specific FrontPage software process you can use at a Web site.

This chapter is designed to help you use a few techniques that aren't essential to the process of building the site but that may be valuable in helping your site reach its full potential.

You'll learn how to make FrontPage Explorer aware of other programs on your system that you can use for editing files. We'll take a look at how you can gain insight into the techniques used at other Web sites. We'll explore some techniques you can use for collaborating with others working on your own site. And we'll look at how to handle the inevitable changes that will be thrown at your Web site, ranging from information that needs to be replaced to moving from one server to another.

Finally, and perhaps most importantly, you'll learn a few tips about to gain more from the hard work you're spending on your Web pages.

WORKING SMARTER

FrontPage's wizards aren't the only smart tools you can use for improving your Web site. Software already on your hard disk and pages at other Web sites can be valuable, too.

Use the Best Editor for the Job

FrontPage Explorer recognizes many of the file types used in a Web site and creates an association between the file's extension and an application. When you double-click on a recognized file from the folder view in

Explorer, the correct application is opened. For example, GIF files are associated with Image Composer, so Image Composer opens any time you double-click on a file with a GIF extension.

You can change the associations for existing files or add new ones. To see a list of the current associations, open FrontPage Explorer, select **Options**, and choose the **Configure Editors** tab shown in Figure 8.1.

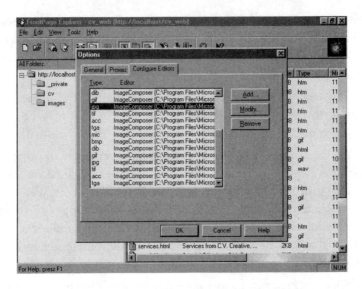

Figure 18.1 The list of files associated with editors.

FrontPage does not inherit the associations between files and applications stored in your Windows configuration. It maintains a separate association. It may sound like a silly thing to do, but it's actually necessary because in FrontPage you will be using files in a different way than you normally will. For example, HTM and HTML files are associated with a Web browser in the Windows configuration. But when you're running FrontPage, you don't want to view a Web page, you want to edit it. So HTM and HTML files are associated with the FrontPage Editor.

FrontPage sets up editors for the file types used by its main applications—FrontPage Editor and Image Composer. As you begin to work on new file types, like WAV sound files and AVI movie files, you will need to configure new editors. To configure a new editor for WAV files, open FrontPage Explorer, select **Options**, and choose the **Configure Editors** dialog box. Select the Add button. You'll need to type in the file extension and a description for the program. Use the **Browser** button to navigate through your system to find the program you'll use to edit files with this extension. The dialog box in Figure 18.2 shows the correct selections to configure the Windows 95 Sound Recorder as a WAV file editor.

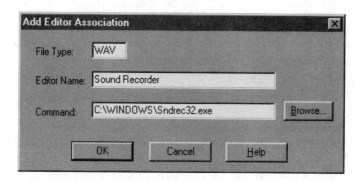

Figure 18.2 Adding an editor for WAV files.

If you're happy using FrontPage Editor and Image Composer for your graphics, you won't need to change the editor. But you may want to use a different editor for only some files. For example, you may want to keep Image Composer as your editor for GIF graphics but select a different editor for JPG files. You can select any file type you want to change, click on **Modify**, and then navigate to the program you want to use instead.

After you confirm the changes, the next time you open files with this extension in FrontPage Explorer, the file will open in this program instead.

Learn from Others

The World Wide Web has become such a creative environment because sharing is easy. If Web designers are architects, then every Web site proudly bears its blueprint in the lobby. Any page displayed at a public Web site can be examined, dissected, and even regenerated into a new Web site.

Virtually every browser provides commands for viewing the HTML source code for a Web page and for saving the file to disk. Any time you visit a Web site that you find interesting and you want to learn about it, use your browser's **File Save As** command. After the file is stored on your hard disk, you have a choice of how you'll open it. If you feel it could be used to create pages you'll want to use in one of your Web sites, after it is stored on your hard disk, use FrontPage Explorer's **Import** command. You can now open the file with FrontPage Editor, and any changes you make or links you build with the page will be part of your Web site.

If you are planning to look at the page only to gain an understanding of how a certain technique was created, you can open it directly from FrontPage Editor. Before you spend too much time capturing other people's work, it's important that you are aware of the limitations on reusing this work.

Any reuse of protected intellectual property or trademarked material in a public forum may be interpreted as infringement on the owner's rights. The clever use of HTML tags to create interesting effects it not protected by law, just as a phrase is not protected. But a distinct design may fall under the protection of trademark or copyright laws. While some copyright holders are willing to grant individuals the right to use their property for personal uses, like private Web sites, others are not.

Normally, only the graphics used in a web site are copyrighted or trademarked. But if you emulate the overall look of a popular sight, you could find yourself infringing on intellectual property. For example, some Web sites put enormous resources into their unique style. You may think imitation is flattery, but they may think it's cause for a restraining order.

Use HTML files on the Web for learning, not for stealing.

All the while, you can learn a little just from reading through the HTML tags, much of the page's original look won't work without the graphics. You can save graphic files using most browsers, too, but be especially wary when you download other people's graphics. All photographs are protected by copyright (even the photographs of an amateur). And anyone who spends 10 minutes creating a GIF image in PC Paintbrush has created a work of art that is their property. They may not mind if you use it, but you are legally not entitled to reuse in any public forum unless you have permission.

In Netscape Navigator, you can save graphics in Web pages you are displaying by selecting **View**, **Document Info**. The top half of the screen will show a list of all the files, including each graphic file. Click on the file name to see a display of the file in the bottom of the screen. Right-click on the file name, and Navigator will open a menu with an option to save the image to your system, as shown in Figure 18.3.

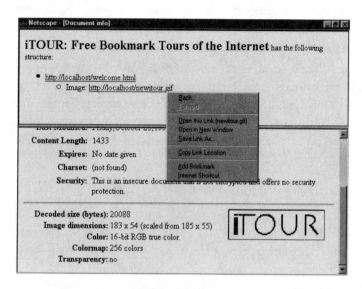

Figure 18.3 Saving graphics with Netscape Navigator.

In Microsoft Internet Explorer, the process is easier. Move your mouse pointer to the image and right-click. A menu will open with the option to save the file.

Annotate Your Tags

When you look at the HTML code used by some of the most successful sites on the Web, one technique you'll find used frequently is annotations within HTML code. In Chapter 16, we saw how annotations are used to hide JavaScript and VBScript code from browsers. Annotations can also be used to make notes to yourself and to your co-workers. Typical uses for annotating your pages are

- To remind yourself to add text, graphics, or a form.
- To explain the purpose of the HTML tags you've entered.

- To explain the purpose of an external program you've inserted, such as a Java applet.
- To convey a comment to co-workers who will work on the page.

You can insert an annotation at any spot in a page. You have two choices for annotating the page. FrontPage provides a comments command, and you can also use the **HTML Markup** command.

FrontPage's comments command displays the text when the page is open in FrontPage Editor but not when the text is viewed in a browser. You add this type of annotation by selecting **Insert, Comment** and typing a phrase in the text box that opens. FrontPage uses a WebBot to insert the comment into the page. The following is the HTML code that FrontPage creates to display the phrase "update this page" as a comment.

```
<!—webbot bot="PurpleText" preview="update this page" —>
```

The second method for annotating a page is to use FrontPage's **Insert, HTML Markup** command and enter text in the syntax normally used at Web sites for annotations. HTML tags that begin with the punctuation mark (!) character are ignored. So it has become common to use them in annotating pages. In fact, an exact syntax has come into common use. The following tag would be used to add the comment, "update this page."

```
<!—/update this page—>
```

When FrontPage displays tags using this syntax, an exclamation point appears in the page. Figure 18.4 shows how FrontPage displays a page where a comment and an HTML markup command is used with this phrase.

CHAPTER 18—Perfecting Your Web Site

Figure 18.4 Comments can be seen but markup tags can't.

Because a WebBot is used, the icon becomes a **robot** icon when the mouse points to the text. In Figure 18.4, the **exclamation point** icon represents the markup tag. You'll notice **markup tag** icons in many of the pages you download from Web sites since this tag is very widely used.

You may want to use this technique instead of the comment tag if you're working with other sites that don't use FrontPage. Adding the correct in FrontPage Editor is performed with the **Insert**, **Html Markup** tag. You'll need to type in the correct syntax, including the opening and closing brackets for an HTML tag. Figure 18.5 shows the correct way to add tags for inserting the comment "update this text."

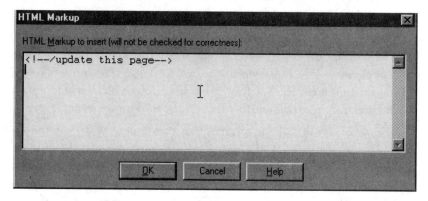

Figure 18.5 Adding a comment with the HTML Markup command.

Unfortunately, FrontPage will insert some additional tags to the command that aren't widely used on the Web. While the **HTML Markup** command is offered as a way of inserting HTML tags that you can't add to your page with any other FrontPage command, FrontPage's additions may undermine the purpose of the tags. In order to prevent FrontPage from attempting to error-check the tags, it needs to mark them as excluded from normal FrontPage processing, so it "wraps" the tags in a different WebBot. Using **HTML Markup** to insert a comment as already shown will generate this HTML code.

```
<!—webbot bot="HTMLMarkup" startspan —><!—/update this page—
><!—webbot bot="HTMLMarkup" endspan —>
```

These tags will not cause problems for browsers or servers processing the page, but they won't be understood by humans who are familiar with HTML syntax. If you are using comments to annotate pages that are being used by people without FrontPage, you may want to open the HTML pages with a word processor and insert the comment tags without the additional markup.

Keeping a To-Do List

FrontPage has a better tool for helping a team collaborate on a Web site than the HTML annotation tags. But like the Comments WebBot, it also requires that FrontPage be running on the system of each team member.

The To-Do list can keep track of all unfinished jobs at a Web site. It can be used by everyone who has administrative and authoring privileges at a Web site—you can even use it just to help you keep track of work you want to remember. But the To-Do list allows you to assign a name to each task so it's an excellent tool for groups working together.

Some of the FrontPage wizards that create new Webs use the To-Do list to guide you through the process of finishing the site after the wizard gets it started. A few FrontPage commands add entries to the To-Do list, too. For example, the **Replace** command adds replace instructions to the To-Do list if you don't complete the process of running a **Replace** command, as shown in Figure 18.6.

CHAPTER 18—Perfecting Your Web Site

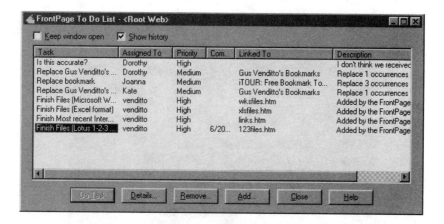

Figure 18.6 The To-Do list.

To display the list, select **Tools, To Do List** from the FrontPage Explorer, FrontPage Editor, or Image Composer. New tasks can be assigned in any of these programs too, by clicking on the **Add** button. You can keep the To-Do list readily available if you select the option **Keep Window Open**.

WARNING

The To-Do list won't always be visible when you've selected the **Keep Window Open** option. It will recede to the background when you work on another open application. Press **Alt-Tab** to find the **To Do List** icon on the menu of all open applications.

You can show tasks that were marked as complete by clicking on **Show History**. When you want to remove a task from the list of active tasks, select it and click on **Complete**. You will have the option of marking it as finished (thus sending it to archives) or deleting it from the To-Do list entirely.

When your list gets long, you may want to sort it by clicking on the header for any of the categories. Click on **Date**, and the tasks are sort chronologically. Click on **Priority**, and tasks marked as a **High** priority are moved to the top of the list.

You add an item by opening the To-Do list and clicking on the **Add** button as shown in Figure 18.7. If you use the list only as a reminder, you can probably enter just a few words in the Task field. But if you are working in a group, you can use the Description field to provide detailed instructions on what needs to be done or to respond to other comments made.

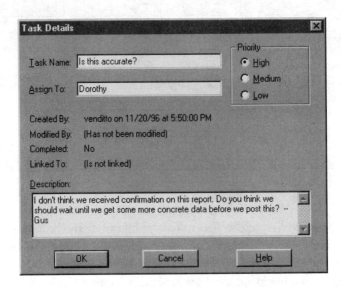

Figure 18.7 Adding items to the To-Do list.

You can change the name of the task or the description by selecting the task and clicking on **Details**. A dialog box opens with the same options as you see when using **Add**.

When a task is added to the To-Do list by FrontPage in the middle of an operation, you can have FrontPage pick up the action back where the job needs to be finished. Click on the **Do Task** button, and FrontPage will resume the operation at the point where the work was left off. Tasks that you add as notes will not have an active **Do Task** button; the button will be grayed out for these tasks.

MOVING YOUR SITE TO A NEW SERVER

Nothing is permanent, especially on the Web. One of the great benefits of using FrontPage is that it simplifies the process of moving a Web site. Normally, moving a Web site can be a long drawn-out process requiring every single URL in every HTML file be rewritten to reflect the directory

Chapter 18—Perfecting Your Web Site

structure of the new location. FrontPage makes moving a snap when the new server runs FrontPage server extensions.

All you need to do is connect to the old site with FrontPage Explorer and select **Export**. The dialog box will prompt your for the new name. FrontPage will move the files and then recalculate the hyperlinks and make any changes that may be needed in referring to URLs. You can track the steps FrontPage takes by watching the status menu in the bottom of the screen.

TIP You can export the Web either from a copy on your disk or from the copies on the server. It's a good idea to always have a copy of your Webs on both your local system and the remote server.

When you need to move your site to a new Web server, you may be faced with the bad news that the server is not running the FrontPage server extensions. Unfortunately, you'll need to invest some time and effort to make the transition smoothly. You may want to start by referring to Chapter 2. The section entitled "What You Need from a Web Server" explains the issues you'll face.

In short, you'll need to:

- Eliminate all WebBot components from your pages.
- Change clickable image maps from WebBots to the new server's format.
- Move your pages to the new server.

Eliminating a WebBot from a page is easy; you just delete the small **robot** icon on the page representing the underlying HTML tags. But replacing the WebBot with new code is a major undertaking. You'll need to obtain scripts in CGI, Perl, JavaScript, VBScript, or Java, depending on the application in order to provide the function your WebBot provided. FrontPage doesn't provide help in creating these new scripts aside from the VBScript and JavaScript wizards described in Chapter 16.

TIP Follow these same techniques when you want to convert pages you create for others who maintain Web sites on servers without FrontPage extensions.

The WebBot that generates clickable image maps, however, can be duplicated by FrontPage, and it's described in the next section. You can also use a FrontPage wizard to help you move the files; it's described in the following section.

Fixing Image Maps for Servers without FrontPage Extensions

By default, FrontPage uses a WebBot to generate clickable image maps (as described in Chapter 8). But you have two ways to replace them for servers without the FrontPage (FP) extensions. Both methods are selected using the FrontPage Explorer. Select the **Tools**, **Web Settings** command and open the **Advanced** tab on the dialog box, which is shown in Figure 18.8.

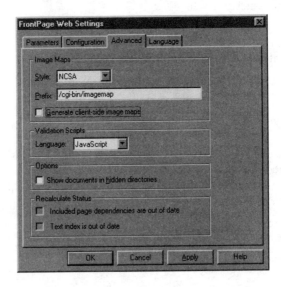

Figure 18.8 Changing the style of image maps for a server.

Chapter 18—Perfecting Your Web Site

The easiest choice is to select client-side image maps. The code for client-side image maps is contained completely within HTML tags, and no server action is required. In addition to being easier to maintain, client-side image maps place no burden on the server, and they execute more quickly. The drawback is that older browsers do not understand the client-side image map HTML tags.

Server image maps using CGI processing are more common throughout the Internet. If your new server does not support FrontPage extensions and you want your site to be accessible to the widest audience, you'll want to specify the server on the **Web Settings** command before you move your site.

First, you'll need to know whether the server conforms to one of the major standards—NCSA, CERN, or Netscape—in order to choose the correct Style for the image maps. And, you'll need to know the directory where image maps (the files that specify the map coordinates inside the graphic) are stored on the server. FrontPage Explorer will make a guess on the folder, but a Web administrator may have created a different folder for your site. You may need to ask your Web administrator for the correct folder name.

TIP

Be sure that you confirm the name of the folder where image maps should be stored on your server. The links to the graphics will not work if FrontPage has the wrong name entered under Web Settings.

After you enter the correct server style and folder, click on **Apply**, and FrontPage Explorer will begin the process of revising all image maps on the Webs managed by this system. Before it makes the changes, it will ask you to confirm that you want to do this right now by displaying the dialog box shown in Figure 18.9.

379

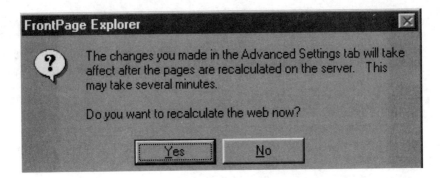

Figure 18.9 Confirming changes to the image map server style.

If you enter **Yes**, FrontPage Explorer will change the HTML tags inside pages that contain image maps and generate image map configuration files. When you publish the file to your new Web site, you'll need to move these configuration files in addition to the HTML and image files in your Web site.

WARNING

Server-side image maps may not work properly on servers running FrontPage extensions. You'll need to select FrontPage for the server style so that the HTML tags specify WebBots for image map processing before you publish the pages on a FrontPage-aware server.

Moving Files to Servers without FrontPage Extensions

The process of moving Web files to a server begins by opening the Web site in FrontPage Explorer. When you use the **Publish** command in Explorer, FrontPage will always attempt to communicate with the server you specify. As long you have an active TCP/IP connection that can reach the server, and you enter the correct server address, FrontPage will be able to determine if the server has FrontPage extensions installed. So if you're not sure if your new server has the extensions, it doesn't hurt to try to move your to the new server using the **Publish** command. If the extensions are not found, FrontPage starts the Web Publish wizard. This wizard can move the files using FTP, the technique used by most Web administrators to communicate with remote servers on the Internet. If possible,

CHAPTER 18—Perfecting Your Web Site

the wizard will use Windows file transfer, although this technique will work only with Windows NT servers across a network connection.

When you're sure the remote server is not running FrontPage server extensions, you may want to use an FTP program instead of the wizard. The wizard always attempts to move every file in your Web. When you want to update just a single file at the Web site, you'll be better off using an FTP program. Figure 18.10 shows WS_FTP, a popular shareware FTP program connected to a Web site.

Figure 18.10 Using an FTP program to move Web pages.

The FrontPage Web Publishing wizard will attempt to manage every aspect of the file transfer process. It starts to run when you attempt to connect to a remote server, and FrontPage determines that it cannot communicate with the server extensions.

When the wizard is not able to establish a network connection, it begins by asking you to choose between a local area network connection and a dial-up modem connection, as shown in Figure 18.11.

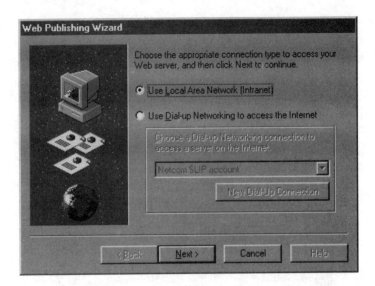

Figure 18.11 The Web Publishing wizard begins the TCP/IP connection.

When you select **dial-up connection**, the wizard will start the Windows dial-up networking software to dial the modem and log in to the Internet account. Once the Internet connection is activated, you'll be prompted for the name of the host. This is the server where the Web site is hosted and is often an FTP address. The following is a typical host name for a Web server:

```
ftp.internetservice.net
```

You can also use the IP address (for example, 199.55.199.55). FrontPage will then look for the server and confirm that it's active. In most cases, you'll need to enter your user name and password for connecting to the server (this is not the same user name and password you need to access your FrontPage Webs).

You'll then be prompted for the remote server and the folder where you have write privileges for your Web pages. The wizard asks for this in two text boxes, as shown in Figure 18.12. The first text box asks for the UNC path (Universal Name Convention), which is the directory where your files are stored on the remote server; the Web administrator will need to give this to you. The second text box asks for the URL, which is the address that a browser uses to display pages at the site.

CHAPTER 18—Perfecting Your Web Site

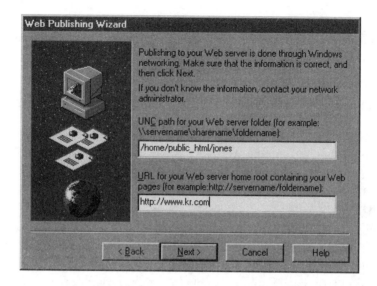

Figure 18.12 Specifying the address for the Web directory.

When you've entered the address of a valid Web site where you have write privileges, FrontPage will transfer all the files in the Web, including folders you've created.

WARNING

If you and someone else are collaborating on this site, the FrontPage Web wizard could overwrite a file at the Web site with an older version of the file. The solution is to use an FTP program rather than the wizard to move files to the site. The FTP program will allow you to change only individual files instead of the entire Web site.

MANAGING CHANGE AT YOUR SITE

Web technology is becoming more popular because it is flexible enough to keep pace with changing conditions. When you need to update information for broadcast to an entire organization or all your customers, rather than print new documents and mail them, you make the change to a file and then publish it at the site.

Managing those changes can become a full-time job. Fortunately, FrontPage has a few tricks you can use to reduce the time you'll spend keeping your site up to date.

Replacing Text in Every Page

Most word processors have a find-and-replace tool that makes it easy to keep documents updated. Whether you need to correct a misspelled name or change the location of a meeting, find-and-replace helps us all cope with the torrential rate of change. Enter the old text to be found and then insert the new text to be replaced, and in seconds, the document is accurate.

A Web site isn't a single document, however. You'll repeat the same information in many documents. Fortunately, the find-and-replace command in FrontPage Explorer is able to search through each page at a Web site and replace every occurrence of text.

TIP

To replace text on more than one page, you need to run the **Replace** command from Explorer. The **Replace** command in FrontPage Editor applies only to the text on the current page.

You run the command by opening a Web in FrontPage Explorer and selecting **Tools**, **Replace**. The dialog box shown in Figure 18.13 opens.

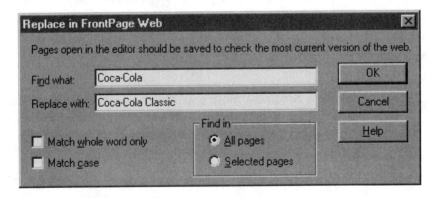

Figure 18.13 Replacing text in more than one page.

CHAPTER 18—Perfecting Your Web Site

The **Replace** command gives you the standard options for a find-and-replace command. You can choose to make the search case-sensitive, and you can restrict replacements only to words that are a complete rather than a partial match.

You have the option of changing every page in the site or just selected pages. If you want to limit the replace operation to only a few pages, highlight those files in FrontPage Explorer. You highlight more than one file using the same technique you would use in other Windows file lists: hold down the **Ctrl** key as you click on each file name with the mouse. As long as you hold down the **Ctrl** key, you are able to highlight more files to the list. When you've selected all the desired files, select **Tools**, **Replace** and click on the **Selected Pages** option.

After the **Replace** command executes, a dialog box will open, offering the option of reviewing each change before it's made in FrontPage Editor or deferring the change by placing it on the To-Do list. This dialog box will keep track of the status of each change, as shown in the dialog box in Figure 18.14, so that you can take your time and make sure each change should be made.

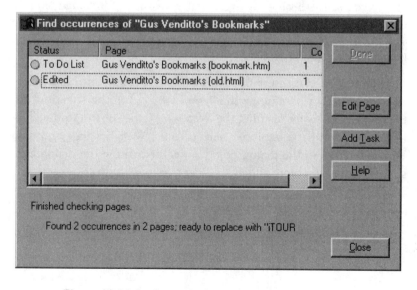

Figure 18.14 Confirming replacements before they're made.

If you aren't sure a change should be made, add it to the To-Do list. FrontPage Explorer will add the item to the To-Do list for this Web to remind you that you may want to take action at a later date.

NOTE

The **Find** command works the same way in FrontPage Explorer; you can find text on all Web pages or on selected Web pages. After the text is found, you can display the page in FrontPage Editor or add the Find results to the To-Do list.

Changing Text That Changes Often

The **Replace** command is useful for fixing mistakes or making changes that you couldn't anticipate needing to make. But some changes are predictable. You know you will need to periodically change dates for scheduled events or the prices of products described at the site. You may know that a name or address is going to change soon, but you don't have the new information.

FrontPage provides a tool for making such predictable changes that's superior to the ordinary **Replace** command. The Substitution WebBot allows you to store values for text that you'll want to change later. Rather than insert the actual information into your Web pages, use the Substitution WebBot. The page will display the current information whenever you open the page.

Before you can insert the Substitution WebBot into your page, you need to create a parameter that you can use for the substitution. You begin the process by opening the Web where the substitution will be performed in FrontPage Explorer. Select **Tools**, **Web Settings** and open the **Parameters** tab in the dialog box. Figure 18.15 show the dialog box after several parameters were added.

CHAPTER 18—Perfecting Your Web Site

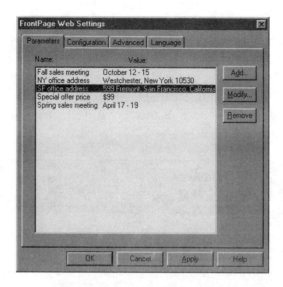

Figure 18.15 Parameters for the substitution WebBot.

For the name of the parameter, use any word or phrase that will help you identify the purpose of the text. For example, "price for Web site special offer." For the value of the substitution parameter, you can add up to a full paragraph of words and numbers (for example, "The special price of $199 is being offered on all new orders.").

Add the substitution parameter's name and the initial value by clicking on the **Add** button, as shown in Figure 18.16.

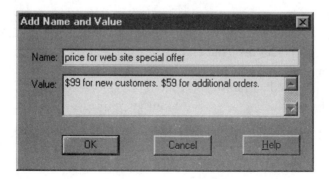

Figure 18.16 Adding a substitution parameter.

After you enter the text, click on **Apply**, and FrontPage will update the indexes for the current Web. You can now use this parameter in a page. Display the page where you want to include the Substitution WebBot and move your cursor to the spot on the page where the text should appear.

Select **Insert**, **WebBot Components**. The list of available WebBot components opens. Select **Substitution**. A dialog box opens with the list of choices, as shown in Figure 18.17.

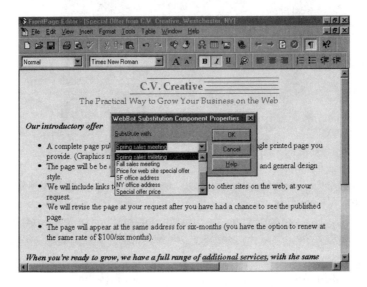

Figure 18.17 Inserting a Substitution WebBot.

The text will appear in the style currently in effect at this position. After the text is inserted, you'll see the friendly WebBot **robot** icon whenever your cursor passes over the text, indicating that this text is patrolled by a WebBot; you can't edit the text on the page. To make any changes to the text, you'll need to return to FrontPage Explorer, display the Parameters dialog box again, and select the **Modify** option.

You can change the appearance of the text. You can choose any style, header, or color for the text. But you cannot create a link to the text.

Gaining More from Your Hard Work

A Web site isn't just a series of chores. It's an investment in the future of your organization and your own career. Try the following techniques to gain a little more payoff from your efforts.

Register Your Site with Search Engines

If some of your sites are on the World Wide Web, you'll want to make sure others can find them. The Web search engines—InfoSeek (www.infoseek.com), AltaVista (www.altavista.digital.com), Excite (www.excite.com), and Lycos (www.lycos.com)—are visited by millions of people every day. Each is looking for information out of the millions of publicly available Web sites.

The search engines have robot programs that comb the Web servers, looking for material to add to their databases, but it can take months before you're noticed. One way to speed up the process is to go to the sites and register. You can register for several at once by visiting the Web site at www.submitit.com. This Web site provides links to the places at the search engines where you register.

After the search engines know about you, their robot software will visit your site and gather information used to create the listing for your pages. You can help some of the sites do a better job if you add keywords to your page. Keywords are added as *meta tags* to the header of your pages. Some of the search engines will be able to add these keywords to their index to improve the likelihood that you'll be found when someone searches on your category. A combination of factors is used by each search engine in determining which pages appear first, including the occurrence of words in headers and the number of times a word appears in a page. For example, if someone is looking for "trucking services" at a Web site, the pages that have the word "trucking" in both a keyword meta tag and the body of the text three times will come up before a page that displays "trucking" just twice in the body of the page. Adding keywords to your page is no guarantee that your page will be found more often at search sites, but it can't hurt.

The keyword meta tags are added to the page by selecting **Page Properties**. When the Page Properties dialog box opens, select the **Custom** tab. In the bottom half of the window (the user variables half), click on **Add**. The dialog box shown in Figure 18.18 opens.

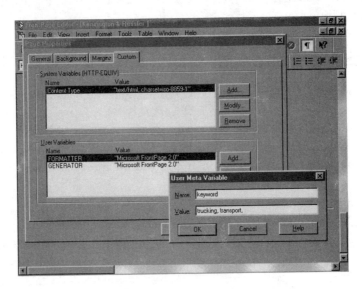

Figure 18.18 Adding keyword meta tags.

Type **keyword** in the Name text box. In the Value text box, type the words that you want to be associated with your page. For example, in the trucking business, you would want to add **trucking**, **transport**, and any other term a customer might use to find you.

Add Your URL to Your E-mail

It's become common practice to add Web site URLs to stationery, business cards, and even e-mail messages. When a complete URL appears in e-mail, many users will be able to visit the site simply by double-clicking on the address. That's because many e-mail programs recognize Web addresses and provide a link to the browser on the user's system. This technique works equally well in corporate intranets and the public Internet. So if you're trying to drum up traffic for your site, this is one way to do it.

Create a Temp Web for Housecleaning

You can't rely on the Windows Recycle Bin to recover lost pages. When FrontPage Explorer deletes a page, there is no way to get it back. That can make it difficult to keep your Web site tidy.

If you want to remove some pages that you're not planning to use but you feel there's a small chance you may need the page again, export it to a temporary Web folder. You can create a temporary Web using FrontPage Explorer's **New**, **FrontPage Web** command. Name it anything you like.

If you use it regularly to clear out old page designs that you can't use anymore, it will pay off in the long run. Anytime you are looking for ideas, skim through the ideas you were going to throw away. You may find a small gold mine.

Index

Numbers and Symbols
3D effects, 195, 202, 230
8-bit files, 24-26. *See also* GIF (Graphics Interchange Format) files
24-bit files. *See* JPEG (Joint Photographic Experts Group) files
< and > (angle brackets), 50, 249
! (exclamation point), 171, 342-343
_ (underscore), 283

A
access
 to servers, 31, 90. *See also* permissions
 to Web pages on intranets, 36
 to Webs, 79-83, 296-298. See also #haccess.ctl file
Access, Microsoft, 363-365
Access Web Publishing wizard, 364-365
active hyperlinks, 147, 155
Active X Control Properties dialog box, 314-315, 315
Active X controls, 27, 312-314, 314-316
Active X environment
 compatibility with Java, 332-333
 described, 331
 vs. other scripting languages, 330
 VBScript requirement for, 333-334
Add to the Current Web option, 103
adding. *See* creating
Administrator program, FrontPage Personal Web Server, 90-91
administrator rights, 80
agenda. *See* Meeting Agenda template
alert messages, 336, 337-340, 344-345
aligning
 cell contents, 227-228
 images, 138-139
 Java applets, 319
 tables on pages, 226-227

ALINK tag, 147
Alt-Tab key combination, 88
anchor links. *See* bookmarks
angle brackets (< and >), 50, 249
animations
 creating GIF, 322-324
 development tools creating illusion of, 318
 GIF89a extension, 59, 135
 inserting clip art, 135
 Microsoft GIF Animator, 320-322
 overview, 319
 Shockwave presentations, 320
 text, 322-324, 325-326
annotating HTML tags, 371-374
Arrange dialog box, 196
Arrange menu, 191-192, 206
AU files, 324
authoring rights, 90-91
AVI video files. *See* video clips, full-motion

B
background color. *See also* colors
 protected Discussion Web opening page, 296
 selecting
  images as, 153-154
  non-image, 155-156
 text color and, 150
 transparent GIF images, 58, 164-169
banners, 238
Bibliography template, 110
blur effects in images, 208
bold text, 127
Bookmark dialog box, 141-142
bookmarks
 creating, 141-143
 in Frequently Asked Questions template, 112
 in Product Description template, 112

393

in Webs created by Personal Web wizard, 105-106
Boolean operators, 285
borders
  frame, 246
  image, 137-138, 139-140
  table, 221, 229-230, 229-231, 232
bounding boxes, 188-189, 194
broken links, 51, 121-122
browsers
  collecting name of from forms, 267
  flexibility in displaying HTML documents, 21-22
  as HTTP clients, 20-21
  incompatibilities
    with fonts, 133
    with frames, 245, 248
    with multimedia, 305
    with VBScript, 342
  installing plug-ins, 309
  JavaScript objects, 335-336
  MIME support, 25-26
  nested tables and, 233
  previewing pages under development in, 122-125
  redirecting to new URL, 340-342, 348-350
  as requirement for viewing Web pages, 7-8
  resolving IP addresses, 16
  saving Web page graphics in, 370-371
  script execution, 62
  switching between FrontPage applications and, 87-88
  updating screen display in, 88
browsing rights, 80
bulleted lists, 127-128, 129

C

Cell Properties dialog box, 225-226, 230
cells, table
  aligning contents of, 227-228
  automatic expansion of height of, 223
  cell padding, 231
  cell spacing, 232
  changing width of, 225-226
  clickable images in, 217-218
  formatting, 221-222
  spanning others, 228-229
  splitting cells, 234
  width of, 224
CGI (common gateway interface) scripts, 26, 32, 254, 265-266
check box form fields, 261
Check Box Properties dialog box, 261
child Webs, 117
Class A through C networks, 13
Class ID, Active X control, 313, 315
clickable images
  advantage of using, 57
  vs. image maps, 140-141
  for navigation bars, 277-278
  in table cells, 217-218
client. *See* browsers
client-server model, 9, 20-21
client-side image maps, 170, 378-379
clip art, 134-135, 153-154, 161
code, HTML. *See also* HTML tags
  in blank pages created with Normal Page template, 109-110
  editing WebBot properties in, 276
  for execution by WebBots, 170-171, 254
  learning by viewing Webs created by others, 369-371
  as underlying Web pages, 21-24, 47
  VBScript vs. JavaScript, 348, 350
Color dialog box, 158-159
Color Lift tool, 203-204
color schemes, 150-152, 159-160
colors. *See also* background color
  adding to Webs
    checking system color palette, 148-149
    color highlights in text, 156-157
    custom, 158-159
    horizontal lines, 160-161
    HTML color tags, 149-150
    overview, 147
    selecting, 155-156
  copying in images, 207
  Discussion Web pages, 295
  form field label, 257
  number available in GIF vs. JPEG formats, 57

Index

page elements that can be colorized, 147-148, 152
   in shape special effects, 203-204
   sprite, 206-207, 210-212
   in tables, 230-231
columns
   frame, 240-241, 245-246
   table, 222-223, 224, 228-229
comment tag, 354, 355, 371-374
composition guide, 186-187, 193-194
compression, file, 59, 214-215
connections, Internet
   cost of dedicated, 39
   speed of host service, 43-44
   testing, 84
Copy Web command, 45
copying colors in images, 207
copyrights, 370
Corporate Presence wizard, 102-103
Create Hyperlink dialog box, 143, 173, 174-175
creating
   alert message in JavaScript, 337-340
   color schemes for reuse, 151-152
   custom colors, 158-159
   decorative text from graphics, 133, 175-177
   forms, 254-257
   GIF animations, 322-324
   HTX database results page, 361-363
   icon for Image Composer, 183
   IDC files using Database Connector wizard, 357-360
   image maps, 169-175, 171-175
   keywords, 389-390
   links
      bookmarks, 141-143
      clickable images vs. image maps, 140-141, 169-170
      href tags, 50-52
      for image map hot spots, 173, 174-175
      to other pages in Web, 143-144
      to other Web sites and URLs, 145-146
      overview, 140
   lists, 127-128
   sprites
      shapes, 197-202
      text, 192-193
      text shadows, 195

table borders, 229-231
tables, 221-223
tables of contents, 285-286
temporary Web folders, 391
To-Do list entries, 375-376
Webs. *See also* wizards, FrontPage
   in Editor vs. Explorer, 109
   naming new Webs, 98-101
   opening new Webs, 96-98
   without wizards and templates, 68
curved shapes, 198
custom grid (for frames), 243-244, 245-246
Customer Support Web wizard, 103-104

D

data files. *See also* Office 97
   inserting into Web pages, 27
   MIME in enabling use of many types of, 25-26
   saved as HTML files, 351-352
Database Connector wizard, 357-360
Database Results template, 361-362
databases, connecting Webs to
   activating queries, 360-361
   creating IDC files, 357-360
   customizing HTX database results, 361-363
   IDC format for SQL queries, 356-357
   Microsoft Access files, 363-365
   overview, 356
deleting
   bookmarks, 142
   borders from tables, 229-231
   cells from tables, 229
   comment tags from spreadsheet files, 355
   hot spots from image maps, 175
   points on lines created with spline tool, 201
   rows and columns from tables, 223
   sprites, 190
   WebBot components, 377
   WebBots, 276
directories. *See also* folders
   display of default HTML files in, 48-49
   organization of Webs, 52
   Personal Web Server default, 91
   UNC path, 382
directory lists, creating, 127-128

395

Directory of Press Releases template, 110
Discussion Web wizard, 104-105, 291-296
Discussion Web wizard dialog boxes, 292-296
Discussion Webs. *See also* protected Discussion Webs
   creating, 104-105, 291-296
   customizing page appearance, 298-301
   described, 287-288
   disadvantages, 290-291
   Feedback Confirmation template, 110
   linking to newsgroups, 288-290
   overview, 287
   User Registration template, 114
disk space
   discussion Web message files, 105
   host service charges for extra, 44
   minimum required on Web server, 39
dithering, 148-149, 159
.DOC files (MS Word), 120
domain names
   automatically directing browsers to new, 340-342
   common zones, 17
   host services and, 44, 45
   matching to IP addresses, 15-17
   registering, 37, 45
   storing Webs in Root Web and, 99
   in URLs, 17-19
domains, remote vs. local references and, 52
download.htm file, 103
downloading files. *See also* FTP (file transfer protocol); *specific entries under* URLs (*universal resource locators*)
   automatic installation of Active X controls, 313
   multimedia, 305
drawing shapes, 197-202
Drop Down Menu Properties dialog box, 262-263
drop shadows, 195
drop-down menu form fields, 262-263, 271-272
Drop-Down Menu Validation dialog box, 271-272

E

e-mail
   adding URL to messages, 390
   transferring from Web site domain to other accounts, 44
e-mail address mailto links, 111, 145-146
Edit Frame Attributes dialog box, 247
Edit Frameset Grid dialog box, 245-246
Edit menus
   Bookmark command, 106, 141
   Database submenu, editing HTX pages, 357
   Image Hotspot Properties, 175
   Image Properties command, video clips, 327
   Java Applet Properties command, 319
   Select All command, identifying sprites, 188
editing
   custom grid (for frames), 245-246
   form fields, 256-257
   frame set pages, 249
   HTML list properties, 128-129
   HTML tags, 54-55, 249-251
   HTX pages, 357
   images, 172
   VBScript source code, 347
   WebBot component properties, 276-277
   Webs, 85-86
editors. *See also* FrontPage Editor; graphics editors
   opening alternate, 84-85, 178-179
   selecting most appropriate, 367-369
8-bit files, 24-26. *See also* GIF (Graphics Interchange Format) files
emphasis formats, 127
Employee Directory template, 110
Employment Opportunities template, 111
encryption. *See* SSL (Secure Sockets Layer) protocol
error messages for broken links, 51
events, 336, 344
Excel spreadsheets, 353-355
exclamation point (!), 171, 342-343
exclamation point icon, 373

Index

Explorer. *See* FrontPage Explorer; Internet Explorer
extensions. *See* FrontPage server extensions; HTML extensions

F

Feedback Confirmation template, 110
Feedback Form template, 111
fields. *See* form fields
file associations, 368
file formats
    graphics, 57-60, 182
    MIME-compliant, 25
    for multimedia files, 61
File menus
    Composition Properties command, 187, 194
    Export command, 267
    New command, 109, 243
    New Folder command, 115
    New, FrontPage Web command, 68, 97
    Open FrontPage Web command, 81, 97, 115
    Page Properties submenu, 151, 153-154
    Preview in Browser command, 122
    Publish command, 116
    Save As command, 121
file names
    server naming conventions and, 100
    in URLs, 18, 99
files. *See also* data files; graphic files; HTML files; source files; Web pages
    adding types to be edited, 85
    changing default size of Image Composer, 186
    compression of, JPEG vs. GIF, 59
    controlling access to, 79-83
    conversion to HTML of MS Word .DOC, 120
    creating links to nonexisting, 143-144
    displaying specific Web site, 18
    excluding from searches, 283
    image map, 171
    image map configuration, 380
    importing from other Webs, 106-108
    links and missing, 51-52
    making available for downloading, 102-103
    MIME encoding of 8-bit, 24-26
    opening in FrontPage Editor, 85-86, 121-122
    saving. *See* saving files
    sending form results to, 266-267
    size of multimedia, 305
    that should never be edited, 78-79
    transferring. *See* FTP (file transfer protocol)
    viewing in FrontPage Explorer, 71-72, 72-73
filter effects in images, 207-210
folders. *See also* directories
    automatic creation of, 76-79
    created by Blank and Normal wizards, 108
    for files to be excluded from searches, 283
    managing, 75-76
    matching Web names to, 99
    in preparing to publish Webs, 115-116
    renaming, 100
    temporary Web, 391
font format tags, 56
Font Properties dialog box, selecting font size, 130-131
fonts. *See also* HTML styles
    adding shadow effects using, 195
    changing size of, 130-132
    form field label, 257
    for pages on intranets, 56, 177
    removing formatting, 133
    selecting, 132-133
form fields
    adding, 254-255, 255-256. *See also specific form fields*
    Discussion Web, 294
    editing, 256-257
    properties
        changing, 258-259
        check box, 261
        drop-down menu, 262-263
        overview, 257-258
        push button, 263-264
        radio button, 261-262
        scrolling text box, 260-261
        text box, 259-260
        for validation of data, 269-270
Format menu
    Font command, 130, 133, 156-157
    Paragraph command, 126-127

Remove Format command, 133
formatting
    documents, HTML tags as controlling, 22
    form field labels, 257
    text
        with fonts, 130-133
        for form results, 267
        with styles, 125-129
        with text sprites, 192-193
    timestamps, 282
forms. *See also* form fields; forms handlers
    for constructing SQL queries, 356-357, 360-361
    creating, 254-257
    as enabling interactivity with Web sites, 26
    in Feedback Form template, 111
    overview, 253-254
    for searching Web sites, 282-285
forms handlers. *See also* scripts
    configuring, 264-267, 361
    page displayed after form completion, 268-269
    purpose, 254
Forms Properties dialog box, 265-266
forums. *See* Discussion Webs
frames
    adding columns and rows, 245-246
    adding source files, 247-248
    for Discussion Webs, 295
    displaying message replies in Discussion Webs, 104-105
    editing and refreshing pages, 251-252
    HTML tags, 238-239, 239, 239-242
    naming and fixing problems, 249
    options for, 242
    overview, 237
    purpose, 237-238
    selecting frame templates, 244-245
    source files, 242
    starting Frames wizard, 243-244
Frames wizard, 239, 243-244, 249
<FRAMESET> tags, 240-241, 249, 250
Frequently Asked Questions template, 112
FrontPage Editor. *See also* templates, FrontPage
    appearance of Web pages in, 87
    avoiding lost files in, 121-122
    moving between Explorer and, 85-86
    refreshing Web view after editing, 76
    saving Web pages as templates in, 95-96
    setting permissions for Webs, 79-83
    shortcut keys for menu commands, 120
    toolbar, 86-87
FrontPage Explorer
    features, 66-67
    vs. Internet Explorer, 65
    moving between Editor and, 85-86
    opening Webs in, 67-70
    screen display, 68-70
    views. *See* views, FrontPage Explorer
FrontPage Image Composer. *See also* graphics editors
    features, 181-183
    fonts installed by, 177
    interface elements and tools, 183-185
    loading, 183
    setting other graphics programs as default, 84-85
    sizing images in, 185-187
    sprites. *See* sprites; text sprites
FrontPage, Microsoft
    programs within
        listed, 65
        switching to and from browser, 87-88
    script construction in, vs. UNIX scripting languages, 26
    Windows systems supporting, 15
FrontPage Personal Web Server
    giving others access to, 90
    purpose, 37
    services performed in background by, 89-90
    on shared corporate networks, 42
FrontPage server extensions
    described, 31-33
    determining if available on server, 380-381
    forms and, 254
    image map hot spots and, 141, 170-171
    moving Webs to servers not supporting, 377-378, 378-380, 381-383
    obtaining from Microsoft, 32
    provided by host services, 43
    requesting installation of, 33-34, 117
FrontPage Software Developer's Kit, 95

Index

FrontPage Web Settings dialog box, 378-379
FTP (file transfer protocol)
    adding functionality for, to Webs, 103-104
    moving Webs, 45, 365, 381
    Publishing wizard vs., 118
FTP sites, creating links to, 145-146

G

gateways, Internet, 12
Getting Started dialog box, 67-68, 96-98
GIF89a extension, 59, 320-322
GIF (Graphics Interchange Format) files. *See also* 8-bit files
    animated, 322-324. *See also* GIF89a extension
    automatic conversion of other formats to, 182
    best uses of, 57
    compression ratio, 59
    for custom horizontal lines, 161
    described, 58-59
    transparent background colors, 58, 164-169
Glossary of Terms template, 112
gopher servers, creating links to, 145-146
gradiant ramps, 205
graphic files. *See also* images
    as background images, 153
    controlling size of, 137-138
    converting to GIF and JPG formats, 182
    as decorative text, 133, 175-177
    formats, 57-60
    MIME encoding of, 24-26
graphics editors
    changing default setting from Image Composer, 84-85, 178-179
    creating decorative text in, 175-177
    selecting best, 177-178
groups, sprite, 191-192
Guest Book template, 112

H

#haccess.ctl file, 78, 79
hardware
    of clients receiving multimedia files, 304
    for connecting to Internet, 10, 12
    for Web host, 39, 41

header styles, font sizes vs., 131
helper applications, 308. *See also* Active X controls; players, multimedia; plug-ins
home page
    naming
        creating new Webs and, 98-101
        publishing Webs and, 118
    organization of Webs around, 49
    renaming when moving Webs between servers, 107-108
    wizard for creating blank, 108
Horizontal Line Properties dialog box, 160-161
host services
    rental by corporations with intranets, 36
    shopping for, 42-45
    SSL availability, 101
hosts
    limitations of some, 29-30
    options in selecting, 37-38
    shared on corporate networks, 41-42
    static IP addresses as requirement for, 14, 30
    total control of, 38-41
    types of
        ideal, 33-36
        stripped-down minimum, 30-31
        well-equipped, 31-33
hot spots
    adding links to, 173, 174-175
    defining, 171-174
    editing links to, 175
    requirement for FrontPage server extensions, 170-171
href tags, 50. *See also* links
HTML conversion wizards, 353
HTML editors, changing default, 84
HTML extensions
    font sizes, 131
    FrontPage support, 24
HTML files
    data files saved as
        advantages, 351-352
        Microsoft Access tables, 364-365
        from Office 97, 352-353
    displaying form results on Web sites in, 267-268
    intellectual property rights and, 370

retrieving at URLs, 48-49
HTML (Hypertext Markup Language), 21-24, 47. *See also* code, HTML
HTML list styles, 128-129
HTML Markup dialog box, 355
HTML pages. *See* Web pages
HTML styles, 125-126. *See also* fonts; HTML list styles
HTML tags. *See also* code, HTML
   annotating, 371-374
   color, 149-150
   comment, 354, 355
   editing, 54-55
   entering using FrontPage vs. word processors, 23
   exclamation point (!) in, 171
   extended, risks in using, 55-56
   formatting Web pages using, 52-54
   for frames, 238-239, 239-242
   for links, 50
   purpose, 22
HTTP (hypertext transport protocol), 18, 20-21, 54
HTTP servers. *See* FrontPage Personal Web server; server software
HTX files, 357, 361-363
HyperDocument Page template, described, 112
hyperlinks. *See* links
hypertext transport protocol. *See* HTTP (hypertext transport protocol)

I

icons
   for Active X links, 315-316
   exclamation point and markup tag, 354, 373
   for Image Composer, creating, 183
   plug-in, 311-312
IDC (Internet Database Connector) files
   creating using Database Connector wizard, 357-360
   described, 356-357
   generated by Microsoft Access, 363
If-Then Conditional Section dialog box, 362-363

Image Composer. *See* FrontPage Image Composer; graphics editors
Image dialog box, 134-135
image editing toolbar, 172-174
image editors. *See* FrontPage Image Composer; graphics editors
image map configuration files, 380
image maps
   clickable images vs., 140-141
   creating, 169-175, 171-175
   moving Webs between servers and, 377, 378-380
Image Properties dialog box
   Alternate Representations settings, 136
   Appearance tab
      aligning images, 138-139
      border thickness, 139-140
      sizing images, 137-138, 166-167
images. *See also* GIF (Graphics Interchange Format) files; graphic files; JPEG (Joint Photographic Experts Group) files; sprites
   adding links to, 140-141
   aligning, 138-139
   alternatives in displaying, 135-137
   animated, 59
   background, 153-154
   blending, 164-169
   borders surrounding. *See* borders
   colors, 16- vs. 24-bit, 148-149
   copyright laws and, 370
   in forms, form field functions and, 257
   FrontPage features for handling, 163-164
   HTML tag displaying, 57
   inserting
      clip art, 134-135
      from FrontPage CD-ROM, 133-134
      Software Data Sheet template, 113
   moving when importing Webs, 107
   reusing, navigational toolbar, 277-278
   scanning into Image Composer files, 181-182
   scheduling display of, 279-282
   sizing, 185-187, 194
   zooming and panning, 187
<IMG> tag, 57
Import Web wizard, 106-108

Index

importing
  color schemes, 152
  databases, 358
Include WebBot
  inserting, 279
  updating pages and, 278
index.html file. *See* naming, Webs
Insert command
  in enabling interactivity with Web sites, 26-27
  multimedia files, 61
Insert Hyperlink dialog box, 145-146
Insert menus
  Comment command, 372
  Form Field command, 254
  Horizontal Line command, 160-161
  Html Markup command, 373
  Hyperlink command
    bookmarks, 142
    images, 170
    links to other pages in Web, 143
  Image command
    described, 134
    file format conversion, 182
    GIFs as transparent backgrounds, 166
  Other Components submenu, Active X Control command, 314
  Script command, 62
    JavaScript wizard, 337
    VBScript wizard, 345
  Video command, 326
  WebBot Components command
    described, 276
    Include WebBot, 279
    Search WebBot, 284
    Substitution WebBot, 388
    Table of Contents WebBot, 285
    Time Stamp WebBot, 281
Insert Table dialog box, 221
intellectual property, HTML tags and, 370
interactivity with Web sites, 61. *See also* multimedia; scripts
  gathering user input. *See* forms
  methods available, 26-27
  overview, 60
internal links. *See* bookmarks
Internet. *See also* World Wide Web
  connecting to, selecting ISPs, 10-12
  granting Web access over, 83
  intranets vs., 9-10
  as technique for connecting computer networks, 8-9
Internet Assistant wizard, Excel, 353-355
Internet Database Connector files. *See* IDC (Internet Database Connector) files
Internet Database Connector Wizard dialog box, 358-360
Internet Explorer
  Active X technology, 331, 332-333
  displaying available MIME types, 310
  frame set pages, 251
  HTML extensions, 24
  Java interpreter, 316-317
  JavaScript interpreter, 333
  MIDI support, 325
  nested tables, 233
  overview, 65
  saving graphics in Web pages, 371
  text animation with marquees, 325-326
Internet Service Providers. *See* ISPs (Internet Service Providers)
Internic, database of Internet names and addresses, 16
intranets
  access to Web pages on, 36
  advantage of VBScript, 334
  fonts in pages on, 56, 177
  forms in collecting team member reports, 260
  vs. Internet, 9-10
IP (Internet Protocol) addresses
  controlling Web access by specifying, 83
  described, 12-13
  determining
    if static or dynamic, 13-15
    specific, 84
  matching to domain names, 15-17
  purpose, 12
  for Web servers on corporate networks, 41
ISPs (Internet Service Providers)
  information required from, for installing server software, 39-40

401

selecting, 38-39
italics, 127

J

Java, 330, 332-333
Java Applet Properties dialog box, 318
Java applets
    adding to Webs, 316-319
    as enabling interactivity with Web sites, 26-27
    potential advantages for multimedia, 305
JavaScript
    adding to Web pages, 335-342
        displaying alert message using, 337-340
        as object-oriented language, 335-337
        redirecting browsers to new URL, 340-342
    advantages, 334
    described, 333
    as enabling interactivity with Web sites, 26
    vs. other scripting languages, 330
JPEG (Joint Photographic Experts Group) files
    best uses of, 57
    conversion of inserted files to, 134, 182
    converting to transparent GIFs, 165
    saving, 213
.JPG file extension, 59

K

keyword meta tags, creating, 389-390

L

labels, form field, 256
lines
    curvey, 198-201
    horizontal, 160-161
LINK tag, 147
links
    colors of, 147, 155-156
    creating
        bookmarks, 141-143
        clickable images vs. image maps, 140-141
        href tags, 50-52
        for image map hot spots, 173, 174-175
        to other pages in Web, 143-144
        to other Web sites and URLs, 145-146
        overview, 140
        wizards in Explorer vs. Editor and, 101-102
    in creating tables of contents, 286
    described, 50
    directing users to location of Active X controls, 313-314
    directory structure and, 52
    from Discussion Webs to newsgroups, 288
    to e-mail addresses, in Employment Opportunities template, 111
    within frames, 247-248
    HTTP as enabling jumping between, 20-21
    to IDC files, 360
    internal. *See* bookmarks
    precision of, requirement for, 21
    viewing in FrontPage Explorer
        all for specific URL, 71-72
        described, 66, 68-70
        inside pages, 73-74
        repeated, 72-73
Liquid Motion Pro, 317-318
List Properties dialog box, 129
list styles. *See* HTML list styles
lists. *See also* drop-down menu form fields
    creating, 127-128
    scrollable. *See* frames
local references, 52
localhost server option, 99
Low-Res images, 136-137

M

Make Transparent tool, 167-169, 215
margins
    frame, preventing resizing of, 248
    tables as providing, 219
marquees, 325-326
Meeting Agenda template, 112
menu lists, 127-128
message forums. *See* Discussion Webs
meta tags, 389-390
methods
    Javascript, 336

Index

VBScript, 344
MIC graphics format, 182
Microsoft Corporation
   extension of HTML by, 24
   in scripting language controversy, 330
Microsoft GIF animator, 320-322
MIDI (Musical Instrument Digital Interchange) files, 61, 325
MIME (Multipurpose Internet Mail Extensions)
   configuring servers for multimedia, 305
   displaying list of types configured, 309-310
   in distributing multimedia, 307-308
   in encoding 8-bit files, 24-26
monitors. *See also* resolution, monitor
   display of colors on, 148-149
motion pictures. *See* video clips, full-motion
moving
   images
      on pages by dragging and dropping, 134
      when importing Webs, 107
   sprites, 189-190, 206
   text in blocks, 196
   Webs to server. *See also* publishing Web sites
      directory structure and links in, 52
      FrontPage server extensions and, 32, 45, 377
      between host services, 45, 376-383
multimedia
   adding file types for editing, 85
   adding to Webs, 61
   animations
      creating GIF, 322-324
      Microsoft GIF Animator, 320-322
      overview, 319
      Shockwave, 320
   defined, 303
   distributing
      Active X controls and, 312-314, 314-316
      files requiring Active X controls, 314-316
      files requiring plug-ins, 311-312
      Java applets and, 316-319
      MIME and, 307-308
      plug-in players, 308-310
   inserting in tables, 221
   overview, 303
   planning distribution of
      client issues, 304-305
      download issues, 305
      server issues, 305-307
   sound, adding, 324-325
   video files, adding, 326-327
Multipurpose Internet Mail Extensions (MIME). *See* MIME (Multipurpose Internet Mail Extensions)

N

naming
   color schemes, 151
   form fields, 258
   frame set pages, 249
   Webs, 98-101, 118
navbar.htm, 103
navigation bar
   created by Corporate Presence wizard, 102-103
   displaying same on every page, 277-278
   image maps as, 170
nesting
   HTML tags, 53
   tables, 233-234
Netscape Communications
   extension of HTML by, 23-24
   in scripting language controversy, 330
Netscape Navigator
   Java interpreter, 316-317
   JavaScript interpreter, 333
   MIDI support, 325
   nested tables, 233
   plug-ins, 309-310
   previewing pages under development in, 123-124
   saving graphics in Web pages, 370-371
   testing frames in, 238
networks. *See also* intranets
   establishing Web server on corporate, 41-42
   Internet as technique for connecting, 8-9
   in IP address system, 12-13
New FrontPage Web dialog box, 98
New Page dialog box, 144, 243
news servers, 289
newsgroups, 145-146

403

NNTP servers, 289
Normal Page template, 109-110
Normal style, 125
Notepad, Windows, 250, 251
numbered lists, 127-128, 129

O

objects
    JavaScript, 335-336
    VBScript, 344
Office 97
    Active X technology and, 331-332
    receiving data files from, 352-353
    saving Excel spreadsheets with Internet wizard, 353-355
    synergies with FrontPage, 351
opacity
    3D effects with shapes, 202
    drop shadows for text, 195
    in overlapping sprites, 206
    of patterns and fills, 206
ovals, creating, 198

P

Page Properties dialog box
    adding keyword meta tags, 390
    creating color schemes, 151-152
    reusing color schemes, 160
pages. *See* Web pages
paint tools, 210-212, 212-213
panning Image Composer images, 187
Paragraph Properties dialog box, changing text styles, 126-127
passwords for text box form fields, 259
Patterns and Fills tools, 204-206
percentages specifying table width, 224-225
permissions
    for child Webs, 117
    setting, 79-83, 90-91
Personal Web wizard, 105-106
photographs, copyright protection of, 370
pixels, 138, 224
players, multimedia
    browsers and, 305

Java scripts as reducing need for, 317
    streaming server applications and, 307
Plug-In Properties dialog box, 311-312
plug-ins
    Active X advantage vs., 313
    adding files requiring, 311-312
    described, 308-310
    as enabling interactivity with Web sites, 27
    Image Composer support of Photoshop API, 182
    Java scripts as reducing need for, 317
    MIME types and, 25-26
polygons, creating, 201-202
Practical JavaScript Programming, 335
Preview in Browser dialog box, 121-122
printing hard copies of Web pages, 125
privileges
    minimum required of hosts, 30
    for Web users. *See* permissions
_private folder
    Discussion Web source pages, 299
    excluding files from searches, 283-284
Product Description template, 112
Project Web wizard, 106
properties. *See also specific objects*
    JavaScript object, 336
    VBScript object, 344
protected Discussion Webs, 294, 296-298
protocols in URLs, 18
proxy servers, 9
publicizing Webs, 389-390
Publishing Web dialog box, 116-117
publishing Web sites
    child Webs, 117
    moving Webs to server
        directory structure and links in, 52
        between host services, 45
        preparing server, 115-116
        transferring files, 116-117
    naming home page, 118
    overview, 8, 114-115
    without FrontPage, 117-118
Publishing wizard, 118, 380-383
push button form fields, 263-264
Push Button Properties dialog box, 263-264

Index

R

radio button form fields, 261-262, 271
Radio Button Properties dialog box, 261-262
Radio Button Validation dialog box, 271
RAM (random access memory)
    conserving, 90
    minimum required
        for Web host, 39, 41
        for working with multiple applications, 88
RealAudio files, 61, 306
recall spline tool, 202-203
rectangles, creating, 197-198
registration page, Discussion Web, 296
remote links, 52
removing. *See* deleting
renaming
    folders, 100
    home page, when moving Webs between servers, 107-108
    To-Do list tasks, 376
repeated links, viewing, 72-73
Replace in FrontPage Web dialog box, 384-385
replacing text, 384-386, 386-388
resizing
    Explorer windows, 70
    fonts, 130-132
    frames, preventing, 248
    sprites, 189-190
resolution, monitor
    HTML and, 22
    image size in pixels and, 138, 185
    system color palette and, 149
    viewing pages at different, 123
results files
    configuring, 266-267
    creating secondary HTML file, 267-268
    HTX, 357, 361-363
RGB palette, 149-150
robot pointer, 256
Root Web. *See also* child Webs
    creating folders for publishing Webs, 115
    setting blanket permissions from, 79-80
    storing Webs in, 99-100

rotating
    sprites, 190
    text for animations, 322-323
rows
    frame, 240-241, 245-246
    table, 222-223, 223

S

Save As dialog box, 121-122
Save Results Component. *See* WebBot Save Results Component
Save Results WebBot, for processing Guest Book entries, 112
saving files
    avoiding lost files when, 121-122
    data files as HTML files
        Excel spreadsheets with Internet wizard, 353-355
        Microsoft Access tables, 364-365
        Office 97 data files, 352-353
    deleted from Web in temporary Web folder, 391
    graphic file formats supported, 182-183
    HTML source code on other Webs, 369-370
    from Image Composer, 213-215
    image map, 171
    JPEGs as GIFs, 165
    before previewing pages in browsers, 124
    Web page graphics in browsers, 370-371
    Web pages as templates, 95-96
    when editing frame set pages, 250
    when switching applications, 88
Scheduled Include dialog box, 280-281
Scheduled Include and Scheduled Include Image WebBots, 280-281
scheduling display of Web pages or graphics, 279-282
Script wizard
    JavaScript, 338-340, 340-342
    VBScript, 345-348, 348-350
scripting languages, 329-330
scripts. *See also* CGI (common gateway interface) scripts
    adding to Web pages

405

JavaScript vs. VBScript, 334
overview, 61-62
scripting language advantages, 334
FrontPage support for, 26
replacing WebBots with, 377
as requirement for form processing, 253
scroll bars, enabling frame, 248, 250
scrollable lists. *See* frames
scrolling text box form fields, 260-261
Scrolling Text Box Properties dialog box, 260
search engines, registering Webs with, 389-390
Search Page template, 113
Search WebBot, 113, 282-285
searching for text
on Discussion Webs, 293
Search WebBot, 113, 282-285
Secure Sockets Layer (SSL), 100-101
secure Web sites, creating links to, 145-146
selection sets, sprite, 191
Seminar Schedule template, 113
server software. *See also* FrontPage Personal Web Server
installing and configuring, 39-40
retrieval of default HTML files, 48
servers. *See also* hosts
in client-server design, 9
Discussion Webs demands on, 290
domain name, 15-17
file names vs. platform, 100
moving Webs to. *See* moving, Webs to server; publishing Web sites
multimedia demands on, 305-307
news, 289
selecting when creating new Webs, 99
service.cnf file, 78
Settings for Saving Results of Form dialog box
sending results to file, 266-267
specifying page displayed after form completion, 268-269
splitting results between files, 267-268
shadows
with shapes, 202-203
text, 195
Shape dialog box, 197
shapes
adding 3D effects using, 202-203

creating, 197-202
warping, 209
Shockwave presentations, 320
shortcut keys
for FrontPage Editor menu commands, 120
for switching applications, 88
sizing
images, 185-187
Java applet windows, 319
scrolling text box form fields, 260
tables, 223-226
software. *See also* graphics editors; word processors
Active X controls and data files, 312, 313
on client systems receiving multimedia, 304
downloading. *See* FTP (file transfer protocol); *specific entries under* URLs *(universal resource locators)*
for establishing TCP/IP connections, 10-11
HTTP server, 33-35, 39
included with FrontPage. *See* FrontPage, Microsoft, programs within
Software Data Sheet template, 113
sorting To-Do list entries, 375
sound files. *See also* MIDI (Musical Instrument Digital Interchange) files; WAV files
adding to Webs, 324-325
playing in background, 325
types of, 61
source files
frame
adding, 247-248
<FRAMESET SRC> tag, 250
importance of, 242
for Java applets, Java Applet Properties dialog box, 318
for IDC files, 357
spacing around objects. *See* white space
spline tool, 198-201. *See also* recall spline tool
Split Cells dialog box, 234
spreadsheets, Excel, 353-355
sprites. *See also* text sprites
colors, 203-204, 204-206
creating new shapes, 197, 197-202
described, 187-189
moving and resizing, 189-190

Index

selecting multiple, 191-192
sending behind others, 206
touching up, 212-213
warps and filters, 207-210
SQL (Structured Query Language) queries
    activating, 360-361
    creating IDC files for, 357-360
    IDC format and, 356-357
SSL (Secure Sockets Layer) protocol, 100-101
streaming audio and video software, 306-307, 326
styles, 125-128
Substitution WebBot, 386-388
Survey Form template, 114

T

<!-##Table##-> tag, 354
Table of Contents template, 114
Table of Contents WebBot dialog box, 285-286
Table menu
    Cell Properties command
        aligning cell contents, 227
        cells spanning others, 229
        changing cell width, 226
    commands, 221-222
    Insert Row/Column commands, 223
    Insert Table, command, 233
    Insert Table command, 221
    Select Cell command, 226, 229
    Table Properties command, 226-227
tables. *See also* cells, table
    adding, rows and columns, 222-223
    aligning
        cell contents, 227-228
        on page, 226-227
    controlling size of, 223-226
    creating, 221-223
    creative design of, 234-236
    Microsoft Access, 364-365
    nesting, 233-234
    overview, 217
    as page design tools, 217-220
tables of contents
    creating, 285-286
    for Discussion Webs, 293

tags. *See* HTML tags
Task Details dialog box, 375-376
TCP/IP (Transmission Control Protocol/Internet Protocol), in connecting to Internet, 10-11
teach yourself... Visual Basic, 343
Telnet programs, Publishing wizard vs., 118
Telnet servers, creating links to, 145-146
templates, FrontPage
    for frame set pages, 243-245
    for HTX format, 357
    opening, 108-109
    overview, 93-94, 108
    types of, 109-114
    wizards vs., 94-96
testing
    frames in Netscape Navigator, 238
    Internet connection, 84
text
    aligning in table cells, 227-228
    animating, 322-324
    color of
        vs. background color, 150
        highlighted, 156-157
        selecting, 155-156
    displaying while graphics download, 136-137, 251
    formatting, 125-129, 130-133
    graphics as decorative, 133, 175-177
    replacing, 384-386, 386-388
    searching on Webs, 113, 282-285, 293
Text Box dialog box, 259-259
text box form fields, 259-260, 270. *See also* scrolling text box form fields
Text Box Validation dialog box, 270
Text dialog box, 192-193
text sprites
    arranging, 195-196
    creating, 192-193
    fitting text into available space, 193-194
    shadow effects, 195
    warping, 209-210
3D effects
    with shapes, 202
    in table borders, 230
    with text, 195
threaded replies, 293

threads, discussion forum, 287-288
Time Stamp WebBot, 281-282
To-Do list
    deferred changes of text on, 385-386
    maintaining, 374-376
    opening, 144
    _x_todo.html file, 78
toolbars
    Forms, 255
    FrontPage Editor, 86-87
    FrontPage Explorer, 69
    Image Composer, 184-185
Tools menus
    Color Picker command, 207, 212
    opening To-Do list from, 144
    Options command
        changing HTML, graphics, or multimedia editors, 84, 178
        configuring editors, 368-369
        default size of Image Composer files, 186
        enabling/disabling display of Getting Started dialog box, 97
    Paint command, 210
    Permissions command, 82
        protected Discussion Webs, 297
    Replace command, 384
    Shapes command, 197
    Show FrontPage Editor command, 85
    Show Image Editor command, 85, 183
    To Do list command, 375
    Web Settings command
        changing image map style, 378
        substitution parameters, 386
transparent GIFs
    as background colors, 58, 164-169
    saving files as, 215
24-bit files. *See* JPEG (Joint Photographic Experts Group) files

U

UNC (Universal Name Convention) path, 382
underscore (_)
    in folder names, 283
    formatting text as, 127
Universal Name Convention (UNC) path, 382

UNIX servers, filename restrictions on, 100
updating Webs
    frame source files and, 242
    Include WebBot and, 278
    informing visitors of changes, 281-282
    overview, 383-384
    Publish (Explorer File menu) command, 117
    replacing text on all pages, 384-386
    table of contents updates and, 286
    temporary Web folders and, 391
    What's New template, 114
URLs (universal resource locators)
    adding to e-mail, 390
    contents of, 17-19
    in creating links, 50-51. *See also* links, creating
    directing users to Active X controls, 313-314
    folder name and, 99
    for frame source files, 242, 247-248
    for FrontPage extensions
        for downloading, 33
        list of hosts supporting, 43
    for HTTP server extension downloads, 32
    for Internet Explorer downloads, 65
    for Internic, 16
    for Liquid Motion Pro information, 318
    MIC images, for purchasing, 182
    for Microsoft GIF Animator downloads, 321
    for multimedia streaming servers, 306
    for plug-ins, 309
    redirecting browsers to new, 340-342, 348-350
    retrieving files from, 48-49
    for search engines, 389
    viewing in FrontPage Explorer
        all links to specific, 71
        described, 68-69
        files referenced by, 71-72
    for W3C, 19
    while awaiting domain name registration, 45
user input, gathering. *See* forms
user names, collecting from forms, 267
User Registration template, 114

V

validating form data

Index

drop-down menus, 271-272
nonstandard characters in field names and, 259
procedure, 269-270
radio buttons, 271
in text box fields, 259-260, 270
VBScript
    adding to Web pages
        displaying alert message, 345-348
        overview, 343-345
        redirecting browsers to new URL, 348-350
        tags inserted by, 342-343
    advantages, 334
    described, 333-334
    as enabling interactivity with Web sites, 26
    vs. other scripting languages, 330
VBScript wizard, 343
video clips, full-motion
    adding to Webs, 61, 326-327
    hardware issues, 304
View menus
    Folder view command, 115
    Forms Toolbar command, 255
    HTML command, 54, 277, 347
    Hyperlinks Inside Pages command, 73
    Options command, 310
    Repeated Hyperlinks command, 72
    Source command, 251
viewers, multimedia. *See* helper applications; players, multimedia; plug-ins
viewing
    HTML source code on other Webs, 369-370
    HTML tags, 54-55
    links in FrontPage Explorer
        all for specific URL, 71-72
        connecting Web site files, 66, 68-70
        inside pages, 73-74
        repeated, 72-73
    MIME types installed in browsers, 309-310
    pages
        at different monitor resolutions, 123
        under development in browser, 122-125
    sprites, 188-189
views, FrontPage Explorer
    folder vs. hyperlink, 74

    options, 71-74
    refreshing after working in FrontPage Editor, 76
    switching from hyperlink to folder view, 74-75
virtual hosting, 44
viruses, Java vulnerability vs. JavaScript immunity to, 333
visited hyperlinks, 147, 155
VLINK tag, 147

W

W3C (World Wide Web Consortium), 19-20, 24, 239
WAIS databases, creating links to, 145-146
warp effects in images, 207-210
watermarks, 153
WAV files, 308, 324
Web pages. *See also* files; home page; HTML files
    adding keywords to, 389-390
    appearance in FrontPage Editor, 87
    code underlying. *See* HTML (Hypertext Markup Language)
    creating
        blank, 68
        with frames, 242-252
    Discussion Web, setting colors, 295
    displaying
        alternates to frame set pages, 248
        on remote sites in browsers, 18
    formatting using HTML tags, 52-54
    internal links. *See* bookmarks
    for intranets vs. Internet, 9-10
    preventing display on searches, 283
    printing hard copies of, 125
    replacing text on all, 384-386
    reusing, 277-279
    saving in temporary Web folder after removing from Web, 391
    scheduling display of, 279-282
    viewing
        in browser while developing, 122-125
        links within, 73-74
Web. *See* Webs; World Wide Web

WebBot components
  deleting, 377
  editing properties of, 276-277
  inserting, 276
WebBot Include Component Properties dialog box, 279
WebBot Registration Component, 297
WebBot Save Results Component
  as default forms handler, 265
  selecting as forms handler, 265-266
  sending results to file, 266-267
WebBot Search Component Properties dialog box, 284
WebBot Timestamp Component Properties dialog box, 281-282
WebBots. *See also* WebBot components
  described, 275-276
  excluding tags from FrontPage error-checking, 374
  for Guest Book entries, 112
  image map execution by, 141, 170-171
  informing visitors of updates, 281-282
  for inserting tables of contents, 285-286
  noframes display, 251
  Project Web wizard, 106
  robot pointer and, 256
  Save Results Component, as default forms handler, 265
  scheduling page or graphic displays using, 279-282
  for searching Webs, 282-285
  for user registration entries on Discussion Webs, 114
  wizards vs., 94
Webs. *See also* child Webs; Root Web
  announcing changes to, 114
  connecting to databases, 356-363
  creating. *See also* wizards, FrontPage
    in Editor vs. Explorer, 109
    naming new Webs, 98-101
    opening new Webs, 96-98
  determining domain name servers for, 16-17
  frame source files and, 242
  generated by Access Web Publishing wizard, 364-365

  importing existing, Import Web wizard, 106-108
  moving to new server, 45, 376-383
  opening in FrontPage Explorer, 67-70
  organization around home page, 49
  public vs. private, 31, 36-37
  publishing. *See* publishing Web sites
  registering with search engines, 389-390
  searches of text in, 113, 282-285, 293
  sharing and controlling access to, 79-83
  table of contents, 285-286
  updating
    Publish (Explorer File menu) command, 117
    What's New template, 114
welcome.html file. *See* naming, Webs
What's New template, 114
white space
  around images, 139
  around table cell contents, 231-232
wide area networks, replacement by intranets, 9
windows
  Image Composer, 184
  resizing FrontPage Explorer, 70
Windows, Microsoft
  Control Panel
    checking type of IP addresss, 14-15
    color palette settings, 148-149
  HTTP servers included with, 89
  software for establishing TCP/IP connections, 10-11
  Sound Recorder as helper app, 308
WINSOCK.DLL, 11
wizards, FrontPage
  for creating scripts, 62
  in Explorer vs. Editor, 101-102
  FrontPage Editor, purpose, 108-109
  FrontPage Explorer
    Blank, 108
    Corporate Presence, 102-103
    Customer Support Web, 103-104
    Discussion Web, 104-105
    Import Web, 106-108
    Normal, 108
    Personal Web, 105-106
    Project Web, 106

Index

Publishing, 118
overview, 93-94
selecting appropriate, 101
speed of creating Webs in, 94
vs. templates, 94-96
vs. WebBots, 94
word processors
    entering HTML tags in, 23
    FrontPage Editor similarities to, 119-121
words, adding emphasis to single, 127
workgroups
    forms in collecting team member reports, 260
    Project Web wizard in creating Webs for, 106
    To-Do lists and, 374

World Wide Web
    rules governing, 19-20
    structure of, 7-13
World Wide Web Consortium (W3C). *See* W3C (World Wide Web Consortium)

X

_x_todo.html file, 78

Z

zooming Image Composer images, 187
specific entries under URLs (universal resource locators), 1
specific form fields, 1
specific objects, 1

About the CD-ROM

The CD-ROM contains graphics, animated graphics, and a graphic utility you can use to create your own animations for a web site.

Microsoft GIF Animator

The graphics utility is Microsoft GIF Animator, a Windows program that makes it possible to create GIF animations using a single image or a series of images. The program's features are explained at length in Chapter 15. To install the program, display the folder for the CD-ROM and double-click on the file **GIFSETUP.EXE**. A setup program will guide you through the process of installing the software and adding a program icon. In addition to the software, Microsoft GIF Animator will install sample animation graphics on your hard disk in a folder titled:

`\Multimedia files\Graphics\Web\Animations\Microsoft GIF Animator`

Microsoft GIF Animator is offered by Microsoft for personal use at no additional cost. The software is offered as is and no technical support is currently being provided. The software is subject to the terms and conditions expressed in the license agreement which appears during the setup process.

Images

The Images folder on the CD-ROM contains ten files in the color TIF format that you can open with Microsoft Image Composer. These images are samples from the MetaPhotos library of digital artwork and are offered on a royalty-free basis by MetaTools Inc. for use in web pages, desktop publishing, multimedia shows, print ads, brochures and more. (Re-sale of the images is strictly prohibited). To order more images from the MetaPhotos library, visit the company's web site at http://www.metatools.com.

At the site you can purchase photo images in libraries that cover a single topic. The samples are numbered according to their volume number. For example, volume 22 includes religious symbols, volume 24 covers wide-angle photography, and volume 25 is comprised of professionals at work.

The files are numbered; and the following is a description of each image on the disk.

- 0050005.TIF, a pair of shoes
- 0220061.TIF, a Buddhist statue
- 0250028.TIF, wide-angle view of a donut
- 0260027.TIF, two firemen
- 0280037.TIF, a desktop computer
- 0280065.TIF, a flying twenty-dollar bill
- 0280070.TIF, a baby frog
- 0280077.TIF, an insect
- 0320047.TIF, an iguana
- 0320005.TIF, a dime

The folder also contains the file "license.wri" a file in WordPad format that explains the conditions under which MetaTools offers the photos.